Outstanding Black Women
of Yalobusha County

Their stories and their contributions to a Mississippi Community

Compiled and Edited by Dottie Chapman Reed

Ben,

Thank you for your support. Hope you enjoy!

Dottie Juaye Chapman Reed

March 18, 2023

About the Cover Picture

Aside from my grandmother, Jane Ophelia Williams Pritchard (December 20, 1871 – September 15, 1969) in the white bonnet, the names of the remaining women standing on the courthouse steps in Water Valley, Mississippi in the late 1800's, are unknown. They are also holding similar bags in their hands, perhaps some type of holiday give away. Contact me if you can identify any of them or have additional information.

Table of Contents

Prologue   1

Cousin's Homecoming - Published June 21, 2018   3

Sally Winters Polk - Published August 23, 2018   4

Emma Spencer Gooch - Published September 13, 2018   6

Juanita Bishop-Cox - Published September 27, 2018   8

Readers Weigh In - Published October 11, 2018   10

Mrs. Lillie Caldwell Roberts - Published October 25, 2018   12

Letters From Vietnam Bring Memories - Published November 1, 2018   14

Rosa White Wright - Published November 22, 2018   16

Mother and Daughter Played Key Roles
in the integration of Water Valley High in 1966 - Published November 29, 2018   18

Annie Givens and Joann Bratton - Published December 13, 2018   23

Readers Weigh In   II - Published December 27, 2018   25

Mae Turner White and Bettye White Milledge - Published January 10, 2019   29

Margie Wilson Avant - Published January 24, 2019   33

Segregation Side Effects   - Published February 7, 2019   35

Joyce Hall Judson - Published February 21, 2019   38

Ethel Hudson Morgan - Published March 14, 2019   41

Dorothy Smith Kee - Published March 28, 2019   45

23 Strong Chartering the NAACP - Published April 11, 2019   50

Cora Lee Folson - Published April 25, 2019   53

Mable Jenkins Lewis - Published May 5, 2019   56

Ruby Buggs Hall - Published May 23, 2019   58

The Women Who Worked On Dupuy,
Panola And Leland Streets - Published June 13, 2019   63

One Year Later - Published June 27, 2019   68

Segregation Side Effects Revisited - Published July 17, 2019   73

Alma Polk Nicholson - Published July 25, 2019   78

Rachel Campbell Hero- Published August 8, 2019   82

Preserving Our History - Published August 22, 2019   86

Lula Pritchard Chapman - Published September 5, 2019   90

Sharing History to Make History - Published September 19, 2019   95

Ruthie Jenkins White - Published October 3, 2019   97

Recording Yalobusha's Black History - Published October 17, 2019   100

Lucy Martin Kelly - Published November 13, 2019 104
Juanita Polk Fleming - Published November 27, 2019 107
Ruby McKie Turner - Published December 8. 2019 111
All Our Names Were Freedom - Published December 26, 2019 116
Good Triumphs Tragedy - Published January 1, 2020 121
When Race Took The Back Seat - Published January 23, 2020 124
Dr. Louise Baker Brown- Published February 6, 2020 128
Mildred Faye Polk - Published February 27, 2020 133
Annie K. Montgomery - Published March 19, 2020 137
Elvira Hervey Jackson - Published April 8, 2020 141
Mamie Herron Shields - Published May 7, 2020 146
Ora Lee Polk Phillips - Published May 28, 2020 153
Ezra Captain Davidson, Sr. - Published June 18, 2020 159
Two Years Later - Published July 2, 2020 164
Epilogue 170
Acknowledgements 172
About Dottie Chapman Reed 173

Prologue

The Outstanding Black Women of Yalobusha newspaper column started from a hospital bed in June 2018 when I recounted a trip to my cousin George Adams' funeral in Rock Island, Illinois. I felt led to share my account of a moment in the service when my cousin's son explained how much his dad loved our hometown, Water Valley, Mississippi, and how he visited often, never turning down an offer to travel south. However, it was the second speaker, Miller Backstrom, whose story resonated the most. He spoke about how important my mother's Sunday School class was to him and to George. I was shocked to hear my mother's name – Helen Chapman – and how fortunate I was there.

Heading back to Atlanta I felt so proud and began to think about the many black women in my hometown like my mom who molded and shaped our lives in such positive ways that we cherish them and the memories to this day.

I sent my write-up to the editor of the Water Valley paper, The *North Mississippi Herald*. Water Valley is the county seat of Yalobusha County, whose population is close to 13,000. I doubted I would get a positive response given what I had previously seen in the paper.

How wrong I was.

David Howell, the editor, liked what I wrote, and we turned my account into what became the first article of the Outstanding Black Women of Yalobusha column. The goal of the column was to feature the unsung but outstanding black women of Yalobusha County with an opportunity for anyone to recommend or write about someone who had impacted their life or the community in a positive way. Now forty-five articles and two years later, I closed out the column in July 2020, having featured not only outstanding black women living and dead, but also various events that touched the lives of blacks and whites in Yalobusha County.

In the back of my mind was the memory of these women's circumstances - mine too: Mississippi's segregated society that by law and unspoken custom circumscribed so many opportunities we can now take for granted. Yet these women forged ahead in the world they found, making the profound contributions to family and community that these columns illuminate.

In October 2018, the University of Mississippi, the state's flagship school located 18 miles from Water Valley, initiated talks about a collaboration with the column and the Center for the Study of Southern Culture. Happily, those talks bore fruit, and the newspaper column has evolved into Black Families of Yalobusha. Dr. Jessie Wilkerson and her graduate students launched the oral history project in the fall of 2019 by conducting interviews with black residents and archiving them at the university. This second phase of the project is underway, and it is my hope that as the students continue to document black family stories, they will discover more outstanding black women. I will continue to support their efforts and occasionally offer an article of interest. Articles about the column and the oral history project have appeared in *The Albany Southwest Georgian* newspaper. Article 38, featuring Dr. Louise Baker Brown and Article 40, featuring Annie Kelly Montgomery, have been reprinted in *The Christian Index*, the national publication of the Christian Methodist Episcopal Church.

The participation and support from Water Valley natives, Camille Fly Dautrich and Dorothy Wiman, was another positive outcome of this project. They both shared their experiences as white students during the integration of Water Valley High in 1971. Danita Hall wrote about the subsequent closure of the all black Davidson High and her challenging transition to WVHS. In separate and additional articles all three wrote about their favorite outstanding black woman. On her own, Camille gathered her childhood girlfriends who wrote about their black maids, cooks and nannies.

This compilation includes all 45 articles previously published in *the Herald* minus some of the pictures. I have included comments from readers from across the country, black and white - comments that surprised and encouraged me such as this one from my college friend and educator Dr. Earl Richard.

"I love the concept of paying homage to these inspiring ladies from the area from whence you came. I have often said that most of us, and especially our younger generations, ignore our predecessors and their accomplishments far too often. Having worked with young people for many years I find that they too often measure accomplishments by what a person has or has accomplished in very limited ways, such as sports, music, movies, or even in illegal activities. Many of us have been just as guilty by not showing them other means of measuring success and accomplishments.

I applaud you and your efforts in recognizing these strong, intelligent, and often visionary ladies from the past, many of whom would never put themselves out there for recognition, and mainly because they didn't see what they were doing as anything special. To them, they were merely doing what came naturally for who they were and, in many cases, who they are."

Because such comments provide different perspectives, insight and enlightenment, I included a few of them in Article 5 and in Article 11, which summarizes those received in 2018. The comments in this publication begin with Article 12. All of the articles and additional pictures can be found on various websites, **www.blackwomenofyalobusha.com** in particular.

1

Cousin's Homecoming Sparks Call For Information About Black Women From Yalobusha County

My second cousin, George Adams, died recently after a very brief illness. He was one I considered a big brother because of how lovingly he treated me when I was four and five years old. I last saw him at his wife Pearlie's family reunion in Atlanta. He and I just picked right up where we left off as cousins do.

George's late mother, Cleala Mae, was my first cousin. George and I took pictures at the reunion, you know, one for him and one for me. To my dismay, I was unable to locate the photograph before attending the funeral in Rock Island, Illinois. But I found it recently.

George and I talked after my sister Faye's transition on October 25, 2016 because the two of them talked almost every day. Like many of us he had spoken to her on her birthday the day before. Faye kept up with everyone and all the family history. Her death left me the sole surviving sibling of Alvin and Helen Chapman.

Thus, my first and second female cousins let me know that I would be hearing from them more often. Unfortunately, I had to cancel a trip to Chicago in 2016 where I had planned to surprise George's older sister Minnie with a visit.

Upon George's death I had to be there for Minnie and his baby sister Mildred. George had told me where he lived in the Quad City Area as the border cities of Illinois and Iowa are known. It was not an easy trip for me. I was two days into a four-day conference at Clark Atlanta University.

I took a late-night flight to Chicago and after a few hours of sleep, drove the three hours to Rock Island, arriving with perfect timing for George's homegoing service.

When his son, George Adams III spoke, he talked of his father's love for our hometown, Water Valley, and how his dad never ever missed an opportunity to travel home. I was a tad surprised since their earlier home had been in a neighboring county.

The next speaker, a Mr. Backstrom, sounded like a name I remembered from my home church, Miles Christian Methodist Episcopal. He began by talking about my mom's Sunday School class. I was astounded and flattered to hear that she always picked them up for Sunday School and that Mr. Backstrom found the story both compelling and appropriate to share on this occasion so many years later. Instantly, I realized I was in Rock Island that day for a reason. If I hadn't been, I would have missed this tribute to my mom, Helen Chapman.

Later, I learned that a group of Water Valley residents had chartered a bus to attend George's funeral. And other Water Valley natives had come from Davenport, Milwaukee, and Chicago, among other cities. Sorry to say I did not get to see everyone, but I did share with the congregation what George meant to me.

This merging of home folks and families combined with George's love for Water Valley gave me an urge to hear more stories like the one that Mr. Backstrom shared.

Thus, I am soliciting biographies, stories, and pictures of black women of Yalobusha County, Mississippi – your mothers, grandmothers, aunties, teachers, church leaders, excreta who are or have impacted your life or others in a positive way.

2
Sally Winters Polk
The Search Continues for Info on County's Matriarchs

Why this project "Black Women of Yalobusha County?" When thinking of outstanding black women of Yalobusha County, it was easy for me to come up with a list of nearly 100 women. However, my list centers around Water Valley, I know I am missing those from Coffeeville and Oakland, thus I need help.

To date, I have secured several verbal commitments from individuals who are working on bios, stories, essays and memories of women who impacted their lives in a positive way. My plan is to share these accounts with you in some way.

Following the printing, on June 21, of the first article about this project in this publication and in the Tri-State Defender, the second phone call I received concerning it came from an 82-year-old Water Valley native now living in California. She left Water Valley after graduating from high school and now returns often to Water Valley and mentioned having fond memories of her black neighbors, a prominent family. She has agreed to write about her mother, who raised 10 children as a single mom and hopefully will share about her neighbors. I look forward to her stories and others.

In the past, most of us went off to school each day not knowing where or to what addresses our mothers went to work as caretakers, maids, nannies, babysitters, field hands, etc. Yet another conversation about this project with my home-girl here in Atlanta revealed that her grandmother worked for years for a family-owned retail establishment on Main Street, Water Valley. While there was no "whites only" sign, we were taught early on that we could only go in to place or pick up an order, nothing else. No sitting at the counter or in the booths.

A while back I read in this publication and learned from other sources about 100-year birthday celebrations for two outstanding women of Yalobusha, Mrs. Georgia Ann White and Mrs. Sallie Ann Polk. Both of whom I have known as strong, strong role models – not to mention their hats and stylish dress. Hats off to such great ladies!

While I wait for your bios, stories, memories and essays, here are portions of the life story of Mrs. Sallie Ann Polk in her own words at 100 years old recorded in May 2008.

"I was born in 1908. I began school when I was five and finished when I was twenty-three years old. I went to Leigh Branch School and finished at Oakland School in Oakland, Ms. We did not have school buses when we went to school, so we had to walk. It was one mile from home to Leigh Branch and two miles to Oakland School.

When I was younger, I lived on a farm and Papa raised cows, chickens and hogs. I had to do housework, barn and yard work, along with gardening. Most of our clothes were made out of flour sacks. At the age of five, that was a busy year for me because that was the year I started working. Every day was a busy day for me. I had to pull

watermelons, pick cotton, and carry water from a homemade well to the house.

When I was 13 years old, I went to town for the first time. Papa had bought me some shoes, but they were too little, so Papa had to take me to town to try on my shoes. After that I can't tell you the next time I went to town.

For entertainment, I played playhouse, ball and jump rope with grapevines or sneaked and got some of Papa's ropes, but only after all our work was done. When I was growing up there were not a lot of white people around us. The only white people that I came in contact with were Molly and Polly Gilmore."

....And perhaps contact with the Gilmore parents I would think. While Mrs. Sallie Ann had more to say about her wholesome life, her family and her love for God, what she mentioned about being able to go to town to try on shoes could get missed. The norm was that you had to maybe draw a picture of the child's foot and take it to the store. There was usually no such thing as trying on at that time in her life and lives of others.

3

Emma Spencer Gooch
A Political Activist Ahead Of Her Time

As the responses come in about Outstanding Black Women of Yalobusha County I am encouraged by the strength and fortitude of these women past and present and how we, by now participating in this process, might encourage and motivate our youth of today; how we might support our millennials who are working for equal rights and registering voters across the country in preparation for the November elections. My high school classmate, Emma Faye submitted the following essay on her grandmother, Mrs. Emma Spencer Gooch, who stood tall for civil rights and equality for women.

My first recollection of Mrs. Emma was from my seat on the school bus as it stopped on Highway 32 to pick up the riders from the Gooch Farm. I recall her giving instructions to the bus driver, earning my respect that day, not by what she said but how she said it with such authority.

I also had opportunities to observe her and several other women in leadership roles in church and yet the community has just recently come to appreciate how much they accomplished, and in most cases, with so little. So little education, so little money, so little support and in most cases fighting an uphill battle. It astounds me to think of the courage it took to speak up and speak out. I thank Mrs. Emma Spencer Gooch for speaking up and speaking out.

Alas these accounts continue to enlighten this writer. Regarding the land leased to build Davidson Schools by their great grandfather, Lucious Spencer, the Gooch Family has tried unsuccessfully to regain the titles. They are still researching even though the property is now in the hands of a private owner.

"Her life was devoted to her Community and Church. She can be best described as a community and political activist, of course way ahead of her time."

*- Emma Faye Gooch,
Emma Gooch's granddaughter*

Emma and Jim Gooch

Emma Gooch
by Emma Faye Gooch

My grandmother, Emma Spencer Gooch was born March 7th, 1906. Her parents were Maude Virginia Carr Spencer and Lucious Spencer, land owners in Yalobusha County, Mississippi. She was the seventh child of 13. Hard working as a child, she often told stories of how Papa (Lucious) taught them that education and hard work was the key to success in life. Her father leased his land to Yalobusha County to build the first colored school in Water Valley, which was known as Davidson school.

Emma married the late Jim Gooch, a sharecropper on the Alexander Farm, better known as the Gooch Farm and they had six children. She was very instrumental in running the household as a wife, mother, cook, seamstress, bookkeeper, Watkins Saleslady, and Big Mama to all her grandchildren.

In 1971, Emma moved from the Alexander Farm to Martin Street in Water Valley. Her life was devoted to her Community and Church. She was a member of Sanders Chapel Church and served as church secretary for many years. She can be best described as a community and political activist, of course way ahead of her time. This is evidenced by her active membership in the Democratic Voter Registration for African Americans, the Homemakers of America, and a member of Queen Ann Grand Chapter Order of the Eastern Star Inc. and Naomi Chapter Number 9.

Our grandmother was blessed with longevity as we have seen of quite a few other black women of Yalobusha County, living to be 97 years old. Transitioning on January 12, 2004, having impacted my life and my siblings and many others and leaving behind a legacy of well-educated and hard-working descendants.

4

Juanita Bishop-Cox
Survived Tornado, Known For Her Cooking

As each story comes my way it brings new revelations and insights into the strength and stamina of the Black Women of Yalobusha County. Below, Tywanda Harden writes about another pioneering woman, her grandmother, Mrs. Juanita Bishop Cox.

If you were to ask natives of Water Valley about this lady, I'm sure her good southern cooking skills would be a major highlight of the conversation. This lady, known by her grandkids as "Bigma," but to others as Juanita Bishop-Cox, was born October 22, 1931, the third of six siblings and lives in Water Valley.

My grandmother is not only known for her extremely good cooking, having been taught by her mother, but grew up as no stranger to her late father's farm. Hoeing, chopping and picking cotton, milking the cows, churning and making homemade butter, stripping sorghum to take to the mills for homemade molasses, and carrying water from springs, wells, and pumps were all familiar chores. It was years later before Juanita experienced what it was like to have running water from any kind of faucet.

My grandmother grew up attending the Rosenwald Bynum Community Center in Batesville Mississippi, where she walked about two miles to school, being taught by local community teachers. She completed eight years at Rosenwald before transferring to Water Valley's Davidson High School for her last four years of school.

While home was in Batesville, Juanita says that she had no choice but to either ride with someone every day or staying with friends or relatives weekly just to attend school, then returning home on weekends.

> *"She created such strong bonds and kind relationships"*
>
> - Tywanda Harden,
> Juanita Bishop-Cox's granddaughter

Working was never questionable for my grandmother, as she embarked on the role of housekeeping for numerous well-known families including Charlie Lowe, Jimmie Knight, Barbara Brown, Mary Beth Jones, Ruth Wilbert, Lawyer Troop, Earl Fly, Kate Richardson and a few others.

Eventually she decided to take on employment at the chicken plant, what was then called Motts, Inc., a local business in Water Valley since 1989. When asked to describe her job at Motts, she replied in a laughing manner, "Pulling Guts!" For anyone who knows my grandmother knows that she's also the one for good laughs.

After approximately six years at Motts, she left and decided to use her cooking skills providing meals for patients at Yalobusha General Hospital. Her employment and services in cooking then and still is today the nature of her southern hospitality at its best. After that my grandmother worked and taught classes at the Headstart Program based at Everdale Baptist Church and with the Headstart Association of Water Valley. Juanita's last corporate job was on the assembly line at Holley, the automobile parts manufacturer, until the company downsized.

Easter evening, 1984, a tornado hit the city of Water Valley, and as part of my grandmother's daily motherly routines, she had gone to Jones Supermarket, and never made it back home. Tornado winds hit the store propelling a sharp object into her left leg. She suffered a deep wound laceration to her calf that had to be skin grafted.

Juanita recalls, "I spent a total of 74 days in the hospital learning to walk on my left leg again, 17 days at Yalobusha General and 57 days at Methodist of Memphis Tennessee."

She created such strong bonds and kind relationships during her 57 days of hospitalization at Methodist, she jokingly says, "when it was time for me to leave Methodist hospital, I cried, the nurses cried and EVEN the doctors cried. It was the most embarrassing but heart-felt moment."

Today, some of her most asked for homemade dishes are chicken and dressing, pound and caramel cake and fried apple pies. My grandmother has remained a member of the Water Valley Homemaker's Club since the 1960s, and a member of Pleasant Green Missionary Baptist Church since she was nine years old. Because of her many words of wisdom, her never-ending love and exceptional example of womanhood our lives have been truly blessed.

Juanita Bishop-Cox

From Dottie Chapman Reed

While working those many jobs and furthering her career Mrs. Juanita raised five children. She now has nine grandchildren, 16 great grandchildren and two great-great grandchildren. Makes one wonder about the many other children whose lives she touched, especially while keeping house for the many families mentioned above. It would be great to hear how their lives were possibly nurtured and impacted by such a dynamic and assertive black woman. What memories, impressions, morals or experiences were bestowed on them that may still linger in their hearts. The goal of this project is to hear how black women of Yalobusha County influenced lives in positive ways. Could we possibly hear from some of them?

Tywanda mentioned briefly her grandmother's sense of humor. She always had me laughing, however I was more impressed by her style, her independence and self-confidence as a wife and a mother. I now wish I had more of her cooking and am glad it's not too late. I am planning to come home soon.

5

Readers Weigh In

This project, which launched in June, has given me an opportunity to reconnect and give back to my home community of Yalobusha County, while recognizing some outstanding black women. It has also allowed me to meet new people and learn about our history.

The idea and motivation came from remarks that were made at the funeral of my cousin, George Adams, earlier this year in Illinois. People spoke of his immense love for Water Valley and about the impact that one Sunday School teacher had on their lives.

That Sunday School teacher was my mom, thus I thought this might just be the time we pay tribute to many of those black women who impacted lives in such a way that we would still remember. In George's honor I am posting the picture below of the last time we were together in Atlanta.

Next, I would like to share a few of the comments that I have received in response to the features on Mrs. Emma Gooch and Mrs. Juanita Cox. I appreciate and thank those individuals for their comments and for permission to publish:

Comments on Article 3 - Emma Gooch

It was great reading the article you wrote in the *North Mississippi Herald* (I worked there when I was in High School) about Mrs. Emma Gooch. I did not know all the history she had. I remember as a child, buying candy from her. I will look forward to your future articles.

Eddie G. Sanders,
Detroit, MI
Davidson High School Class of 1968

I so enjoyed your article in the *North Mississippi Herald*. It was a pleasure to read about Emma Gooch. What a remarkable lady! I don't know if you have just started doing this or if I have missed some articles. I hope I haven't.

We get the Herald every week as my husband was raised in Water Valley. Our son, Lawton, lives there now. He owns The Trusty Diner.

I look forward to your future articles, looks like once a month.

People's lives are so precious!

Happy Gafford,
Orlando, FL

Comments on Article 4 - Juanita Cox

I so enjoyed your article in the Herald about Juanita. She was such a dear to my parents, Carlisle and John Throop, and to all of us Throop daughters as well. It was many a happy Saturday spent in Water Valley when we got to enjoy Juanita's wonderful fried chicken and more. She took such good care of Daddy after Mama died, and we all appreciate her!

Carlisle (Throop) Parsons Wood,
Oxford, MS

My name is Ruth Throop Wilbourn from Water Valley, MS. My family and I were privileged to have Juanita work for us for several years as well as cleaning, cooking and caring for our parents, John and Carlisle Throop until their deaths.
Juanita is a "member" of our family and always will be. I think one of my favorite dishes of hers would be good old southern fried chicken. To this day when we have fried chicken, everyone will say, "Not as good as Juanita's."

I keep up with Juanita through her granddaughter that works at the Water Valley Courthouse.

Thank you for writing this wonderful article for the Herald. I forwarded it on to my sisters, India and Carlisle and my daughters, Christy and Ashley and they all loved it!

Ruth Throop Wilbourn,
Water Valley, MS

George W. Adams passed away on April 18 and remarks made at his funeral about his love for Water Valley inspired Dottie Reed to recognize some of the black matriarchs from the county. This picture of Adams and Reed was taken the last time they were together in Atlanta.

Comments on All Articles to Date
These stories are fabulous!

When my uncle passed last year, it suddenly occurred to me that my generation of cousins is now the "elders" of our family—and we need to pass along our family/community stories or they will be lost!

Your project is a great example of why that's important. Our youth/young adults need the wisdom women like these have to share.

Adrienne S. Harris,
Swann Consulting
Atlanta, GA
www.swannconsulting.com

6

Lillie Caldwell Roberts
First to Register to Vote in Yalobusha County

Mrs. Lillie M. Roberts was born August, 1931, in Coffeeville, where she was twice married with no children. At 87, she is still an active member of the NAACP and was the treasurer for her local organization for 50 years. According to local reporting some 55 years ago, Mrs. Roberts was the first black to register to vote in Yalobusha County.

The registration office was located in the courthouse in Water Valley, one of the county seats for Yalobusha County. She tells her story in her own words in a 2015 book, Delta Jewels, In Search of My Grandmother's Wisdom, by Alysia Burton Steele.

In the book Mrs. Roberts said her decision to register to vote in the fall of 1962 came out of the blue and at a most precarious and volatile time. White folks made it clear they weren't going to let negroes vote and warned them against even going to the courthouse.

In nearby Oxford – just 18 miles north of Water Valley - James Meredith, the Black Air Force Veteran, had enrolled at Ole Miss, prompting a riot on the campus and worry in white Water Valley, that some of the upheaval and turbulence would flow into their town – especially if Dr. Martin Luther King, Jr., the Freedom Riders or other civil rights leaders were in the vicinity.

During this time, she and her first husband, Joe Caldwell, were working in Water Valley. Mrs. Lillie, as she was known, cleaned homes of whites and did other domestic work until the couple moved to Coffeeville. She was 31 years old and did not have a social security card. When she sought work, she was told she needed the card to get a job and had to ask where to go to get one.

One day, much to the couple's surprise - even bewilderment – a white county supervisor came to their home and encouraged them to register to vote. Given the moment and the place -- 1960s in Mississippi- they were dubious. The Caldwells and their black friends and neighbors were not voting because they were understandably afraid, - paying heed to the constant threats of retribution from the white community.

But the supervisor pointed out that they owned land and paid taxes and therefore had the right to vote. County officials, he said, were taking advantages of them and others by taking black folks' money but refusing to let them register and vote. Having made his pitch, the supervisor bid them good bye. Moments later he turned around and came back. Promise me you will go to the courthouse to register, he told the Caldwells, and he promised in turn that he would meet them there. All he needed to know was the time they were coming.

The next day the Caldwells set out for the Water Valley courthouse. Mr. Caldwell told his wife that since he did not read as well as she did, he would put her in line in front of him. But Mr. Caldwell was going to be prepared. He wore a pair of overalls over his regular pants, so he could carry his 38-caliber pistol in an outer pocket.

Lillie Caldwell Roberts

The couple entered the three-story building, walking side by side to the stares of white workers who had come out of their offices. Perhaps rhetorically, a few asked who they were. Mr. Caldwell never took his hands out of his pockets. They didn't see the supervisor, but his assurances had emboldened them to keep going.

When the Caldwells went into the voter registration office, a Mr. Evans took a dusty book out of a cabinet and laid it on the table. He opened the book and asked Mrs. Lillie if she knew the Constitution of the United States. Yes, she told him, though she admitted she had forgotten details because it had been a long time since she went to school. At Mr. Evans's direction, she read three or four amendments, answered a few questions and pushed the book back to him. Mr. Evans then told Mr. Caldwell that because he couldn't read or write, he shouldn't vote because he wouldn't know whom he was voting for.

But, "I got her registered," Mr. Evans said.

The couple left the courthouse with the same white folks once again staring at them from their office doorways. When the Caldwells got to their pickup truck, Mr. Caldwell told Mrs. Lillie he was going to open the door for her. And in his most chivalrous manner, he did so. In the moment, he made her feel like she was somebody. She was and is "somebody" indeed.

Mrs. Lillie Roberts still lives in Coffeeville, and of that day, she says, the *North Mississippi Herald* newspaper reported that she was the first black to register to vote. While washing dishes a day or so later at the home of a white family, she remembered, the lady of the house came up behind her. "I see you registered to vote," she said. Yes, Mrs. Lillie replied, momentarily worried about what would happen next. But nothing did.

Mrs. Lillie kept her job and remained a registered voter. She believes that several other black residents of Yalobusha County had registered before she did but did not want it made public. They worried they would lose their jobs, especially the school teachers. We all should be proud of the courage that Mrs. Lillie and Mr. Joe exhibited that precarious day in Water Valley.

What a reminder of the sacrifices that have been made in order that we can go uninhibited to the polls on November 6. Better yet, let's run to the polls out of respect for Mrs. Lillie and all the Outstanding Black Women of Yalobusha County!

Special thanks to Fred (Pee Wee) Harris, Davidson High Class of 1966, for telling me about Delta Jewels and Mrs. Roberts. Thanks to Ole Miss Assistant Professor, Alysia Burton Steele, for the permission to share this story and for the picture of Mrs. Roberts. Thanks to noted author, Nadine Cohodas for making a better writer out of me!

Mrs. Lillie was recently recognized at a senior recognition on October 14th in Coffeeville at her church as the oldest actively participating member of Pleasant Grove Church. See that coverage in the October 18th edition of the paper.

From "somebody" to HERO!, Mrs. Lillie May Roberts.

7

Letters From Vietnam Bring Memories
Love and Respect for Veterans Should Bring Us Together

In developing this project, Black Women of Yalobusha County, I have written to at least 25 churches in the county. I have reached out to my high school classmates, cousins and friends soliciting their support. As shared in a previous article I continue to receive comments and encouragement from a wide range of readers and other individuals. The total responses have been overwhelming, and my heart overflows. The project is rapidly developing and growing larger than I ever imagined. I hope you will continue to join me on this journey.

While the purpose of the project is to honor black women of Yalobusha, past and present, who have had a positive impact on the community, as Veterans Day approaches I want to share letters that my brother, Floyd Alfred Chapman, wrote to our mother, Helen, from Vietnam.

If my memory serves me correct, he was drafted in the Army while working in Davenport Iowa, sometime after his high school graduation in 1967. He found himself in the military with three first cousins, brothers, E.L Chapman (Army), Ronnie/Raymond Chapman (Army) and Willie James Chapman (Marines).

Perhaps these letters prompt us to reflect, particularly during this time when America is so divided, and we are literally days away from the mid-term elections. I love and respect our veterans and our country and always will regardless of the issues that so often now are misinterpreted, misrepresented and are pulling us apart.

My oldest son is a second lieutenant in the Army married to a sergeant in the Air Force. My middle son completed four years at West Point Military Academy. I have a host of friends and second cousins active, disabled and retired military. I thank them and all veterans and active duty personnel.

Reprinted below are two letters written by my brother, (Gabby):

April 17, 1969

Dear Mother,
How is life? don't never be worrying about me. If anything bad happen to me the Red Cross will let you know. I just got a little cut or nick it was not bad enough to worry about. I just told Aunt Mary Hester something to be talking about. I just got all of the pictures and was they nice. I am still showing them to peoples. They was real nice send some more if you have the chance.

I could use 2 box too. Tell daddy to send me a picture of him. All the boys want to see a picture of him and his little red truck. Your car is pretty. I want forget you on Mother's Day.
Floyd

Excerpts from a second letter:

Hello Mother how is everything I am fine, don't have much time, am a little sleepy. I been sitting up here arguing with a boy about the Church of Christ. Today is the 18th I know you are getting ready for Christmas. On Christmas Day at 12 o'clock you send up a prayer for me and I will do the same at the same time how did you like my pictures. Today we walk 4 miles in about 30 or 40 minutes to help a company out I was point man and I really made them boys behind me walk. When we get there jets had kill most of them

Page 2: *they had drop booms on them and we caught 8 and they gave up without a fight I was glad of that*

Page 4: *I have wrote you too much now will send you extra money the last of this mt. Do what you want with it Keep your car in good shape I will send the church some money soon I would give a million dollars to see Tomie kids now Well this is about all for now. O yes! I dream the other night that daddy and Mr. Edd Wright came over here (Smile) but daddy was not looking well. tell him to drink some milk for me*

wish I was there (Floyd) Merry Christmas.

It had been a while since I read these letters, and again I come away with even more mixed emotions. As you see, Gabby was not great with punctuation and grammar. I had forgotten about the boxes of canned foods and things we mailed out almost weekly as I am sure most military families, organizations and Americans also did. Postage from the soldiers was free then, and I hope that holds true today.

Gabby and my cousin, Ronnie, were able to get together while in Vietnam for some R & R (rest and relaxation). They both made it home with no physical injuries and so did E.L. and Willie James. However, like so many of our Vietnam veterans, Gabby and Ronnie clearly exhibited mental and emotions scars.

Gabby died the fall of my senior year in college, 1973, of carbon monoxide poisoning emitted from a television in his apartment in Davenport, Iowa. Ronnie left us early as well. Rest in peace you guys!

Floyd "Gabby" Chapman

8

Rosa White Wright
From Legacy to Dynasty

I got my driver's licenses at 15, and one of my short cuts from school was through what we called the North End. I always looked for Mrs. Rosa Wright sitting on her porch at 219 West Lee Street. The same was true when I was much younger and walked home with my Aunt Pit (Betsy Finch).

On our way my Aunt always stopped to chat with Mrs. Rosa, who personified what we do not have any more - neighbors who watched out for the school children and the neighborhood. Legacy is the word that her daughter, Carolyn, a retired Army veteran, used in her account below about her mother, but Dynasty is a much more appropriate description!

From the 11 offspring born to Rosa and Hezzie Wright, have come several college graduates, bankers, entrepreneurs, a chemical engineer, a preacher, an educator, an army reservist, active duty and retired military. They have degrees from Mississippi State University, Ole Miss, and Delta State to name a few.

A great grandson currently attends the University of Kentucky and announces UK basketball. Their accomplishments are beyond remarkable. I am proud to claim some kinship. Her late daughter, Earline and her husband, John Hawkins, never missed an opportunity to encourage me when I was in school, and then they sent a

Rosa White-Wright

courageous first black cheerleader to Ole Miss, who took a victorious stand against using the Rebel flag.

Now another son serves as the Chief of University Police at Ole Miss in Oxford.

And I, the first black Ole Miss Admissions Counselor- the first black hired on the administration level - am more than proud and humbled to have known Mrs. Rosa and Mr. Hezzie Wright.

Now enjoy what Carolyn shares with us about her mother:

> *"From the fruits of her labor our mother's dreams have become a reality and her descendants continue to achieve excellence and give service to mankind and the community."*
>
> *- Carolyn Wright*
> *Rosa Wright's daughter*

A Woman with a Legacy
by Carolyn Wright

Rosa Virginia White Wright, a determined and courageous black woman of the past, began as a sharecropper's daughter, and the oldest child of Hattie and William White. Rosa was taught leadership and how to become a hard worker. She believed in human rights and stood firmly on her beliefs.

Rosa's parents moved from Water Valley, but she remained in Yalobusha County. She raised a family of her own with her husband, Hezzie Wright, and 11 children on the land of white owners, until they were able to purchase their own home on West Lee Street in 1957.

Living in the City of Water Valley, Rosa became a caregiver to those who were elderly, hungry, or without family to help and the sick. She worked occasionally for Peewee and Frances Sartain's Restaurant and often catered for the First Baptist Church in Water Valley.

My mother was there for her family and produced high school and college graduates, something she and my father were unable to achieve. They were born in a time when such achievements for African Americans were not only difficult, but most times impossible. Rosa was determined her family would have a better life.

Spirituality, hard work and education were principles that my mother instilled in our family prior to her death in 1979 at the age of 60. Through our families and our accomplishments, our aim has been to encourage and impact future generations in keeping with our mother's example. From the fruits of her labor our mother's dreams have become a reality and her descendants continue to achieve excellence and give service to mankind and the community. Her legacy lives on and the dynasty reigns.

Thank you Mama!

9

Mother and Daughter Played Key Roles in the integration of Water Valley High in 1966

Turbulence - both foreign and domestic - dominated the 22 months between January 1966 and October 1967. Not only was the nation enmeshed in the Vietnam war, but on the home front African Americans stepped up their drive to ensure the full legal equality promised under the Constitution, including enforcement of recently passed laws designed to grant access to public facilities, housing, education and the ballot box.

A timeline of events from this period illustrates the tumult, with some of the signal moments occurring in Mississippi.

In August 1966, amid the tensions of the time, Mable Hervey hesitantly allowed her oldest daughter, Annette, to join two other high school seniors to become the first black students to attend Water Valley High School. The late Dorothy Boston, Dorothy Neely and Annette made history when they enrolled at Water Valley High, and then became the first black students to graduate from the formerly all-white school in May 1967. What courage it must have taken for this mother to acquiesce in her daughter's desire for a better education, though she surely knew that her child could be a catalyst for integration in the segregated South.

What gave Mable Hervey this strength, when the average mother is so often filled with anxiety simply sending a child to his or her first day of elementary school? Mrs. Hervey knew that the first day for Annette and the other girls could go very, very wrong. Fortunately, it did not.

Here is how Annette describes her mom today and recounts their life experiences in Yalobusha County:

My mother, Mable Alexander-Hervey was born April 27, 1926. She was married to Ned L. Hervey and eight children were born from this union. Her parents, Cleveland Alexander and Hattie Person-Alexander were share croppers. Mable was the 4th of eight children, six girls and 2 boys. She worked on her father-in-law Esley Hervey's farm, at the Motts Poultry factory in Water Valley, and retired from Harley's Tool plant.

My mother was an active member of the usher board at Pine Grove East Church, until her health began to decline earlier this year. She always responded to the request when called upon to usher for funerals and worked with the Mt. Moriah Association. Mom currently lives with my youngest sister, Elgenia McClish in Wichita, Kansas. When she gets the urge to check on the home place my brother, Jesse, a wounded Vietnam veteran, travels from Delaware to accompany her to Mississippi.

When she was more active, her hobbies included quilting, working in the yard with her flowers, canning and freezing food. All the neighbors knew she enjoyed putting up vegetables and would often stop by to give her fruits and vegetables. My mother loved entertaining after Sunday church, getting up early every Sunday to cook dinner before she attended service, and having her sister, Hattie Walls and others stop by to have dinner with her later. Mom often took food

1966

January 10 – NAACP local chapter president Vernon Dahmer is injured by a bomb in Hattiesburg, Mississippi. He dies the next day.

June 5 – James Meredith begins a solitary March Against Fear from Memphis, Tennessee to Jackson, Mississippi. Shortly after starting, he is shot with birdshot and injured. Civil rights leaders and organizations rally and continue the march leading to, on June 16, Stokely Carmichael first using the slogan Black power in a speech. Twenty-five thousand marchers entered the capital.

Summer – The Chicago Open Housing Movement, led by Martin Luther King, Jr., James Bevel and Al Raby, includes a large rally, marches, and demands to Mayor Richard J. Daley and the City of Chicago which are discussed in a movement-ending Summit Conference.

October – Black Panther Party founded by Huey P. Newton and Bobby Seale in Oakland, California.

1967

April 4 – MLK delivers "Beyond Vietnam" speech, calling for defeat of "the giant triplets of racism, materialism, and militarism".

June 12 – In Loving v. Virginia, the U.S. Supreme Court rules that prohibiting interracial marriage is unconstitutional.

In the trial of accused killers in the murders of Chaney, Goodman, and Schwerner, the jury convicts 7 of 18 accused men. Conspirator Edgar Ray Killen is later convicted in 2005.

June - August – Over 150 communities burn during the Long, Hot Summer of 1967. The largest and deadliest riots of the summer take place in Newark, New Jersey and Detroit with 26 fatalities reported in Newark and 43 people losing their lives in the Motor City.

October 2 – Thurgood Marshall is sworn in as the first African-American justice of the United States Supreme Court.

to her sister-in-law and sick and shut-in neighbors. Now at 92, she still loves fishing and goes as often as someone will take her.

My mother believes in education, when she was not able to help me with my math, she would drive me to Mr. John Eddie Wright's house, where he tutored me. She still stresses to her grandchildren that education is one of the keys to success. When asked for her thoughts now about my deciding to attend Water Valley High she says she became comfortable with my decision because she knew that I love to do my best in what I love.

Whatever Mrs. Mable Hervey and Annette Hervey Westmoreland are made of, I hope I have some. In addition to Annette and Jesse, Mrs. Mable has a daughter, Mable Lynn and son, DeRoy who live in Maryland, two sons, Amos and George and daughter, Elgenia all living in Wichita, Kansas. Her daughter Flora passed away in 1993. Flora and I spent a summer working at Headstart together and became fast friends. The union of Mr. Ned and Mrs. Mable Hervey has produced 21 grandchildren, 43 great grandchildren and 11 great-great grandchildren.

I find it perplexing that Annette had not previously spoken at length about her experience integrating WVHS. Here is how she now recalls the experience:

I attended Water Valley High School my last year of high school, 1966-1967. At that time, they were letting certain grades integrate the school, and you did not need your parents' signature, I signed myself up. I talked to my teachers and principal at Davidson High [the school for Black students] and they were okay with it, and I went for it. I decided to go for one reason only: I knew Water Valley High had the best curriculum and classes.

I did not have any major problems at WVHS. I lived on the farm and had to be bussed to school. The superintendent/principal had me sitting on the very front seat of the school bus so the driver could have a clear view of me. I usually had the seat by myself, but one young girl would always sit on the seat with me. I guess she figured out that I was not contagious. My mom was not happy about it when she found out I had signed myself up. However, my dad never showed any negative feelings about me going to WVHS. I have attended a few of the WVHS class reunions, but I always attend the class reunion of Davidson High, because I was with them 11 years.

Annette's telling makes this historical moment sound much too routine. I needed more clarification, and so I asked more questions. Here is what I learned:

Annette heard about the opportunity to attend WVHS from the Davidson teachers and staff. She and Dorothy Neely talked about enrolling together. Annette admits that her mother had some concerns and reservations, while her father and siblings were okay with it from the start. When I asked how the Boston and Neely families – and other black families reacted, she said she heard nothing largely because these families didn't see each other regularly. The girls only went to school and town on the weekend, and because the families didn't go to the same church, the girls only saw their friends at school. However, Annette felt that the black community was supportive overall.

The girls took all of their classes together, and Annette added that the teachers – all of them white - treated them fairly and even with kindness. She truly admired one teacher, Mrs. Harvey.

Annette believed they were adequately prepared to succeed at WVHS because they had done well at Davidson. They also believed that is why the teachers and principal supported them when they applied to attend WVHS. Annette felt that they represented themselves, their families and the black community well and did participate in some extracurricular activities.

When asked about the attitudes of the white student body, Annette described them as "okay." She and the other two girls did not hang out with them at all, and she continued, "As long as they didn't bother us we were okay with being there. " The three made it a point to ignore any racist comments or outward bias. But she noted that while she and her friends sat together at lunch every day in the cafeteria, none of the other students joined them.

Asked if she made any friends that she has maintained to date, she mentioned Linda Winters and Diane Redwine, girls "who had no problem with blacks," she said.

Annette graduated and started college at Northwest Mississippi Junior College went on to Jackson State College and graduated from Spencerian College of Business in Milwaukee, Wis. She earned a Christian Education Diploma from American Baptist College, became a certified Dean for Christian Leadership School through the Sunday School Publishing Board and National Baptist Congress of Christian Education.

Engaged in the greater Milwaukee community, Annette served as a Dean of

Mable Hervey

Annette Hervey Westmoreland

Christian Education, Christian Education Team Leader, Sunday School Teacher and Angel Choir Pianist at Mount Olive Baptist Church in the city. She was also an Associate Dean of the Wisconsin General Baptist State Congress of Christian Education. Annette volunteered with Child Evangelism, an after-school program in some of the Milwaukee area schools. She continues that volunteer work now in Arizona.

When in college she began a 37-plus year career with Miller Brewing Company, retiring in 2010. Annette and her husband, Lee, have four adult children, four grandchildren and now reside in Buckeye, Arizona.

While Annette and her mom handled the integration of Water Valley High almost casually, their apparent calm masked a much more complicated atmosphere behind the scenes - some aspects likely forever hidden. As a freshman in high school at Davidson at the time I knew that all eyes were on the situation. There was an unspoken tension coupled with a lot of prayers that all would go well for them.

Annette, Dorothy B. and Dorothy N. had the courage to be first. Attempts to reach Ms. Neely have thus far been unsuccessful, but I plan to keep trying to reach her. Though I could have attended Water Valley High for my last two years of high school, I chose not to. The white students – who passed me every day on their bus ride to school – made it clear from the faces they made through the windows along with the occasional comment that I would not be welcome.

We are grateful for these brave women and for the mothers, fathers and families who forged ahead in 1967-68. Their efforts were crucial as the school system moved to total integration and Davidson High School graduated its last class in 1970.

A December 2014 article in the *Jackson Free Press* - "Then and Now: When 'School Choice' Creates a Divide" – provides history and context for this complex moment:

Between the 1950's and the end of the century, former Mississippi Governor William Winter, said Mississippians desire for an improved education system increased. During most of the mid-20th century, white

Mississippians supported funding quality public education—as long as schools were segregated racially.

Before the Supreme Court's 1954 Brown vs. Topeka Board of Education case, which declared school segregation unconstitutional, leaders in Mississippi didn't have an interest in "school choice." It wasn't until segregationists lost the battle to keep white public schools white that the attacks on public schools—and the demand for "school choice"—began in earnest.

Avoiding Desegregation

"School choice" is a hot-button political phrase, used in some form since the 1960s. At its most generic, it means giving parents an option of where to send their kids to school beyond the traditional public school of the district in which they live, while still using public dollars, such as with charter schools. In recent decades, "school choice" was a kinder, gentler way to refer to school vouchers, meaning that a family could get a "voucher" for taxes they paid and use the funds at a private school instead, a failed idea that is regaining political traction.

During legal segregation years, it was a ploy called "freedom-of-choice" that Mississippi began to implement after Brown specifically to avoid desegregating public schools. After the 1954 Brown decision, the state of Mississippi first ignored the federal mandate to integrate. But when the 1964 Civil Rights Act passed, Mississippi was at risk of losing its federal funding for public schools if it did not desegregate public schools. In 1965, the state agreed to follow the act, but tried to avoid desegregation in other ways—especially with its "freedom of choice" strategy.

School districts allowed parents to cross district lines when determining where to send their kids to school—black children could go to white schools, but most wouldn't. The African American families who did send their children to white schools were met with the loss of jobs, cross burnings, harassment and eviction. Black families feared for their children's safety in white schools.

"Freedom-of-choice plans left segregated patterns of schooling in Mississippi all but untouched; the reasons had little to do with either freedom or choice," historian Joseph Crespino writes in his book, "In Search of Another Country: Mississippi and the Conservative Counterrevolution."

Private "segregation academies"—which only allowed white students—began to pop up across the state after Brown and especially after the 1970 order from the 5th U.S. Circuit Court of Appeals to desegregate.

The greatest hike in private academies was from 1968-1971, in which they grew from educating just over 5,000 to 40,000 students in the state as the court grew closer to forcing southern schools to desegregate in early 1970."

10

Annie Givens and Joann Bratton
Neighbors With A Special Bond

In Marian Wright Edelman's book *Lanterns: A Memoir of Mentors*, published in 1999, the New York Times bestselling author shares stories from her life at the center of the century's most dramatic civil rights struggles. She was the first and only black female lawyer in Mississippi in the 1960s. In this book she pays tribute to the outstanding personal mentors who impacted her life: Martin Luther King, Jr., Robert F. Kennedy, Fannie Lou Hamer, Medgar Evers, Dr. Benjamin E. Mays, Unita Blackwell and many others. Her life is what this girl and possibly every black girl in the South longed to live, and I love how she has shared it in this book.

While I have several take-aways from Lanterns, I quickly relate it to this Outstanding Black Women of Yalobusha County Project (BWOYC) because she writes about the women she described as community elders – co-parents and mentors in Bennettsville, South Carolina who influenced her life, an extraordinary life.

Marian also noted with appreciation observations from Andrew Young, the former US ambassador to the United Nations, former Atlanta mayor, and civil rights advocate: "God has ways of acting anonymously" - to set the stage for the workings of His Justice. Marian echoes those thoughts: "God chooses the actors, the times, the places, sets the stage, lifts the curtain, and begins the drama," she writes, and continues with this charge: "Our task is to be ready to play our parts and to do the work God has assigned us, without anxiety, according to strengths and gifts we are given."

Can you – can we – answer Edelman's charge affirmatively? Have we completed or achieved this task? If not, do we yet have time? Are we currently using our gifts and talents to make a difference in someone's life? What can we do to bridge the racial divide permeating our country and our communities today? What can we do to alleviate poverty and ensure adequate health care? What can we do to improve the image of Mississippi? Does it matter? Are we content? Are we discouraged or simply just don't care?

As 2019 approaches can we commit to doing something positive to make a difference, if just for a neighbor next door? The story of the latest actor in this BWOYC Project suggests Mississippi at its best. Mrs. Joann Bratton, now 85 years old, had left a voice mail for me on Thursday, November 8, telling me she had read my columns and wanted to recommend a woman if she was not already in my plan.

Mrs. Bratton explained that she lived in Water Valley for a couple of years and had the most wonderful neighbor, Mrs. Annie Givens. Mrs. Bratton now resides in Oxford and told me it would be such a loss if Mrs. Givens was not included in this project.

"You know I am white," Mrs. Bratton said.

"I know," I replied.

"I don't know how you know but that's okay," she said.

And I just laughed.

Mrs. Bratton began to tell me about Mrs. Givens, who lived across the street from her on Wagner Street.

One day while she was away from home a severe storm arose, and she worried because she had left her windows open. When she returned, she found that Mrs. Givens had come over and was able to close all the windows – a testament to the comfort between the Brattons and the Givens. My family lived on the same route further out, where later the street was named Wagner Extended. If memory serves it was not that unusual in Water Valley to find a few black families sprinkled in white neighborhoods closer to downtown. This wasn't the case in every neighborhood - and unlike most towns in Mississippi, thankfully, no harm came to Mrs. Givens going into a white woman's home when she was not there. And yet today we still hear folks speak of the days when we were able to leave our doors unlocked day and night. No more days like that.

Then Mrs. Bratton explained how her little daughter, Dawn, would go across the street to Mrs. Givens' house and Mrs. Givens would always check to see if she had permission to come over. When other white neighbors mentioned that Mrs. Givens was involved in the NAACP, Mrs. Bratton had a ready reply: "If I were black, I would be also."

She believes that Mrs. Givens' late husband was a preacher at a local Baptist church.

When I asked Mrs. Bratton if she would write more about her memories of Mrs. Givens, she explained that she had just finished writing her brother's obituary and her husband is in hospice. My heart breaks for her, and I expressed my sympathy and concern. She also reminded me that she is 85 years old and her memory is not 100 percent.

I told her that I knew Mrs. Givens, and she is definitely on my list of approximately 100 women, most from Water Valley, whose contributions to the black community I would like to learn more about.

While I am researching, I would love to hear from anyone who has more information about Mrs. Annie Givens. I know she was a very active member of Everdale Baptist Church. My mother and I walked past her house on our way home, many, many times stopping to get water, or to watch as she worked in her flower garden. Her facial expression always said to me, "Tell me what you are going to be, what are you doing to better yourself. "

She pushed young folks to the highest standards, and I admit that I often tried to avoid her on the street or whenever I saw her at her church! I knew she would expect a full report on my grades, my activities and my plans. And for this alone she made the list.

My high school classmate, Carolyn Wright, whom you heard from in the Rosa Wright story, was really the first to recommend Mrs. Givens. Carolyn told me when she arrived for church one Sunday and found her name listed to serve during worship that morning, she knew Mrs. Givens had volunteered her. Mrs. Givens was one of the Youth Directors at Everdale Baptist Church. So more to come about her, I hope.

Alas, my mind goes back to Mrs. Bratton. While she is mourning the loss of her brother and caring for, and witnessing her husband's decline, she is nonetheless thinking of someone else. We agree to talk later, and I proceed.

11

Readers Weigh In On Project at Year End

As we say so long to an almost indescribable year, I had no idea that this project would be born and survive for six months, birthing 11 articles featuring ordinary yet outstanding black women of Yalobusha County. Moving into 2019, a university has offered to support this project, and I will share about the partnership as it evolves. The goal is to archive, document, and discover more wonderful history about women who continue to positively impact our lives and community.

Thanks to all the contributors, subscribers and readers. I appreciate your recommendations and continued support, which has been so gratifying. Article five featured comments and further insights about the lives of outstanding women such as, Mrs. Sallie Ann Polk, Mrs. Emma Gooch and Mrs. Juanita Cox. While the editors and staff have captured some the positive local comments, I am sharing here more of those that I have received from across the country.

Comments on Article 1:

Hello Mrs. Dottie, I hope this message finds you smiling because after reading today's newspaper, it brought a few tears and a big smile reading about my favorite uncle George. These are the words I heard from you at the homegoing service. Oh, how I miss Uncle George and I just want to say thanks for writing this.
*Velisa Adams,
Oakland, MS*

Comments on Article 2 - Sallie Polk:

This is awesome. There are so many untold stories that need to be documented. Looking forward to more of your discoveries.
*Pam Simmons,
Tucker, GA*

Comments on Article 5:

Thank you for your great work and sharing this marvelous enterprise with me. I am yet pursuing information on Annie K. Montgomery. In addition to Mrs. Montgomery, there are several other women I hope to share with you. Keep up the good work. You make us all proud and grateful.

Your brother in the continuing cause of freedom and destiny of people of color!
*Thomas L. Brown,
Stone Mountain, GA*

I love your articles. This is so amazing, and I am working on something right now. I would love to write about how my grandma, Cleala Mae Adams, impacted my life. She was so precious to us. I wish she was still here with us. She taught me to follow my dreams and with me being a hair dresser she would often tell me, "Don't you mess these people heads up because they will have my name all over town". There were so many special things she told me, and they stick with me every day of my life. Another beautiful memory of my grandma is when she would tell us, "The Early Bird gets the worm." I didn't really know what that meant at the time. Thank you for everything you said about my uncle George, if he was here I know he would drive all the way to Mississippi to get a paper. He had a good impact on everyone. I miss my dad, Lester, a lot and I can't leave him out as he made me who I am today. Again, thanks for all you are doing! You are a blessing.

Velisa Adams,
Oakland MS

Comments on Article 6 - Lillie Roberts:

After re-reading my comments below I just wanted to say that I also love the positive strength, and actions and accomplishments covered in your article!

Once again, a fantastic and real life informative story of the prejudice and struggles which still exist today! I grew up in NJ for 27 years before being transferred to Florida by DJ in the early 70's to cover Florida, Georgia and Alabama. I really was stupefied to see the signs and ways prejudice still existed in the Deep South. Just another great article!

Jim Brzoska,
Deltona, FL

Hi! Another news breaking and informative article. Thank you for answering the call to bring forth history and heritage that has gone untold.

Thomas L. Brown,
Stone Mountain, GA

I love what you are doing? Now this is history! I live in Oakland MS and I get the paper delivered every week. I told my mama and sisters about what you are doing, and some people only buy the newspaper when it's something happening or big going on. My husband reads it constantly. I see your work every week. We are loving what you do.

Velisa Adams,
Oakland, MS

**Comments on Article 7 -
Tribute to Veterans:**

Very nice touch, Vietnam… couple of thoughts:

Your mother like thousands of black mothers agonized over their sons being there. Proportionately black mothers worried in greater numbers because their sons were on the front lines in greater numbers proportionately. Meanwhile: back in the states black mothers - most mothers -were torn between supporting their sons and not supporting a war they disagree with...

Just some first blush impressions... I really love the column....I'm infatuated with all things Vietnam.

Good work….,
James L. Hull,
Tupelo, MS

Comments on Article 8 - Rosa Wright:

I got so caught up in Thanksgiving preparations and having lots of family visiting, that I've just had a chance to enjoy your latest article. I think it's extremely inspirational to focus on the strong women who have pushed our society forward and made the world a better place. I think it focuses people on what is most important in life—not just chasing wealth and fame for yourself.

I thought of this story as I voted today in the early voting session in the runoff for the Secretary of State. There were strong women—black and white—serving as volunteers at the polls, making sure things are done right. There are still good, strong women making the world work.

Maryann McGuire,
Atlanta, GA

Thanks for the article on Ms. Rosa. I always made it a point to visit her when I went to Water Valley. Leon and William are two of my best friends still. Leon was in my wedding when I got married in Jackson. Keep up the awesome work you are doing! You bring back memories and knowledge. Happy Thanksgiving!
Eddie G. Sanders,
Davidson High School Graduate 1968 -
Southfield, Michigan

Comments on Article 9 - the Herveys and Integration:

Thanks for your article on Annette, Dorothy and Dorothy. I know it took a lot of courage and faith for them to make the decision to be the first to integrate Water Valley High School. Later, two of my classmates at Davidson High School, Martha Hoskins and Carolyn Cook transferred to Water Valley High. Racial tensions were high in the 60s and early 70s. I was a student at Jackson State University when on May 15, 1970 the Mississippi State Police and Jackson City police killed two students on Jackson State University.
Eddie G. Sanders

Annette, thanks for sharing! The article was well written. I would love to have a copy of the paper............Love it! Again, special thanks to you all.
Dorothy Neely Middleton,
Jackson, MS

Comments on Article 10 - Annie Givens and Joann Bratton:

Outstanding job of capturing a valuable part of the country's history for future generations, of all races and gender, to both learn and build from.
Mitchell Payne,
Louisville, KY

I remember Mrs. Annie Givens, she was the Dean of the (Baptist) Association and a good friend of Cousin Elgenia Hervey, whose son stayed around Mrs. Givens all the time; Roy Hervey, who has passed away. Mt. Moriah Association is our District. I had one of the Christian Education cards that she signed as a Dean somewhere, I had not finished High School.
Annette Westmoreland,
Buckeye, AZ

Comments on the Overall Project

I absolutely LOVE your project! Reading about the strong, "pioneering" Black Women of Yalobusha County is so inspiring. And you, you are quite a writer. This has to become a book Dottie. I enjoyed the reading, the education, and then, the "unspoken" questions that creep through...like, Emma Faye's piece about....'What ever happened to the Gooch's land that was so-called 'leased' to the County? Huh?' Ain't somebody due for some restitution, or compensation, or something?" ... Keep on writing.

...... recognizing these articles for the historic jewels that they are. Not only to honor the strong, courageous Women, but the brief stories of their lives give insight into some telling timelines of history in Yalobusha County that may otherwise never be given. This project is remarkable. I've always wanted to do something similar, across genders, in my home of Tunica County. So, as you publish more, let me know. I love reading them.

It appears the university has recognized these articles for the historic jewels that they are.
Ken Weeden,
Raleigh, NC

I'm so happy you decided to write these articles about these amazing women. What can I say but Wow! Excellent! History at its finest. I feel inspired and empowered. These

remarkable women's stories do deserve to be told. In addition, acknowledged for their strength and courage. Thank you for sharing Gabby and Ronnie with us. So many served in Vietnam and never made it back home. I'm so proud of you and please send me Article 10.
Warm regards,
Phyllis Pearson,
South Fulton, GA

Dottie,
Thank you for your articles on the Outstanding Black Women of Yalobusha County. I enjoyed reading them. The women mentioned in your articles had strong faith, courage, determination and the will to succeed. I salute and applaud you for the hard work you have done to share their stories. I look forward to reading your upcoming articles.
Eddie G. Sanders

Hey Dottie, I have sincerely enjoyed all the articles, especially the one about the first black person to register to vote in Water Valley, Mrs. Lillian Roberts. I had heard about her from her cousin, James Wilson, another Water Valley native. When he told me about her being featured in a book, I ordered it right away. And then Annette Hervey, Dorothy Boston and Dorothy Neely were brave indeed to be the first to do something so special as integrating Water Valley High School in their senior year when they could have just stayed put. They broke the ice and made it easier for those who came behind them. I enjoyed the article about Mrs. Rosa Wright, having known her sons quite well. Lastly, your brother Floyd was my Davidson classmate, Class of 66, so it was nice to hear, in his own words, about his Vietnam experience and to appreciate his courage and bravery.
Fred (Pee Wee) Harris,
Seattle WA

Happy Thanksgiving to you and the family. Your articles are talked about all over the Valley. Keep up the good work.
Emma Gooch,
Water Valley, MS

Dear Ms. Reed,
I have been reading your recent contributions to the *North Mississippi Herald* with great interest, both as a new Vallian (I moved to WV five years ago) and as a historian. While the paper does discuss history through old headlines, none of it feels as alive as the profiles you present. More generally, I fully agree with your assessment that the people you discuss deserve a lot more public attention than they have received up to now.
Nicolas Trepanier,
Water Valley, M

In closing, I have included a picture of my grandmother, Jane Ophelia Williams (Taliaferro Pritchard) in the white bonnet on the second row, standing on the steps of the Water Valley courthouse. I hope that someone can identify the other women or the occasion that appears to have been some type of giveaway seeing that they are holding bags in their hands. Please keep your comments, recommendations and stories coming.

With Great Expectations, Happy 2019 to ALL!

Mae Turner White and Bettye White Milledge: Mothers and Mentors

The magic of this project, Outstanding Black Women of Yalobusha County, allows us to identify and tell, in any form, the stories of amazing women, living or dead, who have influenced lives in a profound way.

Wade and Dorothy Mae White's house was always a home away from home for me, and it remains so today. If I need a place to stay in Water Valley, the welcome mat is always out, and the door is always open. The first time I spent the night at the White's house in elementary school, I was in awe of the family dynamics: four girls and two boys.

The baby girl, Alice Faye, was my best friend. Her sisters were so beautiful, and her dad was too funny. However, I was almost afraid of her mom. But because she ran her family with such power and finesse, I was able to see that the key to holding it all together was love and the love of the Lord. Mrs. Mae yet holds that strength, even after having recently lost a third child. Today, you can still see the results of that strength in her daughters, nieces, nephews and grandchildren.

The pain on Mrs. Mae's face is visible when she mentions that her feet hurt now from the 26 years that she stood in water on concrete floors on the assembly line at Mott's chicken processing plant. Why did she and so many others do it? To provide for their families is why – because farming and cleaning white families' homes could no longer secure their basic needs.

Mrs. Mae, though, worked for more than just her husband and six children. In 1969 she lost her sister, Velma Joiner, a mother of seven children – four boys and 3 girls – living in Memphis and ranging in age from 16 to 3. Mrs. Mae took the youngest two girls full-time until they were old enough to start school with their family in Memphis. She probably worked the night shift at the chicken plant to be available to care for the girls during the day. Mrs. Mae became and still is the surrogate mother for the Joiner children. She raised her six and her sister's seven with the help of her youngest sister, Asariner, known as Rene, and her husband, Mr. Wade.

Every weekend following their mother's death, the Joiner children came to the White's house, and it became their second home. Even though their Aunt Rene lived in Wisconsin, she helped transport the children to Water Valley as often as she could. The boys continued to attend school in Memphis during the week. But they looked forward to the weekends, feeling loved and nurtured with cousins and friends they made through the White family.

As soon as Marvin, the oldest son, was able to drive, he and his dad and three brothers came to Water Valley every weekend to be with the girls. The youngest girl, Jackie, went on to play scholarship basketball for Northwest Junior College and DePaul University. She now works in the sheriff's department in Shelby County, Tenn.

Today, Marvin recalls how much he enjoyed the family surroundings, especially the baseball diamond that was in the White's front yard, where kids from all around came to play.

This became so routine, he said, that no one had to tell the kids when it was time to go home. Marvin, who is now retired after 39 years with Humko Chemical Company, described how his cousin, Bettye, stayed with them in Memphis during the summers and jokingly remembered how she made sure they always looked presentable in matching clothes — no stripes and checks together!

Back in Water Valley, Bettye was a magnet for family and friends who gathered at the White compound in the evenings for basketball games, roasting marshmallows, and generally having a great time. And through her example, she imbued everyone around her with hope, aspirations and a strong moral code.

Bettye White Milledge, Mrs. Mae's oldest daughter, is a present day Outstanding Black Woman of Yalobusha County. Her resume overwhelms me. She graduated from Davidson High in 1966, married her high school sweetheart, moved to Chicago, and raised a son and daughter. But Bettye never lost her determination to continue her education. She had earned over 100 hours at Malcolm X College when she transferred to Roosevelt College to complete a Bachelor of General Studies degree in 1979 with a concentration in early childhood education. In 1985, she earned her Master of Science degree with a concentration in administration and rehabilitation from DePaul University.

"Through her example, she imbued everyone around her with hope, aspirations and a strong moral code."

Bettye's career includes several key positions in education in Illinois, Michigan, Texas, Ohio and Georgia. Since 1996, she has worked as the senior regional director for Charter School Administration Services based in Oak Park, Mich. She is also the Superintendent for CSAS Texas Schools. Bettye has been the lead person in the startup of 11 charter schools. Educators in Kansas, Arizona, and Florida have drawn on her expertise. Her extensive volunteerism includes work with Optimist International - as member, trainer, and president of the club and lieutenant governor of seven clubs. She also worked as a member of the Advisory Council on Adult, Vocational, and Technical Education, appointed by former Illinois governor James R. Thompson.

However, her passion is in her educational consulting business, where she mentors young black women and men who want to start their own businesses and/or complete their education. She has successfully mentored many from within the charter school arena, especially encouraging the teacher's aides to complete degrees so they could become teachers or work in administration.

Closer to home, when her son-in-law became so dissatisfied with his work that he had to leave, she coached him on starting his own endeavor: a dental assistant training institute in Georgia. His school, now in its third year and open to those who have finished high school, has graduated three classes and has established strong ties with the medical community, resulting in successful placements for his graduates.

Bettye White Milledge

Even closer, Bettye's daughter, Angelia, is administrative assistant to the chairman of the Paulding County, Georgia, board of commissioners.

Bettye shares her love and the importance of reading with her mentees in workshops and in her training sessions with charter school teachers. Her granddaughter, a junior in high school, passes through the room while Bettye and I are talking and happens to mention that with a few days left in 2018, she has read 30-plus books this year and is still counting.

Reflecting on her childhood in Water Valley, Bettye appreciates the closeness of her immediate family and her Sanders Chapel Church family. Potluck dinners and BTU (Baptist Training Union) meetings stand out. She remembers, too, getting off the school bus and heading to their fish pond, eating plums and blackberries on the way. An even bigger treat was the occasional visit to Mr. Jesse Woodard's fish pond in nearby Panola County, which was always so well-stocked.

Bettye was super active and very popular in high school. She played basketball, sang in the glee club, and was a member of the Honor Society and the Student Council. On the state level, Bettye was president of the 4H Club. She loved high school at Davidson and credits her late teachers, Margaret Burgess Campbell and Mary Louise Campbell, for her love of education. The latter teacher gave her a C in math, and Bettye, accustomed to making only A's and B's, was astounded and asked Mrs. Campbell to explain. She told Bettye that she was trying to slow her down so she could focus and set clear goals.

Bettye was concerned about the second-hand books she and her classmates had to use and how her school closed so that black children could help pick cotton even if it deprived them of extra days of learning. She surmised early on that the white leaders did not care about her education and that of other black children in Water Valley.

Even while she was still in high school, Bettye worked in inspections at the same chicken plant where her mother worked. She also babysat white babies and worked in white families' kitchens. Through these experiences, she saw the way blacks were expected to speak and act in the presence of whites. And it bothered her when she heard how her parents and other black adults had to say "yes sir" and "yes ma'am" to whites barely older than she was, and then be addressed by only their first names. With babysitting paying $3 a day and picking cotton $15 per week, Bettye knew education was a way out.

Nonetheless, Bettye speaks of her genuine love of Water Valley and considered moving back. However, painful memories still linger: the segregated movie theater; the white public pool that closed, it seemed, suddenly, with no explanation; the unspoken worry during James Meredith's attempt to

Mae Turner White

integrate Ole Miss in the fall of 1962. Because my family lived on the outskirts of town, we couldn't see what was happening up town, nor did we children know whatever the adults knew. But we sensed the tension. I remember being nervous and afraid seeing my grandmother on the front porch anxiously whispering about her concerns over what was happening. But the adults kept their worries from us children. We were not allowed to go beyond our front yards for days until this volatile episode was over. I now understand that the Water Valley National Guard Unit was indeed activated and sent up to Oxford, 18 miles away.

Now, the lack of progress and economic development in Water Valley, the largest of the county seats, is disappointing, with only one grocery store, the Big Yank building sitting empty on North Main Street for years and years, and the pending closure of the chicken plant.

Bettye hopes that young people and millennials growing up or living in Water Valley now, will take their education and civic involvement much more seriously, especially registering and voting when eligible. Her deepest yearning is for them to understand that they must control their destiny and not cede it to the decision makers, power players, and those in Water Valley supposedly in charge of the crucial decisions that impact livelihood, identity, education, equal and business opportunities, and health care.

Bettye describes her career path as rewarding and challenging. Yet, she states God prepared her for the challenges, including surviving and recovering from three strokes, the first in 2016. She is planning to retire from CSAS this month for the second time and, is ready for leisure travel and to continue to enjoy her husband, family and friends. She now resides in Hiram, Ga., where she spends as much time as possible fishing. Moving forward, she wants to volunteer for the Boys and Girls Clubs. She just cannot stop giving back. Thank goodness!

If there is a Mae White or Bettye Milledge, who influenced your life and the lives of others in an impactful and positive way, let me know! You can acknowledge, express appreciation, share experiences, funny stories, quotes, philosophies, and more in this column. Your recommendations and comments are welcomed.

Reader Comments

Quaye, you are quite a writer, I have enjoyed reading all your articles. I know the women and /or their families are thrilled that you are recognizing them in such a positive light. Keep up the wonderful work!

Cheryl Johnson,
Lithonia, GA

Margie Wilson Avant
The Powerful Love of a Grandmother

This project brings back many memories for me and I hope for you as readers. I do miss the good ole days, but as we feature outstanding black women of Yalobusha County, perhaps we can bridge some gaps, peak curiosity, or inspire positive actions while paying homage to those who have set great examples of unconditional love and kindness. This week we learn about a radiant personality and longtime friend of my family, Margie Wilson Avant, from her granddaughter, Patricia Avant-Pate.

My Grandmother by Patricia Avant-Pate

I have great memories of my grandmother Margie Wilson Avant, who lived in Water Valley her entire life. She was an inspiration to me and my brothers, Danny and Ray.

Margie was born July 6, 1917, and her parents were Mary Shaw Avant and John Eddie Avant. She lived on Blackmur Drive and eventually relocated to her home on Haynes Street. When I was a child my late dad, Dudley Avant, her eldest son, would take us over to her house early on Sunday mornings.

The moment we walked through the door, the aroma of her delicious biscuits, eggs, gravy and rabbit cooking on the stove greeted us. I would only eat the eggs, gravy and biscuits because I did not like wild game. My grandmother never said a word – she just smiled at me. But she made sure that we ate a good hearty breakfast before taking us to Miles Memorial Christian Methodist Episcopal Church on Simmons Street for Sunday school.

For as long as I can remember my grandmother was a member of Miles CME, where she served as an usher and could often be seen cleaning and straightening up the church. She considered the church a second home and loved every position she held and the friends she made among the congregation. On some Saturday evenings she took me along as she walked to members' homes to collect their church offerings when they were ill or unable to attend Sunday services.

As a child I understood my grandmother was a domestic worker in white homes. However, she and her employers seemed to have mutual respect even in that day and time when she was required to go and come through the back door. She worked for the Ross family and the Herman Wright family, owners of Wright's Grocery on Calhoun Street. My father worked at Johnson Chevrolet for a few years and at Larson's Big Star Grocery for almost 39 years. Her youngest son, my uncle Leslie, is retired and lives in Victorville, Calif.

My grandmother worked long hours every day but as soon as she got home, she would tend the flowers she planted in pots on her front porch. Her immaculate front yard further attested to her love of gardening. She loved fishing just as much and took us kids on many fishing trips. Today my

Margie Wilson Avant

brother Danny is an avid fisherman, while my brother Ray and I fish on occasion. One day we were on the creek bank and my grandmother caught a snake which frightened me, so I was done with fishing for a while.

When Ray was just a toddler, my grandmother would stand him in a chair teaching him to cook, and I would stand at her side watching. To teach me the value of hard work – rather than just giving me a grandmotherly allowance – she would have me over every Saturday to earn a little money by washing dishes, mopping floors, dusting, etc. I was earning my own money and learning the satisfaction you feel after doing a good job.

My grandmother had wonderful friends. She would light up with joy when they came to visit, when they chatted by phone or when she visited with them on the street. Her obvious pleasure in these friendships taught me that having good friends and family is truly a blessing in life. She taught us to always be respectful of others and to treat people the way you would want to be treated.

My grandmother gave my brothers and me valuable life lessons. Even all these years later I see myself using the tools she taught me as a child. Although my grandmother is not here with me anymore I can still hear her voice and remember the good times we had together. I am so blessed and thankful to have had such a woman in my life.

Patricia's description of Mrs. Margie warms my heart as my family also belonged to Miles CME Church. I grew up seeing her in action.

She had a gift, a special countenance, a beautiful smile and such a radiant and pleasing personality. Mrs. Margie set an example that I and many others emulated. She did not drive but often accompanied my mom to church programs across the county. I remember the sidewalk that led to her front door being lined with beautiful aromatic flowers matching the persona of the gracious woman within.

Patricia and Ron Pate retired and recently moved to Olive Branch, Mississippi from Stockton, California. Danny is also retired and resides in Sierra Vista, Ariz. Ray lives in Water Valley.

Reader Comments

You do a beautiful job with these articles. I love reading and learning the history of Black Women's accomplishments that I didn't know about. I know those articles are read all over and appreciated as I appreciate them. Keep up the good work.
Patricia Pate,
Olive Branch, MS

I don't know how you continue to come up with them. You are doing a tremendous job.
Eddie Sanders,
Detroit, MI

Thanks for sharing a view of the life of "Miss Margie"..., through her granddaughter. I feel like I knew her too. I think your project is Awesome!
Ken Weeden,
Raleigh, NC

Just another very enjoyable read down memory lane in the lives of the people from Water Valley.
Jim Brzoska,
Deltona, FL

Segregation Side Effects
I Feel Cheated, Do You?

A recent email about this column from a white woman who grew up in Water Valley made me realize that we were cheated out of knowing each other. She wrote to tell me how much she was enjoying this column and wanted to make sure I was going to include three outstanding black woman who influenced her life. She said she did not believe that our paths had ever crossed.

I wrote her back and told her that I knew her. She was very popular at Water Valley High School and was often featured in this newspaper. I idolized her and her friends when I saw them gather around the ice cream counter at Turnage Drugs after school – something that we black kids could not do.

I am excited that we have connected almost 50 years later and to hear of her appreciation of the black women who impacted her life. Just imagine the friendships that we could have forged had our schools not been separate, the pool, movie theatre and other public facilities not segregated, and diversity encouraged.

We simply had no opportunities to get to know each other. Yet our brothers and friends were fighting side by side in a war. We went to the same college and never knew it. Not only have our lives tread common paths, our careers have also, and we have agreed to share more of our experiences in collaboration. So, stay tuned and join in, if you like.

Here are some excerpts from her emails:

You were talking about the ladies who looked after us – I loved Minnie Jenkins like another mother, and I put up such a fuss when I was little about her not getting to sit at the kitchen table with us at lunchtime that my parents relented! And you can rest assured Minnie was always welcome in the bathroom (unlike The Help.) After Minnie died, her son took her body to Waterloo, Iowa, and buried her there, and we went up there once and put flowers on her grave. I'll never forget that.

-More about Minnie later-

I'll tell you another quick story – when I was real little, we went to the Gulf Coast (probably Panama City) and Mildred Backstrum went along to look after us kids. The owners of the motel where we stayed wouldn't let Millie swim in the ocean. IN THE OCEAN! She had brought a swimsuit, so we all got up early one morning and went down to the beach, so she could swim without getting in trouble. My daddy took movie camera pictures of her swimming....

So glad to read all you had written, but I tell you Dottie, that line about watching us all when we gathered at Turnage's brought tears to my eyes. How awful, when I look back, that you and your friends didn't feel welcome there. We white kids didn't know any better then, but hopefully we do now! (at least some of us, I wish more did.)

> "Sing a song full of faith that the dark past has bought us, sing a song full of the hope that the present has brought us; facing the rising sun of our new day begun, let us march on till victory is won. Stony the road we trod, bitter the chastening rod, felt in the day that hope unborn had died; yet with a steady beat, have not our weary feet, come to the place on witch our fathers sighed? We have come over a way that with tears has been watered, we have come, treading our path through the blood of the slaughtered, out from the gloomy past, till now we stand at last where the white gleam of our star is cast."
>
> *Lift Every Voice and Sing*
> *Songwriters:*
> *Rosamond J. Johnson*
> */ James Weldon Johnson*

The uncanny connections are many. When my new friend mentioned her family's maid, Mrs. Mildred Backstrom, I confirmed that it was her son, Miller Backstrom, Jr. (Bumper), who spoke about my mother at my cousin's funeral in Illinois – which led to the birth of this project. I have since spoken to Miller and we were both overjoyed to make the connection.

I was also reminded that Miller Backstrom, Sr. was a street sweeper in Water Valley, and while this may sound like a lowly profession, I, for one, was always comforted when I saw Mr. Backstrom on the streets. I felt safe when I saw him because I knew he was looking out for me and other black kids as we traveled up and down the streets of this small segregated town.

My new friend and I also discussed the integration of Water Valley High School, the closing of Davidson High, whose last class to graduate – mine – was in 1970. She was in the first class of the merger and the first class to graduate in 1971. She said the following about that school year.

Danita Hall and Patricia Freeman were the smartest girls to come over from Davidson in our class, I know that!

I am not trying to impress you with how close I was to my fellow (black) students, but I have so many fond memories of us getting to know each other. Diane Lewis, our great little point guard, getting between me and a bunch of players from another team who were yelling at us as we sat on the basketball bus. They were throwing gravel at the bus, and Diane stuck her head out the window and yelled (some strong words at them). She was so funny. Another time she said at a team meeting that she didn't understand why Coach McLeod would bandage a white foot, but she never saw Coach Easley bandage "no black foot." That taught us all a lesson, I think.

I remember one of the Gaston girls (Dorothy and Martha) asking me why white girls shaved their legs! And another time, we were putting on scenes from the Canterbury Tales in English class and I was an archer, and I shot an arrow (rubber tipped) down the aisle of the classroom, but it curved to the left and got Martha right in the chest!

I was better friends with the girls than the boys, but I always liked Wesley Kerr, Charles White and especially Roosevelt Gooch. I don't know if he still works at the supermarket or not, but I used to see him in there occasionally when my mother was still alive. He was so proud of his children who were all at Ole Miss.

Anyway, lots of good memories. At one of our class reunions, we met at some B&B out on a little lake somewhere, and after everybody had a little too much to drink, person after person, black and white, got up at a microphone and talked about how we were the first to totally integrate, and we did it well. Not that we didn't have our problems, but we made friends and I hope we set a good example.

When my friend was asked a few years ago to write about growing up in Water Valley, she offered the following:

I would be remiss if I neglected to mention all the wonderful African-American ladies, young and old, who helped raise us. This small army of women often left their own children at home to come tend to us white kids. With exotic names like Etoile, Vinnie, Elnora and Ora Lee, or more ordinary monikers like Minnie, Mildred and Bobbie, they cooked, cleaned, played with us and became part of our lives.

The late Minnie Jenkins helped teach me to read Dick and Jane books while both my parents were working...... I still remember after she died and was buried in Waterloo, Iowa (where her son lived,) we went to visit her grave and put flowers on it. To this day, I wish I had a picture of Minnie, but her memory is steadfast in my heart.

Reader Comments

....that line about watching us all when we gathered at Turnage's brought tears to my eyes. How awful, when I look back, that you and your friends didn't feel welcome there. We white kids didn't know any better then, but hopefully we do now! (at least some of us, I wish more did.)
Camille Dautrich,
Branson, MO

I love your reflections about segregation having cheated you and other kids, both black and white, out of friendships you might have had. And the way you interweave your new friend's reflections is so very touching—and instructive. Excellent!
Adrienne Harris,
Atlanta, GA

Wow. That's amazing! I'm glad that the women felt compelled to share experiences from the eyes of a white person. It was really insightful to read her perspective especially the lunch counter connection. I wonder how many others would share their experiences.
Katreena Shelby,
Jackson, MS

This article is beautiful, you are getting the attention of Blacks and Whites. What an amazing job. I have asked a few young ladies to send in something to you but so far they have refused. One person I asked said she would love for you to write about your Mom and of course I would love that also, it would be a very interesting read. Keep up the good work. We are really enjoying your articles.
Patricia Pate,
Olive Branch, MS

This is a great article. I could identify with it so much. Thanks so much for doing this. This series deserves much more exposure.
Pamela Simmons,
Stone Mountain, GA

15

Joyce Hall Judson
Forever Giving of her Talents and Gifts

Yet again, I am amazed at the strength and accomplishments of the outstanding black women of Yalobusha County, Mississippi. It would be easy to say that Water Valley and its residents are not much different from other small towns in Mississippi or in the south. But now more than ever I am convinced that Water Valley is in a special and highly visible position with opportunities to foster transformative actions that could have far reaching impact beyond our imagination.

I have always hoped that the town's proximity to the University of Mississippi, the state's flagship school, would result in projects that benefit the growth and progress of Water Valley and the surrounding communities. Think about it – the town is only 18 miles from Ole Miss, where renowned author William Faulkner lived and died, famous novelist and Ole Miss law school graduate John Grisham resided and penned his first novels and my cousin, Ray Hawkins, is the chief of the University Campus Police.

Yet, the university still has a statue of the Confederacy at its entrance. I shudder as I think about it, while I write this from home in Stone Mountain, Georgia right under the mountain – which has its own confederate iconography.

Students en route to the university regularly travel on Highway 7 or Main Street Water Valley, passing through on their way to the campus. But rising housing prices around Ole Miss have led more individuals affiliated with the college to consider living in Water Valley. Could the addition of these new residents have cultural, economic and political influence on the area?

To be sure, I am looking at this from afar. I would love to hear other perspectives and am pleased that this project has garnered the interest of the university across four academic departments and the Center for Southern Culture. I am eager to tell you more about it, and I will as things develop.

The focus remains on the women we have learned about to date and on women such as Joyce Hall Burgess Judson, a well-known resident of Water Valley. Annette Hervey Westmoreland, who was featured in the November 29 column and Joyce's daughter, Greta, have submitted the following:

Joyce was born in Yalobusha County to Johnny (Jack) and Clara Chapman Hall. She is the twin sister of John C. Hall, and she has four sisters (three deceased) and four brothers. On her first day of school her mother passed away. Joyce was six years old. She was raised by her grandparents, Leland and Alma Hall. Neither could read or write, but somehow her grandfather was able to teach her the alphabet but not necessarily in the right order. Her teacher was then able to help her straighten out the letters. Her grandfather also introduced her to saving before we knew anything about a 401K plan.

He told her when she worked always to put aside money for a rainy day, even if it

Joyce Judson

was one cent, and, he instructed her, do not go back and get it. Her grandparents taught her well.

Joyce graduated from Davidson High School with highest honors in 1967. She was the Salutatorian and Star Student of her high school class and received the Leadership Award. She earned a bachelor of science degree in home economics in 1974 from the University of Mississippi. This was no easy task for a wife and mother of two children under the age of four. She had to drive from Water Valley to Oxford every semester for class, but she kept the faith and believed in her dream.

In 1982 Joyce earned a master's degree from Ole Miss in science education. She taught 5th and 6th grade science at Davidson Elementary for 14 years until she was told to take a test for the postal service.

Scoring 99.3 out of 100 possible points, Joyce was hired at the Grenada post office as a distribution clerk but quickly began her rise in the service. She was promoted to postmaster of the Taylor post office after only three years with the agency. Aside from her daily duties she also worked as a trainer and was instrumental in helping many individuals get jobs at the post office. Both of her daughters are long term postal workers; one of whom is also currently a postmaster.

Along with her professional career work, Joyce is a member of Bayson Chapel Baptist Church, where she teaches Sunday School and is a member of the Mothers Board. In the past she has served in various other capacities such as youth director. Joyce often bakes for the congregation and the community at large and shares her gifts with the elderly, sick and shut-ins.

She uses her gifts to glorify God by showing love to others. Joyce has opened her doors over and over again to her friends and family when they come back to Water Valley for funerals and special occasions. She loves entertaining and making visitors feel welcome in her home.

Joyce also loves doing crafts for herself and others. And we love working with her when she puts on those great feasts for the church and other local groups. She works with a special team of young women, passing on skills and techniques that she has acquired in cooking, catering, decorating and event planning.

Joyce is much more than a role model for only young women. She mentors and encourages young men, too, letting all young people know they can do anything that they put their minds to with God on their side. She is often helping her children and her five grands to succeed, giving them sound advice on handling finances and resolving personal issues.

In addition to teaching and her later postal work, Joyce started a tax preparation business while still in high school, and she has been serving the community for more than 52 years as a tax preparer. Her daughter Tamara works with her in the tax business.

Simply put, her children, grandchildren and the entire community love Joyce Judson because of her humility and her never-ending willingness to share her talents and gifts with others. She has helped many realize their dreams.

And now abideth faith, hope, charity, these three; but the greatest of these is charity.
   – 1 Corinthians 13:13

Recently, I spent some time with Joyce while in town to meet with the folks at Ole Miss and was able to get specific examples of how she uses her gifts and talents:

• Joyce conducted classes in Oxford, Tupelo and Grenada to help applicants pass the U S Postal exam. She has trained at least a 100 people over the last three years. Joyce still offers assistance to those seeking postal employment.

• At least 14 or more individuals have secured postal jobs after her classes and additional tutoring in locations from Southaven to Raymond. Her former husband, Norwood Burgess, also worked at a post office and her daughter, Greta is the postmaster in Terry.

• Joyce's Tax Services offers free tax services to students and to those who cannot afford to pay. And she gives out care packages to some of her clients. She showed me a photo of the hams she is giving away this tax season.

• Not long-ago Joyce hosted senior citizen movie night for ladies in her home. They came in wheelchairs and on canes and had the time of their lives. The evening even helped one attendee decide to go ahead with the knee surgery that she so feared at age 85. A younger attendee decided to return to a craft that she had abandoned.

• Joyce's daughter, Tamara, and her son, Melvin, are Ole Miss graduates. Daughter, Greta got her degree from Delta State.

• Melvin owns his own investment business under the Primerica umbrella, where he is a regional vice president.

Some would describe Joyce as a workaholic and perhaps the smartest person they have ever met. Servanthood is the word that comes to mind when I try to characterize my cousin, Joyce. My late Uncle George and Aunt Bertha Chapman were her maternal grandparents. I think that some of her brains were supposed to be mine!

Reader Comments

Joyce's work, love, charity and accomplishment makes me question what my contributions to society and the world in general should have been.
Jim Brzoska,
Deltona, FL

You picked a good one this time and I have always admired Mrs. Judson. She is awesome.
Velisa Adams,
Coffeeville, MS

Once again thank you for this great work.
Devon Jones,
Towson, MD

Ethel Hudson Morgan
A Student Remembers A Star Teacher

By Camille Fly Dautrich

It's the fall of 1970, and for Water Valley and Davidson High Schools, it's going to be a whole new world. Total school integration has begun, and now all students, regardless of race, will be learning in the same building.

I can't speak for the black experience, but I know we white kids recognized that those students had given up their school building, the Davidson name and their mascot, the Tigers. We were all now Water Valley Blue Devils, and that was that.

Looking back, I think for all of us it was sort of like moving to a new town, albeit with many of your friends moving with you. Suddenly, we had to get to know a whole new group of people and share classrooms, lockers, the cafeteria and other territories. It's been nearly 50 years, but I know we white kids were pretty nervous, and I can only imagine the experience from the other side.

Still, as Nike says, we Just Did It. We got to know each other, and we got along. It wasn't perfect, but it wasn't terrible either.

Sports, I believe, were a major factor in bringing us all together. Football and basketball, where we were forced (if that's the word) to travel together, eat together, shower together and most of all, play together as a team, were great equalizers and helped forge our friendships.

But some things we didn't do. First and foremost, we almost never hung out together outside of school. No black girls came to my house on weekends to practice putting on makeup and talk about boys, or to load up the car and go to a movie in Oxford. Similarly, I was never invited to any of their houses. But we tried, and in many ways, we succeeded. I will always be proud of that.

Into this situation, which could have been volatile, came our teachers, black and white, who I'm sure were just as nervous as we were about this brave new world we were entering. Many in both races worked hard to keep us together and to make the year a success. In this column, I want to concentrate on Ethel Hudson Morgan, our home economics teacher.

I don't want to make Mrs. Morgan sound like a stereotype, but I'm telling the truth when I say she was small but strong, quiet but forceful and most of all, really intelligent. And she always has had the most beautiful smile. Still, only recently did I learn more about her.

The ninth of 10 children born in Coffeeville to Alex and Onia Hudson, Ethel and her family moved to Water Valley when she was in the third grade.

"My parents didn't have much money," she told me, but "(they) instilled great values in their children. They taught us to love God, work hard and get a good education."

To help with family finances, Ethel started to work for an elderly white lady at the corner of Main and Clay Streets when she was in the 8th grade. She was there every day before and after school through the 9th grade as well. "I left home early enough to stop by her house and prepare her breakfast and lunch," she said. "I left her lunch in the refrigerator for her to eat at lunchtime (and) on the way home from school, I prepared her supper." Then on Saturdays, Ethel returned and cleaned the lady's house.

When she was a little older, Ethel said she worked as a maid or a babysitter and continued doing both jobs throughout the summers when she was home from college. "I could always get a job as either a maid or a babysitter," she explained.

Miss Hudson, at the time, graduated as valedictorian of her Davidson high school class in 1965. She was active in a number of organizations, most notably the New Homemakers of America, which was the all-black equivalent of what was then the all-white Future Homemakers of America.

After integration in the early 1970s, Ethel was instrumental in merging the two clubs. She was chosen to serve on the Mississippi state committee to re-write the bylaws and the constitution of the organization.

Ethel was the branch secretary for the first Water Valley NAACP chapter started in 1970, which by June 1971 listed 70 active members.

Ethel attended Alcorn State University in Lorman, MS, where she continued her outstanding academic record, graduating magna cum laude in 1969 and taking part in several sororities and honor societies, including Who's Who Among Students in Universities and Colleges. She married fellow educator James Morgan in 1968.

Next came Ole Miss, where she received her master's degree in 1973.

While Ethel worked on her master's degree, she also taught at Water Valley High School, where she sponsored the FHA Club (later FHA/HERO when males were admitted) and the junior class.

This is when I got to know her, and I am pleased to say today that part of who I am I owe to her. She taught me a lot about cooking (and by the way, Ethel, I made my one and only homemade piecrust in your class; I've cheated and bought them ever since!) but like many of my other teachers, she taught me a lot more.

Ethel Morgan taught me that you don't have to be white to be a good person. Honestly, I knew that already, but she didn't tell me that—she showed me by the way she lived. She taught me that honesty and hard work are two things that will always stand you in good stead.

On the other hand, she also taught me

Ethel Hudson Morgan

that, in the unlikely event I was trying to copy something off Kim Horan's test paper because I couldn't remember the answer, a well-placed "stink eye" in my direction could shame me enough to miss that question honestly, not answer it dishonestly!

After retiring from teaching, Ethel opened a business, Ethel's Footwear and Accessories, which operated from 1995 to 2002. But the very next year, she faced a much bigger challenge than teaching a bunch of giggly high-school girls or running her own business.

In 2003, Ethel was diagnosed with cancer. I remember being devastated when I heard this because my own sister, Harriet Samuels Nelson, had died of cancer in 1988. But Ethel persevered, becoming a leading volunteer with the American Cancer Society. She served as team captain and later as Yalobusha County Relay for Life chairperson. In 2006 she traveled to Washington, D.C., to lobby with nearly 4,000 other Relay for Life Community Ambassadors, all of them, she said, "energetic, committed people who had been touched by cancer and were passionate about . . . eradicating the disease." Ethel returned to Washington several times to continue this important work. She was named Mississippi Volunteer of the Year 2006-2007 by the Mid-South Division of the American Cancer Society and received four additional awards in 2009.

Ethel has been honored for her work, both with the American Cancer Society and the FHA, and closer to home, she and her husband James were chosen to be Grand Marshals of the Water Valley Christmas Parade in 2017.

Perhaps most important to Ethel, however, is her church, and here, too, she is an exemplary volunteer. "I am a born-again Christian," she said, "and a member of Zion Grove Missionary Baptist Church in Coffeeville. I serve as a Sunday School teacher, an usher, and the correspondence secretary. I also serve as the recording

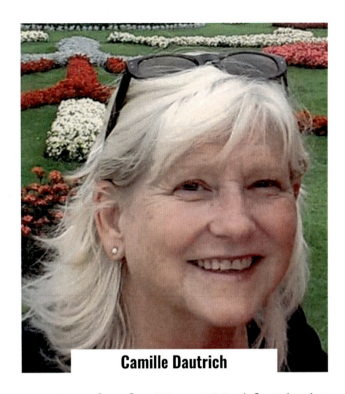

Camille Dautrich

secretary for the Mount Moriah District Missionary Baptist Association, which includes 30 Baptist churches in Yalobusha, Grenada, Calhoun and Panola Counties."

A few years back, my husband Barry and I were visiting Water Valley from Branson, Mo, where we live, and I told him I wanted to see my old Home Ec teacher. When Ethel opened her front door, Barry started laughing. "Camille told me you were OLD," he said. "You're not old at all." He was right. Turns out they graduated from college the same year. Although in my defense, I meant "old" teacher meaning "in the past," not her actual age!

So thank you, Mrs. Morgan, for all you taught me, not just in the classroom but about how to live a good life. Even though I don't see you much, I remember you fondly and think of you often. I heard someone say once about his college professors that while he might not remember many specific things they taught him, he remembered that they taught him how to study, how to learn and how to live. I'm happy and honored to say that many of my teachers and professors taught me those same things, and Ethel, you are most definitely one of them.

Reflections
by Dottie Reed

Camille is the new friend that I wrote about in a previous column, "Segregation Side Effects." Her high school class was the first class to graduate in 1971 following the state mandated integration of public schools in Mississippi. She is a journalist in her own right and has promised to write more soon.

Ethel's work history is even more remarkable given that she was only in the 8th and 9th grades when she prepared breakfast and lunch each day for a Mrs. Walton, a white woman, before going to school. In the summers she cleaned house and babysat for Linda Gordon and another white woman named Mrs. Furhman. In high school she worked for a fourth white woman, a Mrs. Morgan, and then for Dr. and Mrs. Hedges on the weekends.

Finally, every summer when she came home from college, she worked for Ruth and Warren Ray, the owners of Rays Department Store. No surprise that Ethel has been so successful and her life so rewarding. And no surprise either that she had such a positive impact on Camille and numerous other students and also set a great example for her fellow teachers during such a critical time.

The tensions of this moment in Mississippi history hit home to me in February, when a former Jackson area high school principal, a white man now living in Water Valley, called to say how much he was enjoying the column. He said that when freedom of choice ended, and mandatory school integration began in the fall of 1970, he and his staff were in shock – lost really. They were so lost that the black teachers were afraid to discipline the white kids, and the white teachers were afraid to discipline the black kids. After two months, he said to one of his colleagues, a black male teacher "what are we doing?... These are just kids doing what kids do." From that point on all went well.

Reader Comments

I am so grateful that our white school students are involved in writing this history. We need each other no matter what has happened in the past. Under God's eye we are one. Thanks for getting this in the news. This is history and very important.
Annette Westmoreland,
Buckeye, AZ

I feel like I know these people of whom you write. Their stories are transferable to persons that I know here. Keep up the good work and have a great day.
Mitchell Payne,
Louisville, KY

I love this article and Mrs. Morgan! She is the absolute best...at almost everything.
Syreeta Kee,
Coffeeville, MS

A great story about one of my best friends, Mrs. Ethel Morgan. She is Simply the Best. She and her husband Mr. James Morgan are my very, very best friends. Thank you for doing a great, great story on Ethel.
Fred Harris,
Seattle, Washington

This story written by Camille was a really heartfelt thanks to an amazing teacher and friend Ethel. I would think that there were many white students out there that grew up in this period of integration that have had a similar experience and story to relate.
Jim Brzoska,
Deltona, FL

Dorothy Smith Kee
Born to Teach

For such a time as this, the New York Times ran a special section in February entitled "Overlooked" – revisiting 168 years of Times history to provide obituaries for black men and women who never got them. Hard to imagine no obituary for Scott Joplin, the king of ragtime, or Granville T. Woods, an inventor who helped revolutionize modern transportation. They also have a column/newsletter called Race Related, where they are asking folks to share when they first experienced racism.

More recently a friend shared a Times article about 14-year-old Emmett Till and the store in Money, Miss. where he was accused of whistling at a white woman behind the counter in August 1955. The store and the surrounding property, privately owned, are slowly deteriorating, and the family refuses to sell or allow others to preserve the parcel for historical purposes. Money, Miss. - I always thought that name was ironic for a town with barely a 100 people. It is in Leflore County, where a song says Billy Joe McAlister jumped off the Tallahatchie bridge. Years later I remember hearing Bobby Gentry's song while in the family cotton field and thinking no song for poor little Emmett Till and being afraid.

Then I vowed I would never go to Money or to Tallahatchie County. Even when I recruited for the University of Mississippi I never went there. Only 45 miles separates Money from Coffeeville in Yalobusha County. Dorothy Ann Smith Kee hails from Coffeeville – the second largest town in the tri-cities along with Water Valley and Oakland. Her impactful teaching career is a direct outgrowth not only of her parents' significant influence but also their special place in the community.

Clemmie Smith, Dorothy's dad, was dark skinned, and her mother, Clara, could have passed for white, and for that reason alone, the Smith family was often ridiculed and ostracized by whites and even some blacks. When Dorothy, the eldest of seven, and her sisters went shopping with their mom, she recalled, they teased her that they were her maids because she was sometimes mistaken as white.

Clemmie spoke out often against racism and injustice in the late 1960s as a leader of Coffeeville NAACP volunteers. He was well respected by the black community overall, and Dorothy said, many whites viewed him as a threat because he was a civil rights activist. So much so, she recalled that one time an armed ex-con showed up at a march for school integration in Coffeeville, and attempted to break up the march and harm her dad. Fortunately, he failed. She and her family attended church with the family of the ex-con, who had been deputized and ordered to kill her father, Jimmy Matthews and J.T. Miller.

The Smiths owned 100 plus acres of land and were as self-sustaining as much as a black family could be during the 40's and 50's in north Mississippi. These facts alone caused animosity and hostility toward the couple. The family worked every day just to live, raising animals and growing staples such as cotton, soybeans and corn along with truck crops, including watermelons, peanuts and cantaloupes. They picked blackberries and dewberries for extra money, and to save what they earned, Clara made clothes for their seven children. She was both a savvy homemaker and great support to her husband.

Both parents, born in Yalobusha County, completed eighth grade and never had to work for anyone else. Clemmie took classes offered for veterans after being discharged from the army. He received a diploma from the Mississippi Baptist Seminary in Jackson. Though Clara always stayed home to help her family, her sister went away to complete 12th grade because the black school only went to eighth grade. But Clara did not like to be idle, so she repeated eighth grade classes over and over until her late teens even though she had graduated. She didn't look older than her classmates and never minded that she was. Learning new things was the most important thing, a passion that lasted Clara's life time. She was an avid reader, seamstress, crafter, cook, natural remedy researcher, fashionista and game show fan who kept with modern trends until her death in 2013. Clara was also an active member of the Yalobusha County Homemakers Extension, getting her first public job as a traveling nutrition aid at nearly 50 years old.

Though the Smiths were fiercely independent landowners, if they failed to sell enough produce in the fall, they had to borrow money to plant new crops and feed the livestock in the winter. Year after year they managed to prevail and hold on to their land, which was not the case for many other black farmers. Clemmie's granddaughter, Syreeta, remembers how hard her grandfather worked to overcome racial barriers - often manifested in the denial of loans or grants to black farmers.

According to Dorothy, her parents insisted that she and her six siblings adhere to certain standards. They stressed the importance of education and doing well in school. "We were taught to put God first and to read the Bible daily, Dorothy recalled. "Daddy wanted us to be somebody" and she did just that.

Dorothy, who was born in 1946, attended Coffeeville Colored School and credits her first-grade teacher as the first to inspire her to become a teacher. She was so excited she went home and started teaching her siblings. She attended the all-black Central High School and graduated as valedictorian. Her english, science and history teachers solidified her decision to pursue a teaching career.

Dorothy earned a bachelor of science degree in social science with an emphasis in history from Alcorn State University. She chose Alcorn, she said, because a cousin had gone there, and she did not apply anywhere else. Five of her siblings also graduated from Alcorn. The youngest of the seven Smith siblings graduated from Mississippi State University. Dorothy also completed masters' degrees in education and social work from Mississippi State.

She began teaching at 21, just as mandatory integration was taking place in Mississippi. The impending change initially did not faze her, she said. She had learned to accept things as they were and did not "anticipate any animosity from my fellow white associates."

However, she would soon face a new reality. She was married now and expecting her first child. She was out on leave the first few months of 1970, as integration was starting. When she was ready to return to work, school officials told her they were in no hurry for her to come back. She accepted the news at first, but after a couple more trips to see school personnel and then no follow-up, she and her father believed her job was imperiled because of his political activism.

Dorothy and her dad sought counsel with an NAACP attorney, and by February 1971 she returned to teaching, undeterred by the new era of integration. However, she did not return to her previous position but rather was sent to Oakland. Dorothy and her family at first considered this punishment, but it turned out to be a blessing in disguise. The principals she worked under, Buford Sellers and Clinton Jenkins, the faculty, staff and students were some of the best people, in her view, she encountered. She stayed in Oakland for five years before returning to Coffeeville.

By coincidence, six Coffeeville teachers - including my late sister Alma Faye Chapman - lost their jobs in the town as two school systems merged. They sued to get their positions back, claiming the school authorities acted improperly in the way they made teacher selections. In October 1973 four of the teachers - including my sister - were ordered reinstated with back pay. (For details on this case see: https://law.justia.com/cases/federal/district-courts/FSupp/365/990/1414480)

Dorothy taught 7 – 12th grade social studies, history and economics in the public-school system for 30 years. Though she officially retired in 1997, she worked part-time until 2001. However, she remains a presence in her former students' lives. Every time she sees them, they invariably express appreciation for how she taught them and made them feel worthy.

Dorothy says she is proudest that she stayed in an area where her skills were most needed – teaching students from low economic neighborhoods and those who did not desire or could not afford to go to the white private academies that sprang up after the mandatory integration. In a bit of turnabout, Dorothy noted that now many of her students offer their professional services to her.

Dorothy's parents provided her with what I would call a unique and atypical environment: no sharecropping, no servitude or reliance on a bossman. She and her siblings were taught black pride, independence and survival skills. They learned the value and benefits of owning land and saw firsthand the advantages and disadvantages of community service and civic duty. If I were to guess, no more than seven to 10 black families might have owned over 100 acres of land in Yalobusha County in the 1940s. Dorothy is deeply gratified that she and her siblings have held on to every one of the 160 acres that her family farmed. Her mom and dad would be so proud!

The 2015 book Delta Jewels featured Dorothy along with other black Mississippi women, and Congressman Bennie Thompson honored her with a letter of commendation, a certificate and a special mention on his website and Facebook page during Black History Month. Dorothy A. Kee is still teaching!

Through a Daughter's Eyes
by Syreeta Latrice Kee

When my grandmother, Clara Moody Smith, was pregnant with my mother – she would be the first of seven children – she and my grandfather, Clemmie, were in Spokane, Washington, where he was stationed in the Army. They hurried back to Mississippi before Dorothy was born because they wanted her to arrive in their home town of Coffeeville. They appreciated the importance of family, who were nearby.

Clemmie Smith's parents passed away early, and he and his brothers - all close in age - were charged with caring for their younger siblings. Strangely, all three of the ones attempting to run the household were drafted and sent into World War ll.

With no one left to care for the younger ones, an older relative, Leora Ross, moved in to take over the reins. After Clemmie was discharged, he returned to the family home and decided to work the land. Leora, affectionately nicknamed Nola by his children, would remain with them for many years before moving to Chicago with her son.

A family of strong faith, the Smiths encouraged daily Bible reading and participated in all the services and activities at Smith Chapel Baptist Church. But while religious education clearly was important, the couple also emphasized secular education and hard work.

Given that the Smith's oldest three children were girls, Dorothy and her sisters handled many of the farm tasks usually given to boys. They milked cows in the morning before school, fed livestock, chopped and picked cotton and worked in the other fields, vegetable gardens and truck patches.

In good natured fun, Dorothy's siblings crowned her the slowest churner in the south. But she took it as a challenge: The more her family teased her, the more aggressively she churned and the better the butter was. She found an added benefit: She became faster at almost everything, and Dorothy credits this early-learned- and-earned discipline as catalyst for much of what she achieved later in life.

Though many strong women influenced Dorothy, her mother and Nola stand out. She not only admired Clara's sense of style, homemaking skills, kind nature and calm demeanor, but also her ability to stand her ground and to perform manual labor with seeming ease. Dorothy was especially amazed at how well Clara could take the least of things and make the best of things.

Nola kept Dorothy and her siblings in awe when she balanced pots of water on her head walking uphill from the spring, started fires from rocks, taught them to gather and prepare poke salad (sallet) and told them stories of days gone by. It never crossed their minds that she was simply living her cultural history.

In school Dorothy closely observed her teachers, marveling at the way they cared for so many children and were able to impart their knowledge and skill. Three made indelible impressions: Sara James, Elvira Jackson and Henrienne Williams. Though other career options were opening for black women, these teachers inspired Dorothy to follow in their footsteps.

Even though these were lean, substandard times in schools for Mississippi blacks, Dorothy still had fond memories of the many activities she took part in – field days, dramatic productions, oratorical contests and choral music competitions. These provided an outlet while fostering personal development, cooperation and competitiveness. Among the most enjoyable times were those when all the schools in the county gathered, and she would see the same kids she often saw at church events. They kept in touch by writing letters to one another.

Dorothy jokingly says her interest in history began early in life. To keep the kids from hearing "grown-folks talk," older people would send children to other areas of the house when they had company. Inquisitive, Dorothy led the charge to sit under an open window to find out just what this grown-folks business was all about. Despite not always knowing what the things she heard meant, she could repeat them word-for-word and still remembers some of those conversations today. She became the go-to person for family trees, obituary content and more.

Family members even older than her sometimes ask, "How do you remember when that happened?" "I don't," she tells them. "I remember hearing 'them' retelling it while we were eavesdropping outside." Years later, after graduating from Central High School at the top of her class, she would put these skills to use.

Dorothy Kee's (above) impactful teaching career is a direct outgrowth not only of her parents' significant influence, but also their special place in the community. Kee was the first of seven children born to Clara Moody Smith and Clemmie G. Smith in Coffeeville. According to Dorothy, her parents insisted that she and her six siblings adhere to certain standards. They stressed the importance of education and doing well in school.

Dorothy remembers the year she graduated from Alcorn State University - 1967 - as a busy one. She graduated in May, got married in June and started teaching in Coffeeville in August. Dorothy joined her husband's family church, Pleasant Grove Baptist in Coffeeville's Bryant Community where she held numerous positions and participated in several ministries over the years.

However, she still serves as secretary, teen Sunday school teacher and a deaconess. She keeps busy serving on committees, boards and consulting among other things. Dorothy loves to read and encourages others, young and old, to read as well. Some of her other hobbies are watching DIY shows and attempting some of the features, cooking and writing.

She and my father, Nathaniel, have been married for 51 years and have two grown children, my brother, Kevin Erlander, and me, Syreeta Latrice. They have two grandchildren.

Looking back on her youth in comparison to milestones over the years, my mother is marvelously amazed by God's grace, and continues to celebrate His mercy and favor in her life.

Reader Comments

Beautiful! I just love Dorothy Kee!
Joyce Judson,
Water Valley, MS

My uncle in Natchez saw it before we did and called to say one of his friends called him and told him how nice it was and then sent him the link to the e-edition. Calls started coming in from Georgia, California and everywhere after then.

That was a really, really nice article. It is really obvious that you took your time and care with it. My mom says she cannot believe the paper allowed that much space for it.

She said it didn't cross her mind Wednesday -- an older white lady she did not know was exercising next to her and exclaimed loudly, "I'm sitting over here beside Mrs. Kee! She looks just like herself, too." She found out that the lady was referring to her looking like herself in the picture in the newspaper after others mentioned it today.
Syreeta Kee,
Coffeeville, MS

23 Strong Chartering the NAACP
Courtesy Titles Please

Recently a colleague provided archival documents about the NAACP in Water Valley. The earliest record for a local chapter is from 1970. Perhaps it is no surprise that Yalobusha county women - including my mother, Lula Helen Chapman, made up almost half of the membership in the founding branch. Those who know Ethel Hudson Morgan, who was featured in the March 14 column, are likewise not surprised that she was the chapter's founding secretary. "She is the absolute best...at almost everything," one reader noted in a comment on the article.

Water Valley's first branch president was Percy Haywood, Jr. William Holmes was the first vice president, the second, James Morgan, Ethel's husband. Virgia Mae Campbell aided Ethel as the assistant secretary, James Haywood served as treasurer, and Charlie Rogers served as the chaplain.

While I would love to include more of the original members, here are the women listed on the membership roll Ethel submitted on November 2, 1970., in addition to her, my mother and Virgia: Gertie Buford, Margaret Campbell, Essie Carothers, Ruby Fox, Catherine Freeman, Ruby Hall, Luvean Haywood, Annie B. Hervey, Florine Hervey, Louise McFarland, Clotie Love, Bernice Minor, Ella Mae Nicholson, Vira Mae Phillips, Jeannette Rogers, Nettie Rowsey, Janice H. Scott, Leana Mae Toliver, Mary Louise Toliver and Nina White.

I am proud to admit I recognize all but four or five of the founding 50 members. In fact, Mr. Haywood was my high school social studies teacher. It is rather eerie for me to see my mother's name listed. "You never told me your mom was an activist," a friend said.

I had never considered her to be and vaguely recall discussions and meetings around our house. I am also inclined to believe an organized group may have existed before 1971. However, to date no other documentation has surfaced. A January 15, 1971 letter to Water Valley president Haywood provided the Executive Authorization for the branch charter from the NAACP's national board, which had approved it January 11, 1971.

Ethel submitted a subsequent list showing approximately 76 active members as of June 13, 1971. Lest we not forget the FEAR aspect of organizing and becoming a member of the NAACP. Doing so even in the 1970's called for bravery and courage. Many Mississippians in other parts of the state had exhibited the same two decades earlier in a far more dangerous time.

By 1952 they had organized into 19 branches – several in the Delta and western Mississippi. In November of that year members of 16 chapters gathered in Yazoo City for the 7th annual session of the Mississippi State Conference of NAACP Branches. A press release noted resolutions the group approved on many significant subjects: voting, education, police brutality, housing and courtesy titles. They declared that "mob violence, cowardly bombing, intimidations, whether by hooded or unhooded groups, will not deter us. We will not turn back."

We were so poorly thought of that we had to ask for respect through courtesy titles. You may recall Betty White Milledge, who was profiled in the January 10 column, mentioning that as a child in Water Valley, she could not understand why whites were addressed as Mr. or Mrs. and yet those same whites called her parents by their first names. When Ethel sent in that membership list for the Water Valley Branch she was careful to list them as Mr. or Mrs.

The 1952 conference addressed the issue this way:

Whereas, we have for too long a time referred to ourselves as Joe Doe and Sally Roe, and allowed others to refer to us by any other title other than Mr. or Mrs.;

"Be it resolved, that this conference go on record as asking that local branches launch upon a program asking that Negroes, first of all, refer to themselves and to one another as Mr. and Mrs. and insist upon others to do likewise, especially the stores wherein we have accounts and are likely to receive bills."

The perils of organizing were made abundantly clear in Belzoni – where black residents outnumbered whites 2-1 – 18 months after the state conference session. The Reverend George Lee and Gus Courts had formed a chapter and convinced 92 black residents to pay the poll tax, so they simply could register to vote. They both received death threats and tried to take precautions. A letter Courts wrote to the NAACP national office in New York underlined the palpable fear. He explained that he had been forced to resign as president and that other members had been pressured to leave the branch. He hoped for advice and made a chilling request: "any mail sent to me please send in a plain envelope and leave NAACP of [sic]. I have reason for this."

The white resistance turned deadly. While driving home on Mother's Day 1955,

> "Be it resolved, that this conference go on record as asking that local branches launch upon a program asking that Negroes, first of all, refer to themselves and to one another as Mr. and Mrs. and insist upon others to do likewise, especially the stores wherein we have accounts and are likely to receive bills."

Reverend Lee was shot from a passing car. With his face almost gone he made his way to a cab stand. Two black drivers took him to the hospital, where he died. No charges were ever filed. Lee is considered by many as the first martyr of the civil rights movement.

An insight into the difficulties of forming a new branch comes from another activist woman, Cora Britton of Columbia in southern Mississippi. The Marion County chapter formed in 1955, but on March 4, 1958 she wrote the national office in New York about tensions in the community:

"Our branch (Marion County) has been silent for a long time, mostly because of fear. When it was said that whoever belongs to the NAACP would not be given work, they decided to stop for a while."

NAACP records for 1963 show approximately 23 Mississippi chapters with 4,875 members. A report from the Fayette chapter in October of 1966 illustrates the depth of the struggle. The branch presented 16 requests to the county's superintendent of schools and the board of education including that black teachers receive at least the average salaries of the other teachers in the state, that non-teaching personnel be paid no less than $1 per hour and classes have no more than 30 pupils. This branch, too, wanted "courtesy titles" on all communications from the superintendent's office.

While much progress has been made since 1952, the current racially divided environment makes us wonder how much has really changed. We should remember and applaud the bravery of the individuals who often risked their lives and livelihood but continued to fight for their rights despite almost constant threats of retaliation.

In the meantime, perhaps we can find comfort in comments by Jennifer Gunter, the director of the South Carolina Collaborative on Race & Reconciliation (SCCRR).

"People are literally dying over misconceptions of history and race" she said. "I hope to see a reckoning with the past, something that goes beyond apologies. I hope to see the power of conversations and listening transform our understanding of each other." The SCCRR works in South Carolina communities and classrooms to support those seeking greater civic engagement, civil discourse and active understanding to lessen the divides created by our differences.

To whom do you owe your success besides those who brought you into this world? Do you owe anything to anyone beyond your own offspring? Should you offer thanks or try to inspire others to reach their goals by sharing what others have done for you?

In the fall University of Mississippi students will be visiting Yalobusha County to collect oral histories of African Americans in Water Valley, Coffeeville and Oakland. This will provide an opportunity to further document stories and personal histories of some of the outstanding women mentioned above. If you know already that you want to be included, or have suggestions for individuals that we should contact, email me. There will be several local opportunities for you to sign up and participate in the near future. And yes, we are featuring men as I have gotten several recommendations, including Vietnam veterans, my readers would like to see profiled.

My hope is that this project will illuminate the great sacrifices that were made in the past years for all people and encourage us to continue standing up for civil rights and equality for all.

19

Cora Lee Folson
Heartfealt Memories of Cora Folson

"Memories of Cora Folson" meets one of the objectives for this project outlined in my first article back in June 2018. While the primary goal is to honor and share life stories of outstanding black women of Yalobusha County, I asked to hear from the children, adults now, who grew up with black nurses, babysitters, housekeepers, maids and the like in their homes. I said then that I wanted to know about these women and who they worked for when they left their own children at home each morning ofttimes unattended, to feed themselves, do morning chores, to get themselves off to school and elsewhere. These black mothers and grandmothers made this huge sacrifice because these were the only types of jobs, aside from farming, and in a few instances teaching, available to them to help put food on the table and clothes on their backs.

Now I am delighted to learn more about Mrs. Cora and her relationship with the Caulfield family.

I knew her, her son and my late classmate, Willie B. Jones, her daughter, Nancy Telford and her grandsons, Steve and Rickey along with many other relatives. According to the 1940 Census and other available records, Mrs. Cora was born in November 1914 to Robert and Regina Joiner Folson.

She attended school through the seventh grade. By the time she was 24, she worked as a cook and a housekeeper for a Mrs. Pickering while living with her father, Robert, and her 18-year-old sister, Corinne. She died August 10, 1971 and is buried in the Bayson Chapel Cemetery.

Mrs. Cora had four sisters and three brothers. Her sister, Mary Folson Ealy, mentioned in a previous article, worked for many years for the Turnage family, owners of the only drugstore in Water Valley.

When I spoke to Rickey about his grandmother and the article written by one of her employers, he quietly observed that "she raised a lot of them."

Recalling my mother's years of domestic work, my heart connected with his for a moment as I heard that pause in his voice and in our conversation. Perhaps we both wondered what if we could have some of that time back.

Heartfelt Memories
by Dorothy Caulfield Wiman

I was blessed when I was a baby to have a very special lady take care of me. Mama and Daddy worked full time, and I had a sickly grandmother, great aunt, and their cousin who lived in the house. This special lady was Cora Folson. Cora became my best friend and second Mama. I loved her from day one.

Cora usually walked to our house. I remember running to the back door to see her come up the driveway and into the yard. I would holler, "Cora!" She would grab me up in her arms and tell me that I was her baby. I really was. I even remember her giving me a bottle. I must have taken a bottle for a very long time, but I remember lying in her lap and drinking my milk.

Cora had the sweetest smile and was rotund and soft. I loved her softness. She was the best cook in the world. I remember her peeling potatoes and letting me have a taste. She would parboil them and then mash them with the old potato masher that I still have. And, she made the best rice pudding and fried chicken. I remember her making desserts with Karo, and I began to fondly refer to her as "Karo," my Karo; and she called me, "Sweetnin'."

I remember Cora would look at the paper and I would ask her to read it to me. She told me her eyes were bad, but now I wonder whether she could read at all. I know African Americans back then had so few opportunities. It made me very sad when I thought about that.

She stayed with us when Mama and Daddy went to watch Ole Miss in the Sugar Bowl back in 1959. One night, I pulled the tall cabinet over on me and Cora saved me! Thank goodness there were mostly towels in it.

Cora Folson and Dorothy as a baby.

Not only did Cora cook and take care of us, she also ironed. When she ironed upstairs, she would be so hot, because we did not have air conditioning back then. Thankfully, she usually ironed downstairs in Mama and Daddy's bedroom. She kept the house straight, because we kids pretty much destroyed it with our running up and down, playing cowboys, army, baseball, and shooting squirt guns in the house. It's a miracle we are still alive after all that. I'm sure Cora had to tell on us a few times.

Cora worshiped at Everdale Baptist Church. One of the saddest days of my life was when I had to go to that church to say good-bye to her forever. I remember the preacher came from Chicago. He quoted Psalm 23, and the congregation chimed in with their "Yes" and "Amen."

He said, "Cora's not dead! No! She's gone home! She's gone to the city!" My grandmother had made sure Cora knew the Lord as her Savior, because my grandmother was like that. Cora told me before she died, "I'm ready." She was ready, but I was not ready to give her up. The choir sang, "I Need Thee Every Hour," and even though I was thinking, "Yes and amen," I cried my eyes out.

She affected my life for the better, and she loved me unconditionally. I'm so thankful for the sweetness my "Karo" brought into my life. Even though she left us at such an early age, I think of her often even now at the age of 65, especially when I'm mashing potatoes.

Dorothy's heartfelt reflections and the pictures speak for themselves. She describes her love for her "Karo," a reference to mothers and caregivers adding Karo Syrup to sweeten baby milk. To many blacks, however, the sincerity of the "love" that some white families proclaimed for their black domestic workers remains in question. Many sensed that this "love" had limits, offered only as long as blacks stayed in the role whites had assigned them. This was one of the reasons I had a very hard time watching "The Help." I struggled to finish the book and watched the movie only after I saw the cast included superior black actors and actresses. It is like most of the movies about Mississippi that I will only watch once or not at all.

My discomfort and resistance perhaps come from having a mother who worked as a maid, having babysat for white families as a teenager, and having spent seven years at a predominantly white college – whew! Alas, perhaps sharing and examining these memories could lead to transformative thinking and stimulate conversations to make us better people.

Thank you, Dorothy for getting us started and showing us what Mrs. Cora meant to you and how the care and love she poured into you and your family contributed to your success. Dorothy majored in Bible at Belhaven College and taught 1st grade for 21 years. She was a librarian for 10 years and is now retired and residing in Belzoni with her husband, a Presbyterian minister.

Reader Comments

What a wonderful article. Black women have shaped history through the years! I am so glad to be a part of this chain! I plan to do all I can to continue to reach out and help others as long as I am able to do so.
Joyce Judson,
Water Valley, MS

I loved all the articles. I love the authenticity and the passion keep them coming.
Emmitt Jones,
St Louis, MO

You don't know me, but I have lived in Water Valley since 2004. I have gotten the N MS Herald for almost as long as I have lived here and don't think I've ever read something so beautiful as your column. Nice job and look forward to seeing more.
Becky Tatum,
Water Valley, MS

I really enjoyed this article about Ms. Cora, it reminded me so much of the book "The Help". Ms. Cora will really help your readers identify with the struggles of our black mothers and women. It gives us a deeper respect for them and their sacrifices. Keep up the great work!
Cheryl Johnson,
Lithonia, GA

I remember Ricky and Steve. Hopefully, I can talk to them one day. You are doing a great work, and I hope many more African Americans are honored because of your efforts. This has made me want to find out more about my fourth great grandfather and grandmother on my mother's side, who was a slave and indentured servant, respectively.
Dorothy Wiman,
Winona, MS

Mable Jenkins Lewis
A Portrait of a Mother Comes Full Circle

Dear Dottie,

My mother was not a native of Yalobusha County. However, she was a strong black woman who impacted the lives of many. Several years ago, I wrote a narrative in her memory, and I would like to share it with you. I thought you might be able to use it in your column. First, I would like to tell you something about her, and the narrative will follow.

Mable Jenkins Lewis was born in 1923 in the Zemuly community in Attala County to a Baptist minister and his wife. She latched onto the basic tenets of Christianity that her parents taught and modeled for her in the home. Mable sought to live according to these tenets throughout her life.

She worked on the family farm and attended grammar school in community one-room schools until she finished eighth grade. Then, she transferred to Attala Training School in Kosciusko to complete her high school education. In Kosciusko, she and her sister, Ruth, roomed, or as she called it, "light house kept," with her family friends, Reverend and Mrs. John Hollinsworth.

After graduating, Mable began teaching in community one-room schools. During the summer, when school was out, she attended what is now Jackson State University in pursuit of a bachelor's degree.

In December, 1944, Mable married Jerry C. Lewis, who was serving in the United States Army. They immediately began a family, but Mable continued to teach and attend college. After Jerry finished his stint in the Army, they both enrolled at Alcorn A&M State College. After graduating, just as Mississippi started consolidating one-room schools, Mable continued to teach, helped work the Lewis family farm, and care for her children.

She was gifted with a beautiful coloratura soprano voice and sang often at church and for community functions. Through her teaching and singing, and with a gentle spirit, she influenced the lives of many children as well as adults.

FULL CIRCLE

Death came to my mother in March 1980. She had been ill for three months, and we had been warned about the dangers of her operation. Still, we were not prepared.

For the next five or six months my sister and I walked around in a daze. We worked, talked to our husbands and, to the outside world, seemed normal. In our hearts we were not. We really could not believe that Mom was dead.

Mom was my best friend. Though we often disagreed, in her stately, graceful manner she always let me know that she understood and accepted me.

While growing up, many times I wanted to assume a superior air toward children of different races, religions, and socio-economic backgrounds. Mom always brought me to reality with one of her favorite

Mable Lewis

quotes from James Truslow Adams, "There is so much good in the worst of us and so much bad in the best of us that it ill behooves any of us to talk about the rest of us."

When I graduated from high school in the turbulent 60s and announced my desire to attend Ole Miss, Mom did not try to discourage me. She simply stated, "We will send you anywhere in Mississippi that you want to go." This was no easy task on my parents' salaries.

When it seemed as though I would lose my identity and character at Ole Miss while falling in love for the first time and experimenting with the previously forbidden pleasures of adulthood, Mom asked, "Do you want to go somewhere else and start over?"

The day that I graduated was probably one of the happiest in her life.

I remember how happy Mom was when Gordon and I got married. She insisted that we have a wedding. We would have been happy to elope. I remember her encouraging words as I changed during the reception. "You were a beautiful bride," she whispered. I had never thought of myself as beautiful.

Our weekly routine was Saturday morning breakfast. I would call her and request fried eggs, and the two would be ready when I got there. I have not had eggs like that in a long time.

Mom often joked that she would be too old to take care of her grandchildren if my husband and I didn't soon give her some. I don't think she ever accepted the wonderful idea of planned parenthood.

Perhaps the best memory I have of Mom is one of our conversations during her hospitalization. An unexpected group had come to the library where I worked, so I had to stay longer than usual. This meant that I was late getting to visit her. Angrily, I related the incident, and then I said, "of course, every child thinks his mother is special."

"No," Mom replied. "Every child does not think his mother is special. I want you to know, that I'm proud of each of you."

A few weeks later Mom died.

Now, I am in a different phase of my being. Mom is no longer physically with me. I have become the mother. Often times, I hear her voice within me as I seek to nurture and guide the growth and development of my two sons. I hear her saying to me, "You will later thank me for this," and I silently repeat these words to my sons while trying to instill in them my moral and spiritual values. I translate my mother's feelings to them by saying, "I want you to be men of character and integrity. I want you to be men of success and self-discipline."

No, Mom did not see her grandchildren, but they will know her through me.

The giant oak has fallen. Now the sapling is mature, and the little acorns have taken root.

My mother and I have come full circle......

Reader Comments

Is it me or do others feel that your column keeps getting better and better?
Art Boone,
Water Valley, MS

Thank you for sharing Linda's article about her mother. It was so beautiful. I couldn't help but cry.
Patricia Brassel,
Oxford, MS

21

Ruby Buggs Hall
A True Symbol of Strength and Integrity

I am sure if I took a poll, one of every three students who had classes or knew Mrs. Ruby Doris Hall, would have a funny story to tell. She taught high school math, did hair, raised seven children, and was the "cool" teacher everyone liked. Perhaps it was because she had children the same ages as most of us or perhaps it was because her house was a hub of activity where kids and grownups hung out, folks coming in and out all the time. Though her husband's name was Artee Johnes Hall, everybody called him Mr. Billy. He was a barber who loved to go fishing.

Mrs. Hall had that demanding teacher voice that seemed to carry for miles. You never wanted to be embarrassed by her yelling out your name in the hallway. Her oldest daughter, Patricia (Tish), and I were classmates for 12 years and went to the same college. Many times, our moms took us back and forth to campus, and I remember how Mrs. Hall felt so sorry for me when it was raining, which meant that her car would probably get stuck on the muddy dirt road leading to my house. She would bring me down the hill, and then we would all pray that she would make it back up the hill. And she did many times.

Her second daughter, Danita, joined me and Tish at Ole Miss our sophomore year. One day during our senior year Tish told me and a few friends gathered in the dorm that Mrs. Hall was having a baby. We carried on like you would not believe. We had already spoiled the youngest, Yolanda (Lu-Lu). However, we at 20 years old just could not imagine Mrs. Hall having a baby at her age – not that we outsiders even knew her age.

So then came Natasha, whom everyone loved and spoiled even more and watched grow into a smart and accomplished young woman. When Tasha got married a few years ago in Arizona, aside from the opportunity to see everyone after far too many years, I don't know why, but I felt compelled to attend her wedding, and I did.

Danita and Tasha now offer more insight about their mother.

As Remembered by Danita Hall

My name is Danita Hall. I am the second oldest child of Billy and Ruby Hall. I have six siblings, three brothers and three sisters. I say this because I want to lay the foundation of what a remarkable woman my mother was to her family and everyone she came into contact with during the course of her short life time.

Where do I start?

Ruby Doris (Buggs) Hall was born in the small town of Houlka, Miss. on June 6, 1929. She met my father, Billy Hall, who hailed from Water Valley and the two married on February 4, 1951. My father was an auto mechanic by trade, but unfortunately, he hurt his back and became disabled in his early thirties. At the time, my parents had six children—Patricia, Danita, Dennis, Marvin, Tony and Yolanda (the seventh (Natasha) didn't come along until much later). For those who didn't know, my father was denied any and all types of government assistance. As a result, my mother was the sole provider for the family on her small teacher's salary but still sent us to college, although we had to acquire loans, grants and work study, which wasn't always enough. We all managed, though, with my mother's help and graduated with college degrees. The only exception was my youngest sister, Natasha (Hall) Weaver, J.D. She was the smartest one of all of us, and she received a full four-year academic scholarship from The University of Mississippi. My mother had passed away before she finished high school.

Ruby Hall was the epitome of education! She taught 5th and 6th grade math for 37 years! In fact, she taught me for two consecutive years. A loving mother, wife, friend and overall person, she was a beast in the classroom. She believed that every child had the capacity to learn, not get passed along because he or she was a problem kid, or for any other reason. She didn't believe in failure. I fondly remember one incident in her classroom when I was in the 6th grade.

No one in the entire classroom except me and my best friend, Diane (Lewis) Hervey, knew the answers to the problems she presented to us on the blackboard. Back then, teachers were allowed to give a student a "paddling" across their legs while sitting in a chair, which consisted of a maximum of 10 licks. She had the entire class line up for a paddling, except for me and Diane. As she paddled one student after the next, the two of us began laughing at our classmates. She told us to stop laughing. We disobeyed. Needless to say, when she finished paddling our classmates, she called the two of us and gave us a paddling.

I was crushed and humiliated beyond words. How could she embarrass me in front of my classmates?

That, in itself, spoke to the type of teacher she was – she didn't believe in favoritism. She treated all students equally and fairly. However, that didn't stop me from not speaking to her for a solid week after I received that paddling. And, as a side note, I had to address her as "Mrs. Hall" like all the rest of the kids. She wouldn't respond to "Mama" on the school grounds from me or any of my siblings.

Although Mama was hard on us kids in the classroom, our house became the "after school hangout" for most of the neighborhood kids. It didn't matter whether she was our teacher or not, or how old we were. Some of the high schools kids came over to play with us as well, especially for the softball games.

We also played badminton, or croquet in our back yard just about every day after school. However, my oldest sister (Patricia), and I weren't allowed to go outside to play until we finished all of our chores. Our closest friends came to our rescue on some days and helped us out so that we could go outside before it got dark. Diane and I rode our bicycles all over town. When the neighborhood kids and friends would come over, they came through the back door on most days.

My mother wouldn't let a kid pass through without quizzing him/her with a math problem that was appropriate to that particular child's age. What is 7 times 7? What is the square root of 81? If "$x = 10$, and the sum of $x+y = 25$, what is y"?

She never stopped teaching. I truly believed that the kids came through the back door for that reason alone. They wanted to please my Mama by providing the correct answers which gave them a small sense of satisfaction as a Black child. She was very understanding if one of us got a "C" in English or some other course, but you better not bring a "C" home on your report card in math, regardless of who taught us.

My mother worked at other jobs during the summers when school was out. She didn't have a choice, given that she was

Ruby Doris Buggs Hall

the sole provider for our family. She was a proud woman. She wouldn't allow any of us to take on any jobs that required cleaning other people's homes, which was basically all there was in Water Valley at the time. Instead of having a carefree summer off, she worked and worked and worked, making the choice to let us older girls run the house rather than have us work at someone else's home. That was who she was.

I loved my mother like no other. She instilled the following three things in me as we were growing up:

A person is right until proven wrong. If proven wrong, be woman or man enough to say "I stand corrected."

We are not a minority (as a race). You might be a minority if you are the only woman or man in the room (for example), but never as a race.

Be true to yourself.

I took those three things to heart, and it actually helped me in a major way to get through the difficult times at Water Valley High School (1970-1971) during my senior year, which was also the year Water Valley fully integrated all grades--no more white versus black schools. I believe one of the earlier articles that Camille Fly Dautrich wrote said it all.

As for Daddy, he would sit on a stool and cut hair just so he would have a few spending dollars in his pocket and not be a burden to our mother. She hardly ever complained, although I did see her cry one or two times simply from being overwhelmed because she didn't have enough money to provide for us in the manner she felt we deserved. This broke my heart, but as a teenager, I couldn't do anything from a financial perspective.

Besides being a teacher, my mother played on the women's softball team until she had breast cancer and had a radical mastectomy. She would run around the bases like she was a teenager herself.

After the surgery, she coached the team until she could no longer do it. She believed in God and attended Sanders Chapel Church in Water Valley until her death.

I miss her dearly, but I know she is in Heaven teaching math to somebody! You can count on that (no pun intended)!

As Remembered by Natasha Hall Weaver

If I had to choose one word to define my mama, it would be 'strength.' Ruby Doris Buggs Hall epitomized it. And when I say strength, I'm not talking about the strength that comes from lifting copious amounts of weights in a gym; I'm talking about the strength that can only be gained after surrendering your life to Christ and learning to lean on Him for perfect peace when times grow hard. You see as a school teacher in the deep south where wages were perennially at the bottom of the earnings scale, and in a household that was primarily dependent on that meager salary to support a family of two adults and seven children, strength was a prerequisite for survival.

Mama's strength was also evident in the example she set by supporting rather than emasculating my daddy as he unsuccessfully fought the state of Mississippi – several times – for disability benefits after the accident that rendered him unable to work as a mechanic. As a young girl around seven or eight-years old, I remember making the trek to Jackson, MS with my parents as they fought this fight together. Although each denial by the state took something out of them, it also reinforced their resolve to make ends meet for their family no matter what. For Mama, that meant taking summer jobs outside of the house when school was over and 'doing hair' from the house in the evenings and on weekends. For Daddy, that meant becoming a 'shade tree mechanic' and an in-home barber. Together, they grew a garden, raised hogs and fished as much as time would allow. They made sure their family always had enough to eat. They were my living example that there is strength in numbers.

But for me, the greatest show of strength came on the day we learned of Daddy's untimely death. At the time, I was one-week shy of my 13th birthday. Mama was about one-year post-recovery from having a radical unilateral mastectomy. Daddy had left before the sun rose to go fishing with a family friend as was usual during the summer. Mama and I were running errands when the tragic accident occurred (Daddy had a massive heart attack while fishing). We first learned that something might be wrong after returning home; our neighbors had received confirmation but didn't know how best to tell us and only alluded to the 'possibility' of something being awry. After receiving several calls, Mama decided to drive to the sheriff's office to find out the truth herself; simply put, she was strong-willed and had the type of personality that would always rather know the truth no matter how hurtful the truth might be in the end. It was at the sheriff's office where I witnessed Mama's strength in action. As she received confirmation of Daddy's death over the radio system, she broke down and grieved… but she didn't forget to embrace me in the process. During her most vulnerable moment, she had the strength to care for me in her grief – and I've never forgotten that valuable lesson to this day. It was 1985 and Dad was only 57 years old.

Two years later, I witnessed Mama's immeasurable strength again as she was preparing to die. Shortly after Daddy died, Mama's cancer resurfaced and attacked her lungs. When we realized the cancer was out of remission, one lung had collapsed, and the other lung was continually filling with fluid. True to her personality, my strong-willed Mama outright asked her oncologist how much longer she had to live. She explained that she had a minor child and she needed to make provisions for me. And Mama did just that. She didn't want me becoming a ward of the court, so she enlisted the help of my sister, Danita. The two of them hired a lawyer who drafted and finalized her will and made sure I would legally be provided for according to her wishes. She said what needed to be said to each of her children and died in peace. In other words, she handled her business! There was never a time when I didn't respect either of my parents, but when I reflect on the strength and courage it took to make the decisions she made as she was dying, my heart, spirit and soul overflow with happiness and gratitude at the gift provided by my Mama.

Because I was so young when Daddy and Mama died, I often asked God why he took them and left me behind. That was before I understood that each individual has purpose in life. As a wife of almost seven years, and the mother of a 4½-year old son, I'm eternally grateful for the life lessons taught to me by my parents. Because I witnessed the way Mama handled Daddy's disability denial, I learned how to treat my husband in a non-emasculative way. Because Mama was able to comfort me in her time of grief, I've learned to never consider my grief (or problems) greater than anyone else's. And because Mama never forgot that she was a mother – even as she was facing death head on, I've learned that God gave me the gift that is my child, and it's my responsibility to provide for him at all times. I didn't realize it at the time, but both Mama and Daddy were equipping me with valuable life lessons that I would be able to draw from when needed.

Final Thoughts by Dottie Reed

As students at Davidson schools we were blessed to have many outstanding teachers and role models. Mrs. Hall was by far one of the favorites of favorites. We loved her. She was real. She was funny. And she was absolutely intentional about wanting us all to succeed. She made us feel important, that we mattered.

She was a "virtuous renaissance woman," a black woman of unbelievable strength and impeccable character. We were so privileged to have her in our lives and we can, if we are honest, give her credit for inspiring much of our success. Mrs. Ruby Doris Hall exuded confidence, respect and a moral fortitude that touched many lives in a way that we should never forget.

She showed us how to be a professional woman, a wife, and a mother with pride and integrity when segregation was still the norm and well before the women's movement took hold. She chose to work as a cashier during the summers because she did not want her daughters to work cleaning houses for whites. Mrs. Hall passed on November 19, 1987. She was 58. Two years earlier Mr. Billy died on August 14th, 1985. He was 57 years old.

If Mrs. Hall influenced your life or if you are inspired after learning about her from her daughters, can you commit today to do something to make a difference as she did? I know I can, and I will. I invite you to join me in her memory to do more to positively impact our youth and young adults.

Reader Comments

I am sitting just reading your heart warming and inspirational article of people who actually suffered and would have something to be depressed about. Not one negative from either of the two daughters with all they had to deal with in their young lives and all the siblings were productive and accomplished in their lives, because of such a devoted and giving Mother. Please keep warming my heart and teaching me the struggles with these amazing life stories.
Jim Brzoska,
Deltona, FL

I really enjoyed the Hall sisters write up on their mother and father. As a child you don't at times realize or see what's happening right in your face. I knew she was a teacher but did not realize how strong she was. I knew she worked in the evening doing hair in her kitchen. She did my mother's hair and mine. Even though she was a hard worker with a lot of responsibilities since Mr. Hall had a disability, she never showed any signs of her struggle. I remember her as a firm woman always smiling and seemingly happy in her life. Danita and Natasha did a wonderful job giving us a look into their lives.
Patricia Pate,
Olive Branch, MS

I used to hang at her house. She was truly a hero!
Fred Harris,
Seattle, WA

This was one of my favorite articles.
Carolyn West,
Atlanta, GA

22

The Women Who Worked On Dupuy, Panola And Leland Streets

Born and raised in Water Valley, I never knew or never noticed Dupuy or Leland Streets, but my mother, Helen, worked for the Gurners on Panola Street. We often walked on Panola on our way to church on Sundays. When I went to work with my mother, we walked up the Gurners' driveway into the kitchen through the back door.

The homes of white people smelled different to me, and I was fascinated by the size, the furnishings, the books, magazines and the newspapers. When we went to other houses where my mother worked as a maid, I was amazed by the amount and different types of food and the fact that the kids had their own rooms. I was well aware at an early age of the differences: We were Black, and they were White, the haves and the have nots. I played with some of the white kids but understood the friendship could only go so far and at a certain age had to be severed.

A "colored" sign hung on the door where we went to the doctor, and going to the dentist for preventive dentistry was unheard of. If and when we went to the dentist, it was to get a tooth pulled, not to save it. In my early years I knew very little about Water Valley's white community or lifestyles aside from the interaction with the white families my mother worked for or the one family I babysat for in the summer or the white landowners that my dad might have done business with.

Camille Fly Dautrich, a Water Valley native has again obliged us by collecting memories of the women who worked in her neighborhood, the majority of whom I knew and am now pleased to know more about.

She describes a way of life unfamiliar to many of us in the black community. I firmly believe that the sacrifices these women made and the work they did in nurturing these families perhaps made Water Valley a tad better place to live in terms of race relations at that time. Yet now, we are experiencing a rise in overt racism nationally like we have never seen before. When will we ever learn? Will we ever learn? What can we do about it?

So Much More Than "The Help" The Women Who Helped Raise Us
by Camille Fly Dautrich

Growing up with a whole crew of Baby Boomers in the Dupuy/Panola/Leland Streets neighborhood, my friends and I moved easily from one house to another. We knew everyone's parents and everyone's pets. In many cases, we also knew another member of these families – the women who came to our houses, cooked, cleaned and helped raise us. In searching for a word to call these ladies, the most common one might be our "maids," but in truth, they were much, much more.

I've tried to compile some memories of a few of these extraordinary people, who left their own homes and children to take care of us, and I've asked my neighborhood friends to help me. One of the best tributes was from Dorothy Caulfield Wiman, who wrote about Cora Folson. Dorothy's memories have appeared in this space as a stand-alone column, but here are some additional stories about other ladies.

We have many good memories, but unfortunately, we don't have photographs to go with them, so this story is going to be heavy on copy and light on images. Still, we all have pictures in our heads of these women we loved.

African-American friends, please keep in mind that while it might not seem fair that, in many ways, we took these ladies away from you, rest assured—we loved them very much and they taught us many life lessons.

My nearest childhood neighbors were the Throop girls—India, Carlisle and Ruth—and their housekeeper, "Bobbie," Barbara Jean Hervey was a favorite of mine. Bobbie was so classy—pretty to look at and fun to be with. Here's what Carlisle (now Carlisle Parsons Wood) had to say after a sisters' get-together with Ruth and India in Colorado:

"As I write, Ruth and I are sitting on a plane waiting to be towed back to the gate due to maintenance issues. So, I am thinking of our Bobbie who was a best friend to Mama and like another mother to us. Here are a few of my memories of her:

• She sang "O Holy Night" at her church on Christmas Eve, and she would sing it for us before that day.

• She was a wonderful cook. I especially loved her blackberry cobbler, which she made for me on my birthday. I try to make it now, but it never seems as good as hers. And she made potato cakes, which were like fried patties of mashed potatoes with a light crust.

• She taught me to iron, and I think of her when I get the ironing board down.

• I wonder sometimes if Bobbie knew how much we loved and appreciated her. I hope so."

Ruth Throop Wilbourn added, "Yes, Bobbie Hervey was our favorite and was just like a member of our family." India Throop Mount sent a photo of Bobbie to be included with this story.

A little further afield but still in the neighborhood, Genny Wiley Seely wrote about Sarah Brooks. Genny was a few years older than I was and was a best friend to my late sister, Harriet. Here's what Genny wrote:

"We moved to Water Valley when I was four, and the lady I remember keeping me when we lived on Kimmons Avenue was Sarah Brooks. She lived over the hill from us. When she was helping me get dressed, she would warm the inside of my jeans by the gas heater. In first grade, I would read my lesson to her and she would write the teacher a note saying I had done my reading assignment. I remember her coming to the new house on Prospect Drive a few times, but not regularly. By that time, I was in junior high and high school."

During this time, Snooky and Mary Lou Williams and their three children—Charmie, Paul and Ben—moved to Water Valley to run Stubbs Department Store. Charmie (Weeks) remembers the ladies who looked after her hardworking family, both when she was a child and later as an adult.

"Maggie Lee Sanders kept us when I was a toddler," Charmie wrote. "We would drive to the country to pick her up. If I recall correctly, she lived at the end of a long dirt driveway off a country highway. She would hold Paul on her hip while she did housework. I remember her smile and her contagious laugh. Her daughter, Dorothy, was one of the first black children to come into our school system. She was in my class. We were able to reunite at our class reunion last fall."

Later, the Williams and Weeks families relied on Mildred Backstrom to take care of things while they were all at work, first at Stubbs and later at Everett Cock Insurance Agency.

Charmie continued, "Mildred Backstrom lived on the street behind the Crip Tyler family. She was wonderful. When court was in session, Mother would have her cook a big lunch at our house to feed the out-of-town judges. When I moved home, mother and I used her full-time. She would go to Mother's in the morning, clean and cook lunch. After lunch she would walk to my house on Dupuy and clean for me. She would have a wonderful supper ready at the end of the day for us. She was great with Angela and Matt. She moved to the Chicago area as she got older to be with her family. We kept in touch until she passed away."

Camille talking here...

Jane Henry Crow, who at that time lived behind us, often walked down our street with Vinnie Wright, of whom she said, "All I really know is I loved her, and she loved me." One thing I remember about Vinnie myself is that Jane was so little and Vinnie, who was a large woman, would hold out her index finger, and Jane would hang onto it while they walked. They made quite a pair!

All of us in the neighborhood remember Ora Lee Wilson, who with her husband, Snooks, also lived behind the Tylers. She officially worked for Buck and Mary Suratt and their son Bobby (all gone now), while Snooks worked for Mr. Suratt at Blu-Bucks, Ora Lee looked after the rest of us as well in her "spare" time. I remember her babysitting for me at night sometimes, and even though I was probably old enough to stay by myself, I never complained because I loved her company. Her only problem was she wouldn't sit still and watch tv with me; Ora Lee always had to be up doing something. For some reason I remember her ironing our bedsheets, something you would never catch me doing today!

The Throop girls with an unidentified woman.

"Ora Lee was a great friend to Mamma when she was much older," said Jennifer Cofer Flanagan. Ora Lee and Snooks had a son named Buddy who was about our age or a little older, and I remember Mary Brooks Tyler and me sitting in a treehouse in her backyard on summer afternoons, where we could hear poor Buddy being made to practice the piano.

I'm going to digress a little here and tell a story about Buddy, who—when we were small—got bit by a stray dog in front of our house. He rang the doorbell and was out front crying, and my mother brought him inside and set him on the edge of the bathtub, pulled down his jeans and swabbed and bandaged his leg, then gave him a ride home to Ora Lee's. That was a good lesson for me—love, respect and care flow, it turns out, in both directions.

Finally, I'll write about the women I grew up with. When I was a tiny girl, we had a maid named Elnora, and I'm sorry to

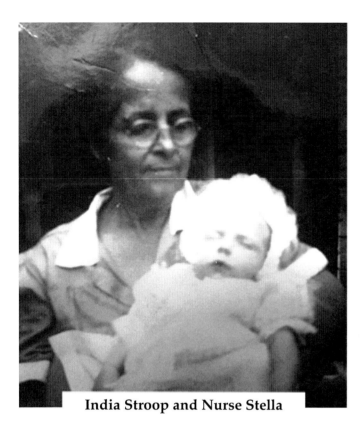
India Stroop and Nurse Stella

say I don't remember her last name. I do remember her as old and grouchy because she fussed at me a lot, especially while she was standing at the ironing board. Some years later, I mentioned to my mother that I couldn't remember Elnora when she was anything but out of sorts, and Mama straightened me out fast. "She loved you so much," she said. Talk about feeling pretty low and pretty guilty. I just hope Elnora is sitting up in Heaven today, knowing that I wish I'd gotten to know her better.

When I was older, Juanita Cox helped my parents a lot as they aged, but the housekeeper I remember best was Minnie Jenkins. Minnie also lived on Dupuy Street, a few blocks west of us, and she walked to work every day. My folks both worked at the bank and my sister Harriet was at school already. So I got to spend a lot of time with Minnie when it was just the two of us. After I went to school, she was always around in the summer and we had our time together then.

When I think of Minnie, what I most remember is that she helped me learn to read. My mother had gotten some beginning readers from Mrs. Afton Smith, longtime first grade teacher. They were about Dick, Jane, Spot and Puff, and Minnie and I worked on them every day so I could show off what I'd learned when Mama and Daddy got home from the bank. I faithfully read along with Minnie and learned every word in those books, imitating Minnie's southern black accent perfectly!

Another great memory of Minnie, that I have recalled many times was when her son and his family visited her from Waterloo, Iowa, and she asked me if I'd want to walk over to her house and spend the morning with her family. We walked over, and it was, oh, so hot. We didn't have air conditioning and neither did Minnie, so when we got ready to head back to my house, her son asked if we wanted a ride. He put me on the front seat between him and Minnie, and his car was air conditioned and oh, so cool. The ride was short, and I hated for it to end because that air was blissful.

When I tell this story about riding in his car, I always say that if he had said, "Little white girl, would you like to ride up to Iowa and live with us?," I would have said, "You bet, let's go!" It wasn't too terribly long after that when we got some window unit air conditioners for the house, and again, it was like paradise for Minnie and me. The only problem was when I got home from school, if Minnie had left and nobody else was home yet, I had to play in the yard till somebody got home. I can remember putting my face up to the mail slot by the front door so I could feel the cool air inside.

This doesn't have anything to do with Minnie, but when I was eight years old, I got a key to the house so I wouldn't have to wait outside for someone else to come home (Harriet usually had band practice, so she and I didn't get home at the same time.) That was a pivotal day in my life to be certain!

This photo from the 1950s shows India and Carlisle Throop (right) along with other unidentified children and ladies.

Eventually Minnie got too old to live alone, and her son moved her up to Waterloo. She'd write us occasionally, long rambling letters that often said "Smile" in parentheses, the way people today write "lol."

But then one day, we got the news that she had died. We didn't get to go to the funeral, but the next summer we drove to Waterloo to visit the cemetery and put flowers on her grave.

I don't have a photo of Minnie, but I have so many good memories—she was part of the village that raised me. Like Elnora, I hope Minnie is up in Heaven secure in the knowledge that I loved her like a second mother. My whole immediate family is gone now—my parents, my sisters Harriet and Barbara—and Minnie. But I'll always remember them with love and thanks for helping make me into the woman I am today.

Reader Comments

You offer an amazing portrait of strong women who contributed a lot to society despite the incredible challenges they faced.
Maryann McGuire,
Atlanta, GA

Once again you have hit another home run! Some of these stories catch me thinking of Mayberry and Andy the sheriff but with integration and all with wonderful lessons and happy memories and good things we could all stand to learn.
Jim Brzoska,
Deltona, FL

This was especially awesome...the reflections from our Caucasian sisters/families....keep them coming.
Dianne Prince,
Orlando, FL

23

One Year Later
Black Women of Yalobusha County

Unbelievable best describes my feelings about how this project has advanced. Several months back my millennial cousin, Jametric Judson, said to me, "You didn't think this would get this big did you"?

I smiled and said, 'No I did not." Though I explained its origin in the first article, I did not mention that I wrote the piece from a hospital bed. Now I can celebrate the first anniversary and a new lease on life. I have not heard that phrase in a long time and am not sure if it is appropriate to use. I am so thankful and give all the glory to God.

I am humble indeed to be writing article number 23 and consider this project a true blessing. While the design is to recognize unsung but outstanding women from a small, little known county in Mississippi – Yalobusha - we are moving forward.

Its location 18 miles from the state's flagship university has placed the county in an interesting position. More and more academicians or folks associated with Ole Miss are moving into the area. Yet a decade or so earlier, drivers would rarely stop in Water Valley, one of the county seats and my hometown, or any place in Yalobusha County; they just passed through.

The county population is around 14,000 with fewer than 4,000 in Water Valley. By the way, there is also a Water Valley in Kentucky and one in Texas - both much smaller than Mississippi's.

While I cannot claim that the circulation of the *North Mississippi Herald* has increased, I can say that this project has opened doors to relationships that were dormant or non-existent. The positive phone calls from white men have been the most surprising and welcomed. The comments from my family and close friends have been empowering even if I have not been able to convince my sons that they could learn more about their mother if they would read my work!

Black men from Water Valley now living in other states have encouraged me to write about their male friends and family members, especially the veterans. The positive comments keep coming. Others keep mentioning writing a book, but I am nowhere near there.

The most perplexing phenomenon is how this project continues to grow – one column leads to another without stress or gaps or a lack of ideas. And there is no shortage of outstanding black women either. I believe I mentioned before that I have never taken a journalism course and barely made it through my second-year English courses, and I have no recollection of taking a math class.

I best leave that alone, for fear that Ole Miss might try to take my degree back. My readers have told me that they look forward to each article, and that one or another has inspired, reminded them of their past or opened their minds or hearts in a new and meaningful way.

This column pulls me into my past while exploring the lives of some remarkably strong black women, and though I feel I am sharing way too much about me, if that is what it takes to continue to move this project forward, so be it.

I do not think that my life has been exceptional in any way. Many others grew up like me in the deep south, in my case so sheltered and deprived that I am embarrassed to say that I'm still learning about how poor and deprived I was. Reminiscing is not always fun and can even be sad and depressing.

This is the reason I am so thankful for the women and men who guided and covered me. I now find it most rewarding to examine their lives more closely. In doing so, we learn more, and we become better. Working with Ole Miss this fall to gather individual and family stories will allow us to dig deeper into the richness of our community and help us understand and appreciate our history. We must record and preserve it for the generations to come.

Following is a portion of my history in my review of former first lady, Michelle Obama's book *Becoming*, where she wrote about being first and black.

Becoming First and Black

I love former First Lady Michelle Obama! After hearing a couple of her interviews about her book, *Becoming*, I asked myself what else could I learn from the book itself. Not much, I thought. So why buy it? Definitely no need to rush to get it. I'll just wait for one of my girlfriends to finish hers. Book sales were off the charts, and her book tour arenas were selling out with overflow crowds.

With another 10-day stay in Fayetteville, North Carolina facing me – I would be staying with my 13-year-old grandson while his Fort Bragg 2nd lieutenant dad is out in the field again – I decided I best get a good book. And I did, finding in *Becoming* Michelle Obama's honest and open account of her life. It prompted deep reflection of my own.

While I was already a great admirer of our former first lady, my respect for the relationship between her and President Obama has also increased. Needless to say, the story of her life is incredible and inspiring, a black girl born and raised on the south side of Chicago becoming the First Lady of the United States of America. Not a dream come true because it was never in her dreams.

I did not expect to personally relate to so much in the book, but what she wrote on page 284 spoke to me: "I was humbled and excited to be First Lady, but not for one second did I think I'd be sliding into some glamorous, easy role. Nobody who has the words 'first and black' attached to them ever would. I stood at the foot of the mountain, knowing I'd need to climb my way into favor."

This called me back to a time when first and black was associated with my name, and I, too like Mrs. Obama asked myself if I was good enough. She writes, "Confidence, I'd learned then, sometimes needs to be called from within. I've repeated the same words to myself many times now, through many climbs. Am I good enough? Yes I am."

The black doctoral student, Dr. Ben Jones, who urged me to apply for the admissions counselor job at Ole Miss in 1974, purchased my first briefcase when I got the job. He left before I could really thank and appreciate him for the gift. That gesture boosted my confidence in ways that I have not forgotten and provided just the encouragement I needed.

I had graduated and turned 22 on August 4th (same birthday as President Obama). I spent the summer of 1974 job hunting and working at my cousin's gas station on Main Street in Water Valley. As I pumped gas and cleaned front car windows, I worried what folks were thinking and found myself questioning my choice of colleges and especially my liberal arts degree. I was even more concerned about being a burden to my parents.

The university job was only the second job offer that I had received by the end of the summer. Even so, I accepted it with serious reservations and felt quite ill prepared to become the first black recruiter for the flagship university of the state of Mississippi. My work study job in the computer center as a student had given me the opportunity to work with the admissions office during registration each semester. I didn't realize that this would enable me to become familiar with the staff and the many enrollment and admissions procedures. Alas, I was afraid, not sure what to expect, what to wear, how to act, how I would be treated, and not sure if I could do the job – recruiting students, and black students in particular, to attend Ole Miss.

After much preparation, job shadowing and practice, I headed out on my own to my assigned high schools, overly concerned about how I would be received, much like how the First Lady felt when she began campaigning for her husband's run for the presidency. Being black and female, I was cautioned directly and indirectly about the likelihood of tension, resistance and racism. I was cautioned about traveling alone across the Delta and north Mississippi to speak to students, counselors and other school personnel about Ole Miss. I had to be careful to avoid restaurants and facilities where blacks were not welcomed. I was also careful to get back home or to my hotel before dark. I had my share of encounters and survived, growing from them all. Yet, I was still quite naive but developed a level of confidence in dealing within the university environment and working across the state of Mississippi and western Tennessee. Perhaps I will write more about my travels and experiences if and when it can serve more definitive purposes.

When Mrs. Obama wrote about her undergraduate experience at Princeton in the early 1980s, again I was able to relate and sadly see similarities to my experience

Dottie Chapman Reed, who graduated from the University of Mississippi in 1974, became the school's first black admissions counselor. She is pictured above on the cover of the Ole Miss telephone directory.

10 years or so earlier: the financial aid package, the work study job, enrolling in the summers to get ahead, and the "effective study" classes in the fall where the majority of the students – black - were taught how to study. (Placement was based on recommendation of your counselor, your entrance test scores or an easy grade.) And the white roommate? The only difference mine did not want to move out. She stayed. Alas, dealing with the classroom antics of white students, the scrutiny of white professors and just being the minority were the biggest challenges.

With the opportunity to write this column and to move forward in developing a project with four Ole Miss PhD's, first and black beckons me and calls me to press on. I have learned as the First Lady did to draw on my inner strength and to keep up the momentum as we see her doing today, for the better good of mankind and our society, to go high when others go low.

I was so naive as a black first and had no idea whether I could be effective or not. In 1974 I was the first black in administration and the only one in the administration building known as the Lyceum. When I prepared to move on in my career and began saying my goodbyes after 3 years, one of my white sociology associates told me that I appeared to be more comfortable on the Ole Miss campus than the average white person. I found that quite disconcerting. He was so wrong. I was never comfortable. I am not comfortable in Mississippi. My mind went back to the first time I met James Meredith, touring the campus with him to see the dorm where he lived, and listening as he recounted his experience, noting the changes on the campus as best he could remember. I also am reminded of the looks sometimes on the faces of prospective white students and parents when this afro-wearing admissions counselor bounced into the admissions office to take them on a campus tour. Most often, I was able to win them over and never heard of any complaints. I also felt a cold strangeness when families asked me to take them to Rowan Oak, William Faulkner's home for a tour. Can you imagine – funny – huh?

As years passed and folks asked me how I recruited for a white school with such a blatant history of racism and discrimination, I resolved that my role/goal became that of convincing students that college was, in my opinion, the best option to get ahead in Mississippi in the late 1970's. Providing admissions, financial aid and college entrance information was what I shared and believed that it would apply wherever students chose to apply. I offered myself as an example, telling them that if I did it, they could, too. I also assured them and sometimes their parents that I would be there for them. In the three years that I recruited, black student enrollment tripled, and I left behind recruiting tools that were duplicated by other white universities and still being used by some today.

The purest irony of my first and black story is that when I graduated in the last Davidson High School Class in 1970, quite disillusioned and anxious about saying goodbye to Water Valley, seeing the world and being on my own, I caught a bus to Detroit with absolutely no intentions of going to college. Much to my chagrin a summer job or fulltime employment did not materialize, and I had to come back home just days before college classes were starting. I had only applied to Ole Miss, through their pre- college program, where I had participated two summers in a row. With no other options, my mother dropped me at the home of a friend, Mrs. Doxey Foster in Oxford, the night before registration opened. Mrs. Foster arranged for Jennifer Jackson, a young woman and an Ole Miss student from her church, to pick me up the next morning and take me to register for college. As Jennifer and I arrived on campus and walked toward

New admission counselors announced

UNIVERSITY — Two pretty, young University of Mississippi graduates are preparing for their first year of travel across Mississippi and other Southern states as Admissions Counselors for their alma mater.

Frances Permenter of Gulfport and Dottie Chapman of Water Valley—both 1974 graduates of Ole Miss—added new dimensions to the University admissions program when they began work recently. Miss Chapman is the first full-time black Admissions Counselor while Miss Permenter is the second member of her family to hold the position.

MISS PERMENTER and Miss Chapman studied sociology while in undergraduate school and they feel the courses they took will help them work with high school students who are deciding where to attend college.

Miss Permenter—who was preceeded at the job by her older sister, Walterine—said "change at Ole Miss" is the key element in the admissions program.

"We've got no hours for women, the freedom to live off-campus, the growing number of activities on campus plus the growth and change of Oxford," she said.

Miss Chapman said she will emphasize the academic points of the University.

"Ole Miss has grown academically, and I plan to tell students about that. Other schools just don't offer students as much," she said.

THE TWO new Admission Counselors are now training and will begin traveling to numerous high schools in October. Later this month, they will attend several fairs—including the Mid-South Fair in Memphis and the Mississippi State Fair in Jackson—where they will open booths to distribute literature about Ole Miss and talk to interested high school and junior college students as well as parents.

Miss Chapman is the daughter of Mr. and Mrs. Alvin Chapman of Water Valley, and Miss Permenter' parents are Mr. and Mrs. Walter N. Permenter of Gulfport.

New counselors

Mike White (left), assistant director of Admissions at the University of Mississippi, and Richard Martin, admissions counselor, discuss travel plans with the department's new counselors, Dottie Chapman (second from right) of Water Valley and Frances Permenter of Gulfport. Miss Chapman and Miss Permenter will be discussing Ole Miss with high school students as they visit schools across the South.

---

the coliseum, we ran into my homegirls, Beatrice Hawkins and Patricia Hall. The three took me under their wings and got me registered. I had no financial aid, no dorm, just a small suitcase, and I wish I could remember how little money I had. I remember I was to let my mother know how much money I needed. I hoped that I would not have to call her because I knew she did not have it, nor did I want her to try to get it.

Though I can't say this is a full circle experience just yet, I am working with Ole Miss this time around, and I will repeat the same words to myself many times now, through many climbs. Am I good enough? Yes, I am.

Thank you, First Lady!

As the Reverend Everett Kimble of Orlando, Fla. puts it: "God would not bring us to it if He did not know we could do it!"

Reader Comments

I could just cry! I appreciate your openness about the challenges you faced every day because of racism. I also appreciate your drawing on your faith and examples of others who faced similar challenges. May God bless you as you continue this wonderful project.
Dorothy Wiman,
Winona, MS

I am so happy that your articles continue to be successful and inspiring. You are doing such a great job of sharing information on these women that would not get the recognition they deserve.
Lillian Dent,
Long Island, NY

24

Segregation Side Effects
Revisted From the Other Perspective

Last November, this column featured an article about the integration of Water Valley High in 1966. In February, in "Segregation Side Effects – I Feel Cheated – Do You?", we presented an account of the total integration of Water Valley public schools when the black Davidson schools and the predominately white Water Valley schools merged. Davidson High School graduated its last class in 1970, and all the future students enrolled in Water Valley High, Davidson Middle and Elementary in the fall of 1970.

I was a member of that last Davidson Class of 1970 and recall a watch and wait state of mind. I was not sure what to expect following the enrollment of the first three black students at WVHS in 1966. If I remember correctly they were followed by a few others in the subsequent years, and all was perceived as peaceful. By the fall of 1970 mandatory integration came as the freedom of choice option ended. I remember feeling relieved that my class and I had been spared the transition. I could not bear the thought of riding a bus with the same white kids who jeered at me every day for almost 12 years as I waited each morning for my bus. In my latter high school years, I could see WVHS from my bus stop, with nary an urge to set foot in the building.

In the meantime, at Davidson we were subjected to a lot of standardized testing, whose purpose I never understood, nor do I recall if it was ever made clear to us students. We also acquired white teachers including a white male guidance counselor.

How ironic, I thought. We had never had a guidance counselor before and now a white one. He was also a minister who went back and forth between the two schools, WVHS and DHS. The majority of Davidson students gave him a hard time, and sometimes I felt sorry for him because he tried really hard to convince us that he had our best interest at heart. He was the lead administrator in the standardized testing. Very few of us sought his counseling advice aside from signing up to take the ACT, which was required to complete applications for college.

Shortchanged, misunderstood and abused is how I and I believe most of my classmates felt in 1969 as we realized we juniors would be the last class to graduate from DHS. The junior class of 1968 had taken the seniors on a trip to New Orleans. It had been a tradition that the junior class sponsor a trip, a picnic or something for the senior class based on what had been given to the previous class.

The administrators decided that we were too immature and rebellious and forbade us to take the seniors on an out-of-town trip. We were sure this was punishment for the way we treated the white guidance counselor Alas, we could not work out a fair solution. We were a small class, fewer than 30 students, and both the senior and sophomore classes of '69 were twice our size. We did not feel that it would be appropriate to ask the upcoming junior class of 1970 to participate in the tradition since they would be heading to WVHS in the fall. Nor would it be fair to offer the senior class of 1969 anything less than a trip to New Orleans or a comparable location. Nor could we accept the administration's assessment of our class.

Financial concerns also played a part because neither we nor the junior class of '70 would be repaid. Ultimately, we ended up not giving the seniors anything, and the tradition was lost with that class, much to our chagrin. Needless to say, our junior and senior years at Davidson were not the most enjoyable. We just muddled through, our days clouded by a lingering sadness, a fear of the unknown and a resentment of losing our school, our teachers and our traditions. Since then there have been some great Davidson school reunions for all classes, but none recently. Some individual class reunions still occur, and the love for Davidson lives on. So in the words of our teacher, Hugh Percy Lark, "We will love our alma mater and to thee be true, Hail to thee our dear old Davidson, Hail oh hail to thee."

Now take a look at what came next as Davidson's junior class of 1970 went on to become members and graduates of the 1971 class of WVHS.

Danita Hall, an exceptional and outstanding woman in her own right, offers her candid perspective. Danita is a Senior Accountant – Finance Department with Youth For Understanding USA.

My Experience as a Member of the WVHS Class of 1971 by Danita Hall

For the WVHS class of '71 it was a very, very tense first month or two of total integration of the previously all white school. Davidson High, the black school was closed, the last class having graduated in May 1970. We would be the first class to graduate following the merger. Everyone (from what I remember) at least had the decency to speak to us, but nothing much more than that until the following happened:

Ms. Rhonda Gardei, who hailed from Florida, was our literature instructor. She was a very petite woman – tanned to the max, with blond hair. She was notorious for dividing her classroom where kids sat to her left and to her right in front of her. She liked to walk down the wide middle of the two sections when she taught. She told us to pick a book to read and bring it to her during our lunch period for her approval.

Well, I chose "Native Son" by Richard Wright. The day I went to get her approval, Trent Howell was behind me to get his book approved as well. She took a look at the book's cover and said yes. A week or two later when I stood at the podium in front of the class to give my oral report, she went off, saying my book was inappropriate and she didn't approve it. [This is why I became very good friends with Trent.]

"Yes, you did," I said.

"No, I didn't, and you need to stop right now and take your seat." She retorted.

"Yes, you did, Ms. Gardei," I repeated, my voice changing by then because I was getting mad.

Then Trent stood up and very politely told her that she did indeed approve my book because he was standing in line behind me that particular day. She was dumbfounded but allowed me to continue. I got an A-plus on the book report in the end.

She had objected to my oral report because she had asked us to include at a minimum the following in the report: Protagonist - Bigger Thomas, Theme, Antagonist and Symbolisms (here we go): I said that the snow represented white people and repression. Everywhere Bigger looked prior to his death was repression -snow and white people. That was pretty much how I felt going to WVHS during the first month or two. It's interesting that "Native Son" recently played on HBO. That report got everyone's attention, needless to say.

Second incident – same instructor. Ms. Gardei asked us to read "The Illiad" by Homer. I had grown a little wiser and knew from my older sister (Patricia) that CliffsNotes were available. She bought this particular pamphlet for me at the Ole Miss book store. Ms. Gardei gave us a test which consisted of four questions. Afterwards she pranced up and down the aisle berating the entire class for failing the test as she was handing our test papers back.

You have to remember that if you get 1-2 right, you fail, 3 gets you a C, and naturally 4 equals an A. Well, she said the entire class had basically failed this test with the exception of one person.

At this point, everyone started looking around at Camille Fly, Trent Howell, Van Hedges, and a couple of others (the academic, white heavy hitters in my class). I sat in the middle section, and I noticed how one would mouth to another, "is it you?" when they were handed back their tests from Ms. Gardei.

He/she would shake their head no. I had no idea who that person was either. After she had passed out all of the test papers, one person was brave enough to ask her to throw out the grade. She said that she had thought about it, but that it wouldn't be fair to the person who had scored 100.

Then she said she would let that person make the decision to throw out the grade or keep it. Again, they all looked around trying to figure out who it was. After some very tense minutes, she finally told them that it was Danita Hall. Mouths dropped open in disbelief. Then she said,

"Danita, do you want to keep it or throw it out?"

"Keep it," I said.

The class was in an uproar. When she got them to be quiet, one person asked me why.

"From what I have experienced and seen thus far at this school, you wouldn't do it for me," I told them. "So help me understand why I should do it for you."

It was an E F Hutton moment at that point. Quiet as a mouse. I truly believe that was the pivot that turned our relationships (blacks/whites) around. After class they wanted to know how I knew all the answers, etc. I became very good friends with Camille, Trent, Dorothy Caulfield, J.C. Womble, Janet Dickey, and a few others.

One white student never really liked any of us and she later organized a 10th class reunion for whites only. One of my very good white friends found out about it, called me and pleaded with me to come. I said no because I thought we had gotten away from all the bigotry, racism, etc, and it was simply the principle of it all. I had attended Ole Miss and had to deal with a lot of racism there and I certainly wasn't going to deal with it 10 years after I had graduated from WVHS.

Yet another white student, perhaps the most popular male athlete, was friendly, but a little on the standoffish side. When we were at Davidson High School, my class was very tight. We never told on anyone –no matter what they did. Patricia Freeman and I were the class leaders, and if we accepted/rejected something, then the entire class followed our suit.

That is why I made the statement in bold above. I knew it would hurt my fellow black classmates, but I had to be true to myself and set an example for my black classmates. I somehow had to prove that I was just as smart and was their equal and that we blacks shouldn't be underestimated, belittled or ignored.

I did get to work in the office since I only had four classes during my senior year. I worked for Mrs. Dale Childress and she was the best. She was a sweetheart and gave me some guidance because she knew what we were dealing with as black students. I have lived on the East Coast since 1982 but when I visited Water Valley, I would go to see her.

I felt that I was cheated out of being the Valedictorian of my graduating class, but that too is another story. Nonetheless, beautiful and lasting friendships came out of my senior year at WVHS. Judge Trent Howell is one of my dear friends. We attended Ole Miss together, and he was the attorney who did the legal work for Mama's will. We have exchanged Christmas cards every year and when I do go to Water Valley, I seek him out if only to hug him and say hello.

He had my back in high school. I will never forget how he stood up for me that day against my English instructor in front of the whole class. His honesty was the catalyst that made my classmates respect me early on during the semester. He was destined to be a judge! I also try to say hello to Janet Dickey at the bank.

More Input from Classmates

Upon hearing that this article was in the works, Danita's classmate Dorothy Caulfield Wiman wrote the following:

"So glad Danita is writing about our senior year. I can hardly believe this year marks our 48th year since graduation. I think it was a wonderful year of meeting new people and getting outside our comfort zone. I think we students had a greater appreciation for each other and a genuine caring for each other unlike previous generations. I'm not saying we did everything right, but I remember our superintendent, Mr. Clovis Steele, addressed us on the first day of school and said something to the effect that there is no black and white and that we would treat each other with respect. Not that we weren't who we are, but that there would be no favoritism. I just wish that I had known black history and understood the deep hurt, profound fear, and humiliation suffered by African Americans. I still have so much to learn, but my dearest African American friends have taught me a lot. They have been very patient with me."

Another classmate, Camille Fly Dautrich, also acknowledged beautiful and lasting friendships in her February article about her experience in the 1971 WVHS Class. While they probably never crossed paths before WVHS, both women developed mutual respect for each other. They grew up on different sides of town, a black side and a white side, and under different lifestyles, one of privilege and one lacking privilege.

Some of the former Davidson students, however, remain scarred from their experience at WVHS. Wounds heal but leave marks as a constant reminder. Time has passed, and the playing field has leveled somewhat. But we still struggle with and suffer from the negative effects of slavery and segregation. Alas, racism and hate crimes are on the rise, but we still have time to make amends, to educate and to reach across the table. It is time for some to offer apologies, to tell the truth, to educate their children and to face the realities.

Remember – our complete history has not been told, has not been printed and is not being taught in our schools. If there was ever a time for truth, it is now. We must exert all efforts to make America whole again.

Finally, I must share the following comments regarding the article that appeared on May 23rd about Danita's mother, Mrs. Ruby Hall. They come from one of her former students, Sean Carothers:

"I just returned home to see a copy of the North Miss Herald laying on my kitchen counter. My wife had apparently gotten it because of an article about a friend's son on the front page. I don't subscribe to it, and I don't keep up much with what is going on in Water Valley.

Danita Hall - Class of 1971

It made me smile when I opened it up and saw Mrs. Hall's picture. The wonderful picture you portrayed of what a fine woman she was, and what a positive influence she made on so many lives was understated. In fact, I don't know if there are words that could do it justice. Mrs. Hall taught me 5th grade I think. Lulu was my classmate and Tony was my friend. I played ball with Tony and Marvin. I was occasionally in their home. Their whole family has always impressed me so. Particularly given the times we were living in. As you know their mother cared for everyone. Care is all I ever felt from her. I have thought so many times of things she said and her demeanor and attitude. She was surely a beacon of light. One of my favorite (memories) that I think about often is her response when someone decided they were sick. Her response would be 'you just sick of living and scared of dying.' I have quoted it often. I consider Mrs. Hall one of the most influential people in my younger years, and as you know, those are the people who mold you into what you become as an adult. I noticed your bio said that you were sharing info about women in the county that have made an impact on the African American community.

Rest assured, Mrs. Hall's impact was much more far reaching than the African American community. I can testify to that."

Reader Comments

For me a little heartbreaking and more so enlightening as to the pain and suffering that prevailed during yours and many other black students time in childhood and as students in learning establishments that were meant for all! Keep these fine articles coming and open other hearts and minds to this tragedy of our times!
Jim Brzoska,
Deltona, FL

I'm excited to read this one. Yesterday had a conversation with teachers about the impact of segregation and integration.
Michael Browning,
Atlanta, GA

I am beginning to see things that I didn't see even then. I pray these articles and this project help us all to grow up in our thinking and to love and appreciate each other as never before.
Dorothy Wiman,
Winona, MS

Alma Polk Nicholson
A Shining Star - A Class Act - A Driving Force

What do you get when two sisters marry two brothers and raise 27 children in the deep south? Shining stars, and one of them is Alma Ophelia Polk Nicholson. As a young girl I admired and idolized many of the older girls in Water Valley, and Alma Polk was one of them. She was always so together - poised, beautiful and confident - and such a lady some would call her "proper." I credit her for keeping me on the right track most of the time because I felt that she expected a lot of me, and I did not want to disappoint her. Today, she still has high expectations for our young people, a signature laugh, and such great diction that you can recognize her by her voice alone. At my request her sister, Mildred, and her brother, Walter, tell us more about their sister.

Our Sister, Alma
by Mildred Fay Polk & Walter (Pap) Polk

Born the 12th of 17 children to James K. and Gencie Marie O. Winters Polk, Alma has lived her entire life in Yalobusha County. The Jim Crow segregation laws and overt racism of her childhood years confined most black Mississippians to sharecropping or picking cotton, and Alma and her siblings persevered through it all. We all chopped and picked cotton as a way for our parents to make ends meet. Like most poor black families, we lived off the land that we sharecropped.

But with such a large family, we found ways to have so much fun that we didn't realize how poor we really were. Alma was one of the many comedians in the family and kept us laughing all the time with her silly snippets of comedy. Out in those cotton fields and in mother's huge garden, Alma and some of us used joy and laughter to survive the hard work and the hot sun beaming down on us during the day.

Case in point: One day I remember being out in the field and the fun activity was seeing who could tell the biggest lie. Not sure today if Alma made this suggestion, but I would not put it past her. Each sibling proceeded to come up with a big fib, and much laughter filled the field on that afternoon. There were many such fun occasions that kept us, it seemed, from ever being bored or overwhelmed with such redundant and back-breaking work.

Growing up poor is not always bad or sad. It was up to us to make the best of what we had before us, and we did that.

We were a church going, Bible believing, and God loving family, thanks to our mother who raised us up in the fear and admonition of the Lord. I was the youngest girl (number 15 of 17), and I remember my mom always preparing something for those special days we would have at church.

I think she saw some talent and maybe some interest in piano in our sister, Alma. So, the next thing we knew one of the oldest and biggest black pianos we had ever seen showed up in our guest room – we called it "the other room." It was so large that a full living room set, a full bedroom set with a 'chifforobe,' and now this huge piano fit inside.

A few weeks after the piano arrived, my mom chose Alma for piano lessons with Ms. Edith Wilson, one of the teachers at Davidson High School in Water Valley. Mom took Alma into town on weekends for lessons, and Alma became the first musician to play for our church, Bayson Chapel Missionary Baptist. One of our cousins, who happened to be an assistant minister at the time, was so overjoyed to have music during the service that he shortened the prayer meetings in order to hear Alma play. She later became the congregation's first official pianist, and for many years she faithfully played for the choir. We never heard her complain about the pay she received, which was probably nil, because she knew that God had her back and her life in His hand.

Most of us attended and graduated from Davidson High School. However, Alma chose to leave high school when she became pregnant by her future husband. But that was not the end of the story. Alma always knew that she made a mistake in not finishing high school, and she dreamed of hearing her name called, walking across the stage, and accepting her diploma from a teacher, principal or school administrator.

She refused to let the dream die.

It wasn't until after her five daughters were grown that she completed her GED. She considered this one of the proudest moments of her life next to being saved and having her children. Alma has often said she was grateful God had afforded her the opportunity to close an unfinished chapter of her past.

Alma and her husband moved to Coffeeville– which is nestled between Water Valley and Oakland – after they married, and she has lived there ever since. As a young woman, she attended cosmetology school in Grenada and became a beautician. She ultimately owned and operated a shop for many years at a time when many blacks did not own their own businesses. Even today she will do a favorite customer's hair. Alma also earned a Certificate of Achievement in Biblical Studies after attending satellite schools in both Coffeeville and Southaven. This was another bucket list item, a goal met to enhance her credentials as a Bible teacher at church.

Back in the day our mom, Gencie, and Aunt Sally Polk took charge of decorating the church each year for the program we called The Lord's Acre Day. This was a time to thank God for the harvest of blessings we'd had in the present year. Parishioners took pride in bringing all the products they had grown and fruits and vegetables they had canned to place before the altar to say 'Thank You Lord' for another successful year of sowing and harvesting. They also offered a "Thank You for keeping us fed for another year. "

After our mother died and Aunt Sally could no longer decorate the altar, Alma and our cousin, Ora Lee Phillips, took over the task. The event is now called the "The Harvest Program" and is held each year on the first Sunday in October. The premise is still the same: to give God thanks for His bountiful blessings for the year.

Now the torch has passed to the next generation, the children of Alma and Ora Lee. Alma has taught this next generation that the fruits and vegetables, the canned items and anything put around the altar should always be fresh from the field. Those in charge must never resort to plastic or artificial foods!

Alma remains a faithful and active member of Bayson Chapel MBC and on occasion still plays piano for the senior choir. She is also a Bible School teacher, the Christian Education Director and Seminar Facilitator

Alma Nicholson

with that take-charge attitude. In this case that means, if she was not appointed to lead an event, she will take charge anyway if she believes it is in the best interest of the whole. She has been an up-front, take charge person all her life, and that includes with the family! Many times, we are TOLD what we are going to do when it comes to the events hosted at her Coffeeville home.

One of the highlights is the annual New Year's Day gathering that is also the anniversary celebration of the many years of marriage of our cousins, Ora Lee and Raymond Phillips. Most years more than 100 people come by for food, fellowship and fun.

When Davidson High alumni, teachers, administrator and friends began having a school reunion, Alma was on the committee along with many others who lived in the Yalobusha County area. She has chaired the Bell-Polk-Winters Family Reunion Committee for the Mississippi team for many years. Alma is also chairperson for the Davidson High Class of 1966 tri-annual reunion, which was held in May this year in Water Valley. It was a great success and was featured earlier in this publication.

Alma loves to travel as long as someone else is driving. The three sisters living in the north Mississippi and south Memphis area

– Alma, Ruth and Mildred - on occasion will hop in a car and visit other family members usually with me, Mildred, at the wheel. We have traveled to Milwaukee, Wisconsin for family gatherings and for my own preaching engagements. We have been – though not traveling by car – to Orlando, Florida and Cincinnati, Ohio just for a few days of fun. Alma has also visited her daughter in Washington, DC.

Usually the three sisters travel together for real vacations. We went on our first cruise in 2003 to the Bahamas. It was such an experience for me - Mildred - that I said I was ready to go again. But not Alma and Ruth - who insisted "once is enough for me." Our cabin was pretty small for three people, so I let my sisters have the two bottom bunks. I'm so glad I did because as we were laying there just talking and laughing and too excited to fall asleep, Alma fell out of her bed. The laughter got louder and longer, and it was even harder to get to sleep after that little mishap. Alma and I did take a second cruise a couple of years later, but Ruth kept her word. She will not get back on a cruise ship.

Alma loves the Lord and tries to get to as many workshops, seminars, and conferences as she can each year to show herself approved unto God; a work woman that need not to be ashamed, and to rightly divide the word of truth. Like me, she has a hunger for the Word of God. Alma wants to know it in order to teach it to others, so they can pass it on to the next generation.

She attends as many Christian trainings as she can get to, that is, as long as she does not have to drive or go alone. Her church work is her main interest at this stage in her life's journey. I know mom would be proud if she was still alive to see the strong God fearing and dedicated servant Alma has become.

Alma is a widow and mother of five daughters, all of them fine, responsible young women. She also has seven grands and eight great- grand children.

Reader Comments

That was really Alma, always fun to be in her presence. Always keeping us laughing.
Juanita Fleming,
Sallis, MS

This is beautiful and she is a special lady. I can't wait until you write about my grandmother, Cleala Mae.
Velisa Adams,
Coffeeville, MS

She seemed very pleased with the article. So I'm happy. Also my brother called and was very pleased with it.
Mildred Polk,
Southaven, MS

Rachel Campbell Herod
Talents and Versatility Reflected in The Fruits of her Labor

With each story I become more aware that while growing up in Yalobusha County in the sixties and seventies, we were surrounded by multi-talented black women with strong constitutions, unfurled strength and a magnitude of fortitude. Women who willingly took domestic jobs in white homes, along with work in the fields and then in the factories to provide for their families.

Prideful women whose parents taught them to appreciate their heritage and the importance of religion and education. Women who still found the time to visit the hospitals and cook meals for the sick and shut-in. Women who were able to endure the harshness of segregation and discrimination while nurturing their own families and who can now enjoy the fruits of their labors. Valerie Herod Belay shares her story of this kind of woman in such fascinating detail that I am awestruck, yet even more inspired.

Sadly, the subject of this article, Rachel Herod, passed away on July 30th. We must carry on these legacies!

The Rachel Herod Story
by Valerie Herod Belay

My mom, Rachel Lee Campbell, was born in Calhoun County and spent most of her early life there. She was the eldest daughter of Mr. and Mrs. Silas Campbell. She had one sister and five brothers. Only her sister, Annie Robinson, and one brother, O.V. Campbell, are living today. Mom's family were proud farm owners and still maintain the family farm today. The Campbell home was a religious household with my grandfather teaching Sunday School and his children joining church at an early age. Mom called Zion Springs Baptist Church in Bruce her church home. Later her own children would recall performing on many Mother's Day programs at Zion Springs.

My mother has a rich and proud ancestry in Mississippi stretching back to the documented birth of her third great-grandfather, Rueben Stephens, in 1836. Mom's maternal lineage originates with the Steen/Stephens families. Her paternal surnames come from the Campbell/Winters families, which can be documented to 1841 in Mississippi. Other descendants of George Campbell, my mother's great uncle, are presently documenting the origins of the Campbell family prior to their arrival in Mississippi. A marker at the

Memorial Garden Cemetery in Banner, an unincorporated town in Calhoun County, states: "This is the resting place of freed Black people and their descendants. The members of the Hawkins, Pearson, Reese, Steen and Shipp families established the Mt. Pleasant Church, Bryant School, a cotton gin, grist mill and a blacksmith shop in Calhoun County." The Steen mentioned on the historical marker refers to my mother's second great-grandfather, William "Billie" Steen.

The families' establishment of a school confirms their belief in the importance of education. Mom attended Bruce schools through the eighth grade, but because the town had no colored high school, Mom moved to Water Valley to continue her education. She lived with her uncle and aunt, Mr. and Mrs. John D. Campbell, until graduating from Davidson High School, where she was a member of the Glee Club.

After finishing high school, Mom married John Watson Herod of Water Valley in 1954. They had five children. Dad was a teacher and later a principal in Water Valley and Coffeeville schools throughout their 63-year marriage. He passed in 2017.

Over her lifetime in Yalobusha County, Mom had several jobs including domestic work like many African American women of the era, a short stint at the Water Valley Poultry Plant and then several years as a seamstress at Big Yank Corporation, where she was a member of the United Garment Workers of America. Mom eventually retired from Borg Warner Incorporated, an automotive parts supplier, at age 62 as a quality inspector.

Mom taught us that rewards would be received in glory. Nevertheless, she received some while living too! My parents were greatly honored to serve as Grand Marshals for the Water Valley Christmas Parade in 2002. Mom was delighted to have her winning squash casserole recipe published in a cookbook in 1980. Finally, Mom's most

Rachel Herod

recent honor was to share her recording, "A Talk with Mom-Rachel Herod," with the StoryCorps.org project.

My mother's artistic bent showed in her hobbies. My favorite was that she sewed all her daughters' clothing, even my pageant gowns! Mom also has a large photograph collection documenting family and Water Valley history. After the Bank of Water Valley was torn down, she shared her pictures of the original building with the Historical Society.

Mom loved to quilt, and she enjoyed quilting with her cousin, the late Leona Cruthird of Water Valley, and my dad's cousin, the late Lunell Stokes Miller of Toccopola. She made close to 100 quilts for family and friends. Every grandchild was received into this world with one of their grandma's quilts and later sent off to college with a quilt especially made to fit those extra-long dorm room beds. In 2010 the Detroit School of Arts mounted a photo exhibit of Mom's quilts for the Visual Arts Major Program.

Mom gave her time, talents and treasures to Yalobusha County, and she fondly recounts her time as a Cub Scout Pack Leader for my younger brother's troop. Mom and Dad also gave money to Water Valley High School to buy computers after dad's retirement.

Mom probably is best remembered for how she gave of her talents. But she is also well remembered for her skills in the kitchen. She enjoyed cooking and canning vegetables from her garden, and she made every type of fruit jelly imaginable! As part of her Christian missionary work, she routinely cooked meals for the elderly and infirm members of Water Valley until she needed those services herself.

As we advance in age, we tend to think about our legacy. If you were to ask Mom what she thought her legacy was, she would say, "My children, grandchildren and great-grandchildren." Mom and Dad had five children, all of whom were college educated. They are pharmacists, teacher administrators, respiratory therapist and safety specialist who attained advanced degrees and certifications in their chosen fields. Four of their children also proudly served in the US armed forces. Mom is extremely proud of each of her grandchildren and their accomplishments. Of the grandsons, two are noted physicians and two are noted chefs. Of the granddaughters, we count a US Army Captain, a State House Representative for Colorado, a restaurant manager, a social worker, a television broadcast journalist and a veterinary microbiologist. Mom's eight young great grandchildren are still dreaming of future careers. I would say that's quite a legacy!

The Graduation List

The schools that Rachel Herod's husband, children and grandchildren attended attest to the impact she had on her family. Simply put, her legacy extends well beyond Yalobusha County and the State of Mississippi.

Mr. Herod – Alcorn State University

Johnny – Northwest Junior College, University of Kansas, Baker College

Barbara – University of Maryland, University of Mississippi

Michael – University of Maryland

Valerie – Mississippi University for Women, University of Southern Mississippi, Spring Arbor University

Tony – Columbia Southern University

Grandchildren's List

University of Alabama, *The University of Kansas, Johns Hopkins School of Medicine, University of Central Missouri, *University of Colorado, Indiana University-Purdue University Indianapolis, *Bowling Green State University, Michigan State University, University of Washington

(*indicates multiple grand-kids attended the college)

Teach Love, Not Hate

I agree with Valerie.

Based on this legacy one can only imagine the contributions that Rachel Herod's great grandchildren will make. Her life story has almost left me speechless. How impressive to be able to document your family ancestry back to 1836 and to have your family's contribution documented and preserved in history. It is no wonder that she poured her talents and skills into growing a beautifully talented and extremely accomplished family. Her children and their offspring are following the examples that she and Mr. Herod and their ancestors set for them and many others.

Mrs. Herod's numerous contributions to the education of black children and the welfare of all of Yalobusha County were mostly behind the scenes. Though often unnoticed, she supported her husband, his staffs, the teachers, the parents and the children for years. Especially now, as she is laid to rest, let us offer one more thank you to Rachel Herod for her exemplary life and her infinite legacy.

As I close this article, I am in some ways regretting energies that I have exerted recently in hopes that my alma mater, the University of Mississippi, was ready to make "a progressive move" to address the racism that continues to fester on and off the campus. Murder and Racism all in one week, just days apart – negative national news again! The insensitive act in front of the Emmett Till memorial really hurt. I wonder if those Ole Miss fraternity boys would have turned out differently if they had more positive influences in their lives like Rachel Herod and the outstanding black women of Yalobusha County. We need to be teaching love, not hate! What say ye flagship university?

Reader Comments

I can't express the depth of gratitude I feel for the wonderful article you composed about my mom. It was beautiful and I had to compose myself before replying to you. You said it would be a nice tribute and it was. I'll make sure that each family member gets a copy of the paper. Now I want to bless you with the words sent to me from a new friend, " May you and your family always have the blessings of God's undeserved kindness."
Valerie Belay,
Farmington Hills, MI

This article came at the perfect time for me. I've been thinking a lot about legacy this week in light of the passing of Toni Morrison, one of my literary heroes. People like Morrison, Ms. Herod, and so many other black women have a profound impact on people, each in her own way. But I don't think they think about their lives and work in terms of legacy. I think they think about their lives and work simply as who they are—the natural expression of themselves as children of God. I can only pray that I am as God-expressed as Toni Morrison and the women you've been featuring in your column. Certainly, your recording of the lives of the Outstanding Women of Yalobusha County is part of your legacy—the natural expression of who you are as a child of God.
Adrienne Harris,
Atlanta, GA

Preserving Our History
To Help Us Understand the Past and the Present

The past is past, right? We can't do anything about it, but we can learn from it and use it to understand the present and perhaps make for better days ahead. The Spanish writer Javier Marias put it so well when he said, "The past has a future we never expect."

2019 has presented challenges and concerns that many of us have never experienced before. The issues are plentiful: racism remains rampant and continues to plague our daily lives. I believe that we can work to relieve some of the current pressures by sharing life stories that show that we have much more in common than most can imagine.

Since I was a student in the 70's at the University of Mississippi, I have felt that the school could do more for Water Valley, especially its black residents, for no other reason than the town's proximity to Oxford. Beyond that, over the last 30 years many of them have earned degrees and taken advantage of other university programs, and more students, teachers and retirees – black and white – have migrated to Water Valley or communities in between. I am biased, I know, and I have said often how special I believe Water Valley and Yalobusha County are primarily, in my opinion, because of the outstanding black women who were the foundation of the community. The life stories of more than 20 have appeared in this column, and we will continue to feature others.

Now I believe we have found a way to connect the community more deeply with the university by using its resources to record and archive oral histories of black families in Yalobusha County. We will be filling gaps, documenting and showcasing untold stories that can be handed down to inform and motivate the generations to come. And we will all be better for it.

It has been said that God has given each of us spiritual gifts, talents, skills and experiences to serve wholeheartedly behind the scenes or in the forefront. Please accept this personal invitation to participate and make a difference. I hope I can count on you. Ole Miss History professor, Dr. Jessie Wilkerson, describes how the process will work below. She and I attended the Homecoming Services at Everdale Baptist Church in July and were so well received that we are planning to visit more congregations on our next trip to Water Valley in September. To participate or for more information contact me or Dr. Wilkerson. Her contact information is listed below.

From the Ole Miss Classroom to the Yalobusha Community
by Dr. Jessie Wilkerson

About a year ago a friend told me about the "Outstanding Black Women of Yalobusha County" column by Dottie Chapman Reed. To say I was rapt is an understatement. Ms. Reed's articles gave me a glimpse into the rich history of black women in North Mississippi, something that I especially appreciate as a scholar who studies the South and U.S. women's history. I soon had the opportunity to read the backlog of articles with curiosity, deep interest, and appreciation, and Ms. Reed and I began a conversation about the possibility of building a collaborative project to document the history of black families in Yalobusha County.

I am a historian and professor at the University of Mississippi, where I have worked for the past five years. One morning over breakfast, during the weeks that I was considering a job in Oxford, I read that several students had placed a noose on the James Meredith statue.

"Where exactly am I about to move?" I thought to myself. "What does it mean to take a position and accept a salary at an institution that has consistently held up, defended, and bred white supremacist policies and actions?" But because I am a historian of the South, I know the story is always more complicated. In my five years here, I have learned and taught about the long history of oppression, but I have also yoked myself to the progressive history that has also always been part of the undercurrent at the University of Mississippi, and the state as a whole. The history of how people, especially black Mississippians, have fought against oppression and envisioned a more just society has become a fundamental part of my research and teaching.

Over the last five years, I have heard stories of how black Mississippians have struggled for fair treatment by and access to an institution that is supposed to be a shared resource. I read about how black women laundry workers at the university, when faced with horrendous working conditions on campus, went on strike in the 1940s and won. I learned that civil rights leader Medgar Evers, before becoming the NAACP director for Mississippi, attempted to enroll at the University of Mississippi Law School in 1950. He was denied, but that did not take away the power of his action: He fought to claim the resources that were his birthright. I heard stories from black Oxonians about how the struggle around James Meredith's integration did not end when he enrolled but continued for a year. Federal marshals went to school and church with Meredith to provide security, a reminder of how loathe many white people were to black people accessing public resources. The university celebrates Meredith's integration as the single-greatest turning point, a break from the segregationist and white supremacist past. But the story of black students who protested a racist climate during the 1969-1970 school year suggests a different story: the struggle was and is a hard-fought slog and continues into the present.

With the help of Ms. Reed's column, I have expanded my knowledge and now know many more stories of resilience across North Mississippi: of black people finding a way to make a living, raise their families, take care of one another, fight for equality, and build community. Such stories are integral to our shared past, and as a historian at the University of Mississippi, I see it as my responsibility to do what I can to document and preserve Mississippi stories, especially those of black people and other marginalized groups.

Dottie Reed is collaborating with Dr. Jessie Wilkerson of the University of Mississippi on an oral history project to help preserve the stories of Yalobusha County's black citizens.

In this spirit, last fall I proposed to Ms. Reed that we collaborate on an oral history project to document the history of black families in Yalobusha County. Oral history is a recording of a first-person account made by an interviewer and interviewee. Recording oral history interviews with regular people about their daily lives and family stories will help us weave a broader story of black families in Yalobusha County, stories that we will supplement with other types of research.

My hope is to work with Ms. Reed to bring public, university resources to the valuable work she has already begun. Our project will rely on relationships between students and faculty at the university and community members in Yalobusha County. I know that we have work to do to gain your trust.

Here is what the project will look like in its first phase: I am teaching a class on oral history in the fall 2019 semester, and I will work with a team of graduate students to document black community history in North Mississippi. Many of the graduate students in the class are working toward their master's degree in the Southern Studies program, an interdisciplinary program that investigates the complexity of the American South. After undergoing training on how to conduct and record oral history interviews, we will work with Ms. Reed to see who might be interested in participating in the project.

As part of that process, Ms. Reed, the team of graduate students, and I will be in Water Valley on Sunday, September 29. In the weeks and months after that, students will record interviews with individuals, asking them about their lives in Yalobusha County and the history of their families in the region (interviews usually last between one and two hours). Students will then transcribe the interview and provide the person with the transcript of the interview and an audio recording. If the person so chooses, we will archive the interview at the University of Mississippi, helping to preserve black history of North Mississippi and making the interviews accessible to historians, students, and community members interested in Mississippi, southern, and African-American history. We also hope to organize an exhibit—online or at a community space—where we can share what we learned and hear your questions.

I and my students take seriously the mission of the university to "devote its knowledge and abilities to serve the state and the world." I train my students to listen for the lesser known stories, those that have been muted in dominant histories of the South, but that are vital to understanding the past and present. The interviews that we collect will help us tell a richer, more diverse, more nuanced story about North Mississippi. We hope that you will consider joining us. If you have any questions for me about the project, or if you know you would like to participate, please don't hesitate to reach out.

Reader Comments

Again, great work. Can't wait to read the other pieces and looking forward to Dr. Wilkerson's findings.
Cecil Moore,
Tucker, GA

You know I'm so proud of your efforts. This is going to be a definite plus to the citizens in the region.
Carolyn West,
Atlanta, GA

This is so tremendous. As you told me of this before, I could not help but recall (the important but not as well know as it should be) "To Be a Slave" by Julius Lester. Oral histories are crucial as they speak with voices ignored or seldom heard!
Vance P. Ross,
Atlanta GA

After reading your article and about Dr Jessie Wilkerson's project I am bursting with joy and pride as to where your great stories of outstanding black women from Yalobusha County is leading you. It is amazing how God is directing your path and shining light on information you are presenting. It is your efforts, concise writing and God that made that connection between you and Dr. Wilkerson. All the best in continuing to heal the wounds of the past and create new insights to improve things for the future.
Lillian Dent,
Roosevelt, NY

Lula Pritchard Chapman
She Wanted The World To Be a Better Place

Adam Evans, who teaches at a Washington, D.C. public high school, reads this column and is planning to use it in two of his history classes. His assessment of the entries thus far drew my attention and gave me pause. "I thought the reflection of writing this sort of history as a reminiscing that isn't always happy was an apt way of describing the pursuit of history as personal, professional, and never-ending. As a history teacher," he said, "it is always a struggle to peel back the larger narrative and focus on the personal. I've been enjoying the manner in which the writers do this, showing that revisionist history isn't changing the past, but changing our understanding of it as we obtain a more full picture of what happened."

Adam is from Athens, Georgia and earned his Master's degree from the University of Mississippi. His astute description of the column captures its intent: to tell the history as we know and lived it. Every story written thus far has opened yet another door.

It has taken a lot for me to be able to write about someone so close to me. Not long after I started this project, James Judson, my cousin Mildred's husband and my late brother's best friend, said that "if you really wanted to write about an outstanding black woman of Yalobusha County, you need to write about your mother, Helen Chapman." She had done more for him and other young folks in Water Valley than anyone he knew, he told me. He mentioned the trips she took them on to the Memphis Zoo, Parchman Penitentiary, Mound Bayou and other places –– trips, activities and training that made an impact on his life.

"When are you going to write about Aunt Helen?" another cousin, Eva Chatman Newton, asked months ago. Much later Danita Hall scolded me after I had already twisted her arm to write about her mother, Ruby Hall. Then, when Valerie Herod Belay wrote a beautiful and well-deserved tribute to her mother, Rachel Herod, I decided I had to do what I have been asking others to do. I guess I was concerned that some would see it as bragging on my part.

A Mother to Me, A Mentor to So Many Others
by Dottie Chapman Reed

My mother, whose 'real name' as they say, was Lula B., had lived more than half of her life when I was born in 1952. To understand her early years, I have sought information from my first cousins, one of whom was there when I was born, Odessa Finch Douglas. "Your dad came to get me to be your nurse when you were born." she said. I entered the world of Water Valley, Yalobusha County *(M I Crooked Letter, Crooked Letter I, Crooked*

Letter, Crooked Letter I, Hump Back, Hump Back I - our childhood chant for learning to spell Mississippi), the fourth child born to Helen and Alvin Chapman. She was forty years old.

"My sister Ann (Annie Clyde), Irene Robinson, Willie Ree Smith and I stayed with Aunt Helen and Uncle Alvin in order to go to high school." Odessa added. "Living with them during the week was the only way we could get to school each day. We stayed for three years or so until we graduated because we lived too far away." Unimaginable – as my parents had three other children (Tomie, Faye and Gabby) when I came along – all of us in a three-bedroom house with no running water, an outdoor toilet, a wood stove for heating and cooking and no air conditioning. That was 10 people!

"Aunt Helen made our breakfast each morning, provided our school lunches and everything else we needed. We walked to church and school when Uncle Alvin did not drive us in his truck, "Odessa continued. "One night during the week Aunt Helen arranged for us to watch television at a white family's home nearby. What a good old time we had! Usually we four girls went home on the weekends. Aunt Helen got me my first job ironing for Lou McNamee. She told me if I saw money lying around where you think they don't know it, do not touch it. She told me that they (whites) will generally test you."

My dad took Odessa to her senior prom, and she was in the same class with the late Rachel Herod, featured in the last article. Odessa said our aunt in Memphis purchased her prom dress, which she allowed Rachel to borrow and wear to the prom in Coffeeville, where her future husband worked at the "colored" high school. When Odessa told me that my mom and dad paid for her senior class ring because her parents, Uncle Buddy (Al) and Aunt Pit (Betsy) Finch, could not afford it, I got emotional.

According to Odessa, the girls thought my parents were rich because they bought a farm with substantial acreage. My father had purchased the land from a white man, Calvin Bruce Gurner, March 19, 1952, and my mother worked for two Gurner families who lived on Panola Street. Odessa's sister, Ann, was assigned to take care of my brother, Gabby, when he started school in 1954. He was quite a handful. One time when the kids were riding in the back of the family truck, Gabby told my mom that if she couldn't drive any faster, he might as well jump off. And he did!

I cannot leave my second cousins out because we grew up together and spent many overnights at my house and theirs. About those youth trips that James mentioned: on my first trip to the Memphis Zoo we traveled on what I called a cattle-gap truck that had make-shift benches in the back. So, there was a lot of sliding and bouncing around. As I have gotten older, it occurred to me that we should have been embarrassed traveling that way. But we weren't. I thought it was funny how we had to pull into those weigh stations on Interstate 55 to be weighed just like cattle.

The chaperones – women and the occasional man – organized kids into groups of five or six, each identified by a little strip of colored ribbon pinned on our lapels. When we arrived at the zoo, we would excitedly eat our bologna sandwiches and drink sodas on the grounds and then take off for the day. None of us can recall any hindrances or restrictions because of the color of our skin. An additional highlight was the drive by of Elvis Presley's home. I think we had snacks for the approximately 90-mile trip home. My cousin Eva remembers that when my mom drove her and three schoolmates on their first trip to the Memphis Zoo, she made them take notes and a write a report for school - evidence of my mom's belief in education.

My next trip with my mother was to the Parchman Penitentiary, traveling once again in the "cattle-gap" truck. We encountered an unexpected delay when prison officials required one of the chaperones, Oscar Gordon, to shave his beard off. Security reasons, they claimed. The first part of the tour took us through a huge kitchen where I saw the biggest vats of boiling water and cooking containers that I had ever seen. In the prison itself, we saw how the men - all of them in striped uniforms- lived and worked. It was a very eye opening, frightening experience, and I realized then that Parchman was a place I never wanted to be.

Completely opposite from the trip to Parchman was our visit to the all-black town of Mound Bayou, in the Delta. I believe my mother's purpose for these trips was to educate and expose us to the world beyond Yalobusha County.

Percy Lee Rogers, a community activist in her own right, recalls making three trips to the zoo as a chaperone, the trip to Parchman and many trips that illustrate another of my mother's roles - mistress of ceremony sponsoring singing programs in various churches across all denominations. Ms. Rogers recalls going to many congregations in north Mississippi and at least one in Canton, just outside Jackson. These programs featured mostly male quartets. One was led by Charlie Rogers. Other prominent groups included the Crowder and Covington families. "I can hardly remember a Sunday when we were not in some church morning, afternoon and evening," said Eva. She recalled that mom kept her, her siblings and mine in church every Sunday night. They had to sing, read the scripture or recite a speech. I, too, became a victim as soon as I was of age.

Aside from sponsoring singing programs, my mother worked with and supported many preachers, most of whom sat at our table for Sunday afternoon dinners. We children couldn't eat until the preacher and the other adults had finished. Percy Lee credits my mom and Mamie Douglas for keeping the AME Zion Church in Water Valley running after most of the male leaders left or passed away.

Even with all this travel, my mom never owned a brand-new car. I remember our having more than one flat tire. I mean we had a lot of flat tires. The very worst came one Sunday on our way to Green Goshen CME Church in what we call the bald hot summer sun. My mom knew how to change a tire. However, we did not always have a good spare, but eventually we would get to the program she was sponsoring. Seems like someone always came along to help us – sometimes black and sometimes white.

When Eva's father, my Uncle Red (Andrew) Chatman, lost his best friend and needed transportation, my mom stepped in to take him wherever he needed to go, picked up his medicines and assisted any other needs. She always visited the sick in their homes and the hospital. During the last months of my aunt Ann Chapman's life, we were at the house in Oakland every Sunday evening. I remember mom giving her last to anyone in need many times when we did not have enough for our family. Our door was always open to anyone in need and to family. Relatives from Memphis, Chicago, Detroit and Grand Rapids spent summers at our house in the fifties and sixties on a regular basis.

My mother traveled often to visit my grandfather, Alfred Pritchard, in Haiti, Missouri, and I was always afraid when we crossed the Memphis-Arkansas bridge. It was high and narrow, and there was always an accident. We would spend the night with relatives in Osceola, Arkansas before driving on to Haiti. Stanhope Cox drove us often as he was an experienced long-haul truck driver. Granddaddy changed his last name to Turner for reasons unknown to me. I suspect he had an encounter with the law in Mississippi – which might also explain how he ended up in that tiny little town.

By 1962 my mother was raising the first of her four grandchildren. By 1968 she had taken in the other three because she did not believe Chicago, where my sister and their mother lived, was safe. We farmed cotton on our land and even did some sharecropping. My mother did it all, chopping the cotton, growing all sorts of vegetables and tending our orchard. She loved to fish and pick blackberries. We helped relatives harvest okra and soybeans, especially when more labor was needed, and time or weather threatened to destroy the crops. It was hard work but so necessary to survive.

My mother plowed her own garden when my dad and brother were too slow for her liking. I tried to do everything my mom or sisters did but plowing with a mule was much too hard. Though I learned to drive the tractor, I was no expert. My mom could pick a lot of cotton, and again I was not good at that either! The kids from town, who would come to pick cotton for us, always picked more than I did. They were getting paid. I was the water boy – or girl – I should say. County officials set the calendar for black students to allow us to miss school to pick cotton when it was time to harvest. I do not need to describe how I and others felt when we were in the hot fields as the buses with the white students, usually heckling, passed by.

My grandmother, Jane Ophelia Williams Pritchard (December 20, 1871- September 15, 1969) also lived with us for several years. Even in her 80s she walked to and from town on the days when she wanted to cash her check and buy her snuff and groceries. She was the fifth child of Samuel Tom Williams and Sylvia Hale, both of whom were born in North Carolina. According to oral family history, Sylvia, my great-grandmother, was the daughter of a Confederate soldier from the Carolinas and an unknown white woman. Because she was born out of wedlock, she was put with slaves and encouraged to pass as a mulatto or mixed. Sylvia's daughter, my grandmother, married Allen Taliaferro

Lula B. "Helen" Chapman and her daughter, Dottie on her wedding day at Burns United Methodist Church, Oxford, MS

in 1895 in Yalobusha County. They had five children. He died in 1903, and she married my grandfather, Alfred Pritchard, in 1906. They had two daughters, my aunt Coree and my mom, the youngest.

Mom worked as a maid for the Gurners, the Porters, the Weavers, the McNamees, the Nolens and a few others that I cannot recall. Mr. Nolen worked in the post office, and though Mrs. Nolen taught at Ole Miss when I was a student there, our paths never crossed on campus. My mother and sister, Faye, also worked at the infamous, but now closed, Mott's Chicken factory as did many of the black women in Yalobusha county. It was horrible. While I never set foot in the place, I knew the conditions were deplorable when I saw the cuts and scratches on my mother's swollen hands after her shifts. The odor on their clothing penetrated. While the pay was good, the wear and tear on their bodies was debilitating and clearly manifested in our black community. Yet this type of employment in the late sixties and seventies moved blacks from the fields into the factories.

My mother understood hard work and servanthood and showed it by her example and leadership. Politically active and outspoken, she maintained her memberships in the PTA and the NAACP. I have come to understand myself better as I have learned more about her. Her keeping us overly active in church, I now see, was the training we needed to get us through life and to promote our spiritual growth towards discipleship and servanthood. Those speeches surely gave us more confidence. Those trips no doubt birthed a desire in us to see what lay beyond Yalobusha County, beyond Mississippi and Memphis – all of it helping us learn or develop organizational and leadership skills that we are using today.

My mother only finished 8th grade. My father could not read or write. Simply put my mother - like the women we have learned about in this column – helped many people, wore many hats, put others first and enriched the community in remarkable ways. I saw another side of her in December 1973, the fall of my senior year in college, when Gabby, now a Vietnam veteran, died from carbon monoxide poisoning in his apartment in Milwaukee, Wisconsin. During this time of deep loss, my mother showed great strength through her faith I never saw her cry, even in this painful moment.

In the early eighties, one or two years into my job with The Wall Street Journal, I was having dinner in the restaurant on top of the World Trade Center in New York. As I looked out at the ships and boats on the Hudson River in awe, I started to cry and remember thinking, "I am just a little black country girl from Water Valley, Mississippi who owes it all to the examples set by my mother and many other outstanding black women."

By this time my mother was terminally ill. She passed away in 1983, before my sons were born. When Cameron, my middle son, was accepted to the US Military Academy at West Point on the other side of the Hudson River, on our first visit I thought of how proud my mother would have been. My cousin, Janie Toliver Curry, who just celebrated her 91st birthday, remembers my mother as a very beautiful person who walked close to God and kept God in everything she did. My mom had a signature song that perhaps sums up her goals in life, her service to mankind and describes her journey to make the world a better place. "There is joy in that land where I am bound," she sang. "Don't you wanna to go to that land where I am bound?"

In her own way she invited us to come along.

Reader Comments

Wonderful article about a beautiful lady! It's the person connections that make theses articles compelling reads. News of your work is spreading. Friends from the Carolinas with distant ties to Mississippi messaged me yesterday asking if I knew your series!
 Valerie Belay,
 Farmington, MI

Your mom was beautiful inside and out. What inspiring women. God bless you for sharing this,
 Effie Chisholm,
 Lithonia, GA

I had to do a lot of blinking of the eyes when I read the article. Your Mom was phenomenal! She looked so beautiful in your wedding photo. Sometimes I wish I could travel back in time prior to my Mama's death so that I could give her one more hug and just simply inhale while hugging her. I have no regrets as a daughter – just wished she had lived longer. Absolutely beautiful article. I had clearly forgotten that Ms. Helen used to pull money from a handkerchief. I smiled... ....I continue to smile at the memories that come out of some of the articles. Keep it up!
 Danita Hall,
 Baltimore, MD

29

Sharing History to Make History

Gratified is the best way to describe how I feel about the response to this column and the stories of outstanding, unsung black women of Yalobusha County. I wish I had time and the space to share all the phone calls, emails and encouraging comments I have received about the 28 articles published so far. If not for this project I might never have seen the 1947 picture of my family. Nor would I have known the impact my mother, Helen Chapman, had on Georgia Barry, a native of Water Valley. After reading the article Georgia called me and sent the following note:

"My name is Georgia Phillips Barry, and I am the second child of Fred and Hazel Phillips. I thoroughly enjoy reading your articles that are appearing in the Water Valley paper. Whenever I saw your mom at church, she would tell me how proud she was of me for my academic honors in college. She would then dig into her purse and pull out a handkerchief with a knot in it. She would pull out a few wrinkled dollar bills and with a hug, encourage me to keep working. I am now a retired school counselor from Shelby County Schools in Memphis. I honor your mom by passing along a hug, a little money and words of encouragement to college students. I will always remember cousin, Mrs. Helen Chapman."

I was so pleased to learn that even after her children had left Water Valley, my mother continued to show love to young people in her surrounding community.

As this project moves into the next phase, - I encourage others to share their stories to motivate our youth, to instill pride and to make the world a better place. Consider it an opportunity to give back, to make a difference. In these days of "see something, say something," "the me too" movement, "Black Lives Matter" and "going high instead of going low," what can you do to make a positive impact in this community? Let's remember: "Each one teach one!"

As previously mentioned, the next phase of this project, beginning in October, will be the collection of oral histories of black families in Yalobusha County. The eventual permanent record will be available to current relatives and future descendants. The *North Mississippi Herald* column will continue and will be used to update you on the oral history portion.

If you need even more encouragement to participate either by writing about a woman who influenced your life in a powerful way or by recording your family history, here is yet another comment, this one from Michigan, about the last article. It illustrates how these stories are making an impact beyond Mississippi.

"Wonderful article about a beautiful lady! It's the personal connections that make these articles compelling reads. News of your work is spreading. Friends from the Carolinas with distant ties to Mississippi messaged me yesterday asking if I knew your series! "

www.blackwomenofyalobusha.com is now up and running, and the previously published articles are posted there. At the end of the month I will be meeting with the various departments at Ole Miss to launch the oral history segment.

We now have the power to write our own stories and record our history, let us not disappoint. Black womanhood was powerful then and is powerful now. We owe it to our mothers, grandmothers, aunts, sisters, nieces, teachers, mentors and friends to shine a light on them for being simply outstanding. Now is not the time to be silent!

Reader Comments

As usual, it was very interesting to hear about the unsung heroes of the past generation—women who made everything work. It occurred to me that you might be interested in the 1619 project. It has a huge impact on many, many people. It blew me away. It makes us see US history in an entirely new way.
Maryann McGuire
Atlanta, GA

I am excited that this "project of love" is finding its legs and coming off the page to touch so many lives in so many ways. Wishing you only good things in the next phase.
Carolyn West
Atlanta, GA

So happy to see things moving along with unbelievable speed. The articles continue to peak my passion for a visit one day to Water Valley!
Jim Brzoska
Deltona, FL

So excited about how well the project is expanding! You are making an impact in the lives of many.
DeAndrea Thompson,
Douglasville, GA

Thank you for continuing to promote and give voice to so many voiceless women of color in Yalobusha County Mississippi. God has given you a novel vision.
Thomas Brown,
Tucker, GA

I thoroughly enjoyed reading about your mother and the lady's perspective of her. From the writing, I was able to glean a bit about her character and her lesson to "pass it on."
Dianne Prince,
Orlando, FL

Just a little note to the editor and crew at the Herald to express my appreciation for giving Dottie Reed a place to educate and inform, and my thanks to her for all the wonderful work she has been doing. I've been reading her column for so long and meant to thank her long before now. I am thrilled to see in her column this week that an oral history project is being started in Yalobusha County. Not having been a resident in Water Valley and Yalobusha County until about 13 years ago, I have nothing to contribute, but lots to learn.
Waurene Roberson,
Water Valley, MS

I read your column every week and while I am both white and not from Mississippi, I am so excited for the African American community of Yalobusha County about the upcoming project. All sparked by your column! I am proud and happy for you and everyone involved, and I applaud you for your hard work and continuing efforts.
Alexe van Beuren,
Water Valley, MS

30
Ruthie Jenkins White
A Quietly Kept First

Ruthie Jenkins White was the youngest of eleven children, born in June 1952 to Mattie Horton Jenkins. Her father, Johnnie Jenkins, and the family lived and worked on the Moore Place Plantation outside of Coffeeville. Sharecroppers, they farmed cotton, peanuts and corn and had a garden. Mattie could read and write, but neither she nor Johnnie had any formal education.

"When I told my children that as a child we worked on the farm, did the same job, came home to eat together and then went to bed together, they thought it strange," Ruthie said.

Ruthie was only three when her mother became very ill. Johnnie Jenkins took the seven older children and left. Ruthie's Aunt Ruth- her namesake – took her in while Mattie was ill. When Mattie got better, she came for Ruthie, and for the next fifteen years or so, it was just the two of them. No one had any information about where Johnnie and the older children were living.

Ruthie attended the black elementary school in Coffeeville - and fondly remembers her first-grade teacher, Dorothy Martin. Her sixth grade teacher, Elvira Jackson, a leading educator, inspired her. And in 10th grade Ruthie found a new passion. "I got really excited in 10th grade at Central High, the black high school, when our math teacher, Alma Faye Chapman, introduced cheerleading. We had never had anything like that before," she recalled. "I signed up immediately, it was something new and I really enjoyed it. We cheered for the day games only."

"I wanted to go to college," Ruthie added, "but I did not have the funds nor did we know who to talk too. I took the ACT in Oxford somewhere. I scored 23 on the ACT [a very good score], and I remember seeing my scores posted at the bottom of my high school transcript and feeling proud."

Ruthie was the first in her family to graduate from high school, and her class was the last to graduate from Central High before mandatory integration began in the fall of 1970 for all the schools in Yalobusha County.

Mattie wanted her daughter to have a class ring and had to borrow the $59 from the white family she worked for – Mr. and Mrs. Lillton Pipkin. Ruthie knew them because when she was younger, her mother sometimes took her as she cleaned the house and ironed the Pipkins' clothes. Ruthie still wears that Central High - Class of 1970 - ring today. She tells her son and daughter that it is made of real gold.

After she graduated from high school, Ruthie reconnected with her older siblings. She learned that Johnnie had taken them from place to place over the years.

Ruthie's first job – one of many after high school – was at Kellwood Pants manufacturing plant, where she worked for eight years. After leaving the plant, she spent a year as a teacher's aide at Coffeeville High, and then she moved to the assembly line at Holley Carburetor in Water Valley, working there for ten years.

Ruthie White

Ruthie got married in 1972 while working at Holley, but her marriage ended after three years. By 1989, Holly Carburetor began major layoffs. Ruthie found another job, this one in Grenada at Pennaco Hosiery. She stayed there until the plant closed eight years later. Ruthie returned to Coffeeville, working as a cashier for four years at the local Piggly Wiggly Supermarket.

All of these jobs totaled 30 years in the work force, but Ruthie was not done yet. On February 11, 2000 the Yalobusha County Board of Supervisors hired her as the county's first black assistant purchasing clerk, responsible for getting supplies for all the county departments. This included the sheriff's office and the courthouses (one in Water Valley and the other in Coffeeville) and covered, among other things, vehicles, guns, uniforms, briefcases, judges' robes, and office supplies. Ruthie supplemented her training for this new position with computer classes from Northwest Community College and obtained various certifications.

Just as she got settled in to her high-profile position, she was told that she didn't need to take any more classes. At the same time, she began to feel pressure to leave her job. She did her best to push that pressure aside and credits counsel from a local pastor for helping her "hang in there," as she put it. Daily Bible reading also sustained her, though to avoid any backlash, she kept her Bible in her desk drawer. Nonetheless, she remained as upbeat as possible.

"Under the circumstances I never dreaded the job," Ruthie said. "And I hoped that I was setting a positive example for my people," she reasoned.

Ruthie retired in good standing from the Board of Supervisor position in 2015, completing 15 years of service to Yalobusha County. She now volunteers as the District Secretary for the Mt. Moriah District Missionary Baptist Association and its 23 member churches. The Association, based in Coffeeville, was organized in 1908 under the leadership of Dr. C.P. Bohannon and celebrated its 111th anniversary in July.

Ruthie remains active at her family church, Hopewell Baptist, and enjoys spending time with her daughter, son and four grandchildren.

Roughly 13 miles separate Coffeeville and Water Valley, and only two months separate Ruthie and me in age. Yet our life trajectories were different. What if someone had told Ruthie that 23 on the ACT meant that she was indeed college material? I was an almost STAR student, scoring the highest in my Davidson High class at the time, but I did not score that high.

What if someone – a teacher, a counselor, a pastor – had given Ruthie just a little push and some encouragement? What if someone had told her about the college admissions process and how to apply for financial aid? That was my first job as a college recruiter! Wish I had known Ruthie then. What if she had been told of other career opportunities? How different her path might have been.

How many more of her classmates might have been able to attend college with proper advice, counseling, mentoring or if given the opportunity?

While the college doors did not open for Ruthie, she forged a career path for which she and her children can be proud. Her mother, too. When the assistant purchasing clerk opportunity became available, she did not ask, as I did, or as First Lady Michelle Obama did in *Becoming*, her award-winning best seller, *if she was good enough*. Ruthie was not afraid to be the first black. She had already paid her dues to become an outstanding, self-assured black woman, an inspiration to her community still.

Reader Comments

I sincerely thank you for the articles. I get inspired reading them. It is amazing that growing up, I never heard about the accomplishments of the Outstanding Black Women of Yalobusha County. I am sure your name belongs on that list!
Eddie Sanders,
Detroit, MI

Another heartwarming story, but a sad one at the same time! Just a small crossing in paths and Ruthie missed you as a friend and someone who would have changed her life! Ruthie had a tough life all around but was and still is an outstanding woman with what she accomplished.
Jim Brzoska,
Deltona, FL

You are right, she had the talent but not the opportunity.
Pamela Simmons,
Stone Mountain, GA

Recording Yalobusha's Black History
Phase One Begins

Spending almost five days on the University of Mississippi campus recently left me with a combination of déjà vu and where am I? It was not my first visit since graduating in 1974, leaving my university job in 1977 or attending the second black student alumni reunion in 2012. But it was at that reunion, when to my astonishment, then chancellor Dr. Dan Jones apologized to Myrlie Evers-Williams and to black alumni. He apologized to Mrs. Evers-Williams for the university law school denying admission to her late husband, Medgar, who had met all the requirements.

And he apologized to us, the black alumni, for years of discrimination and the wrongdoings we experienced. Linda Lewis Jamison and I looked at each other in amazement and disbelief. We confirmed later that he said what we thought we heard. We also feared that some in the audience might have missed the significance of this first-ever apology from the highest paid position in the state.

When the news broke roughly three years later, that Chancellor Jones was asked to resign shortly after returning from a medical leave, I sent a note wishing him well and thanking him for that apology and for all the positive changes he brought to the university.

My visit this time was to meet with Dr. Jessie Wilkerson and her graduate level oral history class. In addition, she and I met with various administrators to discuss the oral history project that we, along with 6 of her students, launched in the Yalobusha County towns of Water Valley and Coffeeville on Sunday, September 29th. I had barely made it back home to Georgia before the latest uproar at the university once again captured national attention. The Institutions of Higher Learning, which had been charged with finding a new leader, announced that it had hired a former IHF commissioner who had been paid as a consultant in the search process. He had not been on the list of candidates under consideration.

Students immediately protested, and the university canceled the press conference to announce the selection of the 18th chancellor. The first picture I saw showed my cousin and Water Valley native Ray Hawkins, the chief of university police, carrying a female student protester out of the room. It was he who announced the cancellation after the IHF officials retreated.

Then I remembered a comment from an administrator I had met a few days earlier – that negative acts inside and outside the university continue to thwart the school's positive efforts.

The previous article in this column, "A Quietly Kept First," featured Ruthie White, who with a high score on the ACT in 1970 wanted to go to college but did not know whom to talk to, nor did she or her family have the money.

Almost 50 years later, on September 27, 2019, Abby Sonnier, a junior public policy

The oral history project in Yalobusha County was launched last month as Ole Miss students visited Spring Hill North Baptist Church and Mt. Moriah District Association. The group at Mt. Moriah included (from left) Rhondalyn Peairs, Michelle Bright, Colton Babbitt, Dr. Jessie Wilkerson, Reverend Larry Hervey, Ruthie White, Dottie Reed, Keon Burns, Brittany Brown and Cecelia Parks.

and leadership major from Louisiana, wrote an opinion piece in the Daily Mississippian entitled, "Higher education isn't accessible to everyone." "I never worried about paying for college," she began. "As an upper-middle class individual, it never crossed my mind that I would not be able to go to college because of financial factors outside my control. Until I got to college, I honestly did not know that people just like me in nearly every way – except financially – had to sacrifice higher education because they could not afford it. Unfortunately, this is the reality for many aspiring students across Mississippi. Thousands of students are deprived of the basic tools they need to pursue higher education, and it is not by accident.

"A sufficient education can only be provided if it is properly funded," she continued. And Mississippi falls short. According to the U.S. Department of Education, she noted, the state spends $33,000 less per student throughout their K-12 public education than the U.S. average ($137,467).

In closing Abby wrote, "I have heard many stories of my peers having to forgo a meal because they couldn't afford it or forgo a shower and lights in their apartment because they couldn't pay rent that month. The state motto of Mississippi is 'by valor and arms'. Wouldn't it be the brave thing – the valiant thing- for Mississippi to allow education and opportunity to extend to (and) to be fully accessible to a whole new socioeconomic group which has never before been allotted this opportunity?"

Hats off to you Abby! How wonderful it would be if the IHL, which oversees all of the public institutions of higher education, paid more serious attention to this new socioeconomic group - the students and children of Mississippi.

Our oral history project in Yalobusha County is forging ahead with this ideal, reaching out, educating, engaging and connecting communities.

Our launch was a great success. The graduate students will conduct oral history interviews of black residents and natives of Yalobusha County. We were able to speak to approximately 150 people at worship services at Spring Hill North Baptist Church in Water Valley and the Mt. Moriah Missionary Baptist District Church Association in Coffeeville. Several individuals volunteered, agreeing to grant interviews to begin immediately. The students who are participating in this project are excited and describe their recent visit and anticipation.

From The Students Preparing To Collect The Untold Stories

Keon Burns

Upon entering Water Valley, we were embraced by the community and held so close that I honestly did not want to leave. The Water Valley community has a rich history that its members embrace and cherish with such fervor. I am ecstatic to learn more about the heart of the Black Community of Water Valley, THE BLOCK! I am so thankful to Ms. Dottie Chapman Reed for allowing me the opportunity to collaborate with the community and immortalize their history.

Cecelia Parks

I had visited Water Valley many times before going with Mrs. Reed, but our trip gave me an entirely new perspective on a familiar place. Hearing stories about attending the segregated schools or hanging out on The Block complicated both the history I thought I knew and my understanding of the changes the town is currently undergoing. I sincerely appreciate everyone we spoke with for welcoming us and taking the time to speak with us.

Michelle Bright

It was such a pleasure to visit with the members of Spring Hill North Missionary Baptist Church and Mount Moriah Missionary Baptist Association and other residents of Water Valley and Yalobusha County a few weeks ago. As a nearby resident of Oxford, I've often considered moving to a smaller town because Oxford's noise and traffic and crowds get to be a bit too much for this country girl at times. During the past 20 years when I've debated with myself whether or not to move to Water Valley, I thought I'd become pretty familiar with the town and it's history. I learned Sunday, September 29, that I was terribly mistaken. It was so cool to hear stories about The Block (Martin Street), but it was sobering to realize that all I'd ever known prior to that day was the white history of Water Valley. My classmates and I are eager to listen to and help you preserve as much of the history of the African American experience in Water Valley and surrounding Yalobusha County as you are willing and able to share with us. We look forward to working with you!

Rhondalyn Peairs

Though I had not been to Water Valley frequently since I returned to Mississippi eleven years ago, my most recent visit showed me that the more things change, the more they stay the same. The main street area stands revitalized with stores, cafes and even an art gallery. Those changes are good. As we entered the first missionary baptist church, a modern building on "The Block," the past rang out in the call and response of the deacons leading worship. It instantly reminded me of the Sunday service and revivals in Black Baptist and Methodist churches throughout the state of Mississippi in my youth. The comforting, participatory and communal nature of the worship was comforting. The traditions continue and I was home.

Colton L. Babbitt

Although I have lived in Water Valley for several months now, the day we spent in Water Valley allowed me to see this town in a new way. I expected and assumed our tour would take us down Main Street, where the First Baptist Church looks down the hill at recently restored store fronts that house new boutiques and restaurants. Instead, I learned about "the block," the historic hub of the black community, and had the privilege to worship at Spring Hill M.B. Church and Mt. Moriah. I am so thankful for the welcome we received at 5th Sunday and to have met so many of my Yalobusha County neighbors. The stories I heard were better than any assumptions I could make, and I look forward to hearing and preserving them through this oral history project.

Brittany Brown

I appreciate the Water Valley and Yalobusha County communities for welcoming us with open arms. Attending church service at Spring Hill North M.B. Church and Mt. Moriah Baptist Association reminded me of my own upbringing in the Missionary Baptist Church. The tour of Water Valley, especially learning about Davidson School and The Block, made me think about my own small hometown of Quitman, MS. What stories, people, and histories are going untold? I'm looking forward to having the chance to highlight the rich history that exists in Water Valley and want to do so with honor, creativity, and integrity.

Lucy Martin Kelly
Still Known By Her Full Name

My angel editor questions why I still insist on using Mr. and Mrs. when I refer to my elders. I cannot avoid it in this instance because the most special thing that I remember about Mrs. Lucy Kelly was we all called her "Mrs. Lucy Kelly."

As a beloved teacher in the Davidson School System, she demanded our respect and honor. As with the majority of the outstanding women that we have featured, I was delighted to learn more about her and respect her even more because of this new information.

Lucy Martin Kelly was born November 18, 1900 in Bryant, Miss. to Barney and Hannah Martin. She joined Pleasant Grove Missionary Baptist Church in Coffeeville when she was 19. The pastor at that time was Dr. C. P. Bohannon, who founded the Mt. Moriah Missionary Baptist Association in 1908. On January 19, 1935 she married Jonah L. Kelly and became a step mom to his six children. Lucy and her husband were farmers and both taught Sunday School. Her great nieces, Maxine and Clementine Booker, lived with the Kellys. After a while Maxine joined her mother out of state, but Clementine stayed with them until she graduated from high school.

Lucy completed her elementary and high school requirements in what appears to be several installments – indicative of the limited educational opportunity for blacks in Mississippi at the time. Records show that she completed her early education at a Coffeeville Extension Center between 1941 and 1944. She was accepted in good standing by certificate to Rust High School in Holly Springs in September 1944 with elementary education to be her major. Records show that she also submitted her information to Mississippi Industrial College in Holly Springs, which is no longer in operation. Lucy received her Bachelor of Science degree in Elementary Education from Rust College on June 2, 1958.

Mrs. Lucy spent the majority her teaching career in the all black Davidson School System. The Kellys were neighbors of the Orice and Beatrice Sims family. According to their son, Lee Russell Sims, she also taught his father, Orice Sims, in a one room log cabin. Lee Russell remembers being in her fourth grade class. "She often left me in charge of the class when she had to step out or during end-of-the-year testing," he said. He laughingly recalls she had a big paddle and loved fried chicken. Mr. Kelly, he added, was like a granddad to him and his 13 siblings and always watched out for them.

Mrs. Lucy was a decades-long member of Mt. Grove M. B. Church, remaining a congregant until her death on November 15, 1986, three days before her 86th birthday. Reverend Jacob Charles Hentz remembered her as "a fine lady and a dedicated servant of God. She worked tirelessly and supported many ministries while teaching in the public school and in the church." She served as president of the Missionary Society and as

Mrs. Daliah McLeod and Mrs. Dollie Ann Henderson on the playground at Davidson Elementary during the time of Mrs. Kelly's tenure.

the educational director. Mrs. Lucy served as the vice president of the Missionary Society for the Mt. Moriah District and was a past matron of Heroines of Jericho Court 160.

Mrs. Lucy Kelly also taught me in fourth grade, and I can still see us standing in line in front of the blackboard for the spelling quizzes. I was terrified of missing a word and terrified of her. But she did have a gentleness about her, and I came to understand that Mrs. Kelly was more smoke than fire. She loved us and wanted us to be successful, and we did not want to disappoint her. Like with most of my teachers, I did not care for moving on to the next grade after getting accustomed to one teacher, and this was especially true with Mrs. Kelly.

Now let's do the math Mrs. Kelly was born in 1900, and I was in fourth grade in 1961. She was 61 years old.

As I have said many times before, we had some awesome educators at Davidson. Just meeting the state requirements probably presented a challenge to all of them. Mrs. Lucy Kelly was one who garnered such respect that most of us still call her by her full name, not due to her age but out of sincere gratitude and admiration. She overcame obstacles and barriers to simply obtain an education, and because she shared that knowledge, we are better for it. There is indeed something special about being known by your full name. We remember her!

Update on Phase Two- Oral History Project

The six students from the Oral History graduate class at the University of Mississippi have completed the first series of interviews designed to document black community history in North Mississippi. These students are pursuing masters degrees in southern studies, an interdisciplinary program that investigates the complexity of the American South.

The students report having had extraordinary experiences while learning about Yalobusha County and the lives of

Mrs. Lucy Kelly

its black citizens. The students are now getting ready to present their interviews, a part of their final class requirements. These presentations will take place on the afternoon of December 7th in Water Valley and will be open to the families of those interviewed and the general public. The location will be announced after final arrangements are made. This informative and educational program provides a great opportunity for younger generations to learn more of the black history of their community.

We are still soliciting individuals to participate in the interview process. We hope that the collaboration between this column and the University of Mississippi history department will continue beyond this semester. Consider this an invitation to support this project and mark your calendar to join us December 7th for the Oral History Event. Stay tuned for the time and location!

Reader Comments

Thanks for the article on Mrs. Lucy Kelly. She was an amazing woman. I remember that she and Mr. Jonah would visit my grandfather, Frank Sanders on Sunday afternoons.
Eddie G. Sanders,
Detroit. MI

Lucy Kelly is my great, great aunt on my dad's side, his grandmother's sister. He just lost a sister this week who was somewhat the family historian. This might perk him up a bit. I got excited just seeing Aunt Lucy's name in the subject line. Thank you so, so much for all you're doing!
Syreeta Kee,
Coffeeville, MS

Enjoyed the article. Very well written. Thanks for caring.
Marilyn Curry,
Holly Springs, MS

Very interesting and I can relate. Going to school in the south we respected our teachers and looked up to them. That relationship does not exist anymore in New York.
Lillian Dent,
Roosevelt, NY

Juanita Polk Fleming
What A Woman - A Superwoman

At this year's July Fourth Homecoming Day Festival in Sallis, Miss., I caught up with Juanita Polk Fleming and her husband, Jesse. They are members of a cooperative that supports the event, now in its 12th year. As Juanita showed me around on a sizzling hot day, I could feel the respect and adoration each vendor had for her as she stopped to make purchases – the very appealing sweet potato pies, cakes and watermelons.

Juanita and I had talked recently but could not pinpoint where our paths crossed while growing up in Yalobusha. Most likely it was at Bayson Missionary Baptist Church, where we attended events as children. Her parents, Will and Sallie Polk, and her Uncle James and Aunt Gencie Polk were lifelong members of Bayson. Juanita is one of 10 children and first cousin to her aunt and uncles' 17 children. Serving God, community service and education remain cornerstones of the Polk families' activities.

At the festival I kept hearing, "Hi, Mrs. Fleming," from all ages, especially from her former students. As a teacher, apparently Juanita molded many successful individuals including her own sons, Jesse, Jr. and Jeffery. Her friend, Linda Lewis Jamison and Juanita's sons, tell us more about yet another outstanding woman of Yalobusha County.

A Defining Reach Beyond Yalobusha
By Linda Lewis Jamison

When Juanita Polk Fleming migrated to the small town of Sallis, Mississippi, the residents had no idea how her electrifying personality would affect them. After graduating from Central High School in Coffeeville, she attended Alcorn State University where she met her husband Jesse. After Juanita graduated from Alcorn in 1970, she taught home economics for a year in the Tunica, MS public schools – before Tunica became the recreational mecca it is today. Then she married Jesse James Fleming, and they homesteaded on his family's farm in Sallis, where Juanita became an integral part of the community.

Juanita began teaching elementary reading at Long Creek School because there were no available home economics positions in the area. Not only did she influence many students in the classroom, but she also served several years as the assistant principal. In addition, Juanita assisted with the state testing program and does to this day, even though she has retired. While she was employed, Juanita also helped with many extracurricular activities such as the annual Spring Fling Carnival and Pageant.

In her retirement, Juanita remains connected to education, serving as the president of the local Retired Educational Personnel of Mississippi. This allows her to continue influencing the students of Attala County. Juanita's former students and co-workers remember her as an extremely thorough, capable, and compassionate educator who sought not only to teach academics, but also to help mold the students into successful, productive adults who possess integrity and high moral character.

In addition to her professional endeavors, Juanita and her husband Jesse have influenced the community in other ways. She has served on the Board of Directors of the Oprah Winfrey Boys and Girls Club and continues to help with their fundraising even though she is no longer on the board. She and Jesse helped found and are active members of the Self-Help Co-op, which provides educational and other assistance to farmers. They also sponsor an annual Father-Son fishing tournament on their private lake. And they partner with their church in a Blessing of the Bikes Ceremony in the spring. This Ceremony, similar to the Blessing of the Fleet, is for motorcycles, bicycles, ATV's and their drivers. Jesse's tenure as the first black on the Attala County Board of Supervisors highlighted the couple's importance to the community.

Along with serving the residents of Sallis professionally and in community affairs, Juanita also participates in the area's religious activities. She is a member of Mount Olive Missionary Baptist Church, where she is the church's announcer. Jesse is a deacon, and she is a deaconess. In this capacity, she helps prepare the communion table and assists with the benevolence the church extends to the needy – members and non-members alike. Juanita also works in other ministry areas such as vacation bible school, transporting friends to and from medical appointments and providing her signature dishes to the sick and shut in.

Juanita truly exemplifies the teachings of Jesus concerning servanthood, and she and Jesse have sought to instill these values in their sons, Jesse and Jeffery, and their grandchildren. Juanita Polk Fleming has been and still is a truly positive, electrifying influence on the residents of rural Attala County and beyond.

Six Lessons From A Teacher
By Jesse and Jeffery Fleming

On Nov. 9th, 1949 Willie and Sallie Polk welcomed their 9th child and 5th daughter, Juanita, to the world. Born and reared in Coffeeville, Juanita graduated from Central High School before going off to college at Alcorn State University. Attending Alcorn State University proved to be one of the most significant decisions that she made as she met our father, Jesse J. Fleming, there. This is also where we (Jesse K. and Jeffery) went to school.

Mom spent most of her professional career as a teacher and assistant principal at Long Creek Elementary in our hometown of Sallis. Although teaching was her profession, the lessons that she taught extended well beyond the classroom. How she lives her life has taught us more valuable lessons than any textbook written. Here are a few lessons from Juanita.

Lesson 1 – Our mom taught us how to serve with her commitment to the Sallis and Attala County communities. She taught night-classes for people who wanted to get their GED, tutored students after school, and taught summer school occasionally. She served as secretary for the Sunday School and church business meetings. Additionally, she spent several years as the president of our church choir. This was before we got fancy and created the "Minister of Music" title. The fact that our father was also a

Juanita and Jesse Fleming are pictured with sons Jeffery and Jesse, Jr.

teacher and superintendent of our Sunday school made them an awesome, evenly yoked couple. She served those who were in need or needed any support. "Don't brag on what you do for others. Let God brag on you," she would say. It's a lesson we grew to understand.

Lesson 2 – She taught us how to survive. Our mother poured into our lives and helped us transition from boys to men. Mom was a home economics major when she was at Alcorn. Dad often said that was one of the reasons he wanted to marry her. She was a great cook, enjoyed cooking and she taught us how to cook.

My brother Jesse paid more attention in the cooking classes than I did. I followed our dad's plan and found a wife who knew how to cook! She probably didn't know that I was comparing her meals to mom's. I can remember the Saturday morning when my mom taught me how to iron. She tricked me into believing that ironing was fun! Little did I know that the joke was on me, as she had just gotten out of ironing my clothes for the rest of her life. I thought she was smiling because she was proud of me. It was not until the next Saturday, when I was ironing again, that I figured out why she really was smiling!

Lesson 3 - She taught us how to show love. Her love started at home, and then it spread. She demonstrated how to have a loving relationship with your family no doubt influenced by coming from a family of 10 siblings with lots of love to go around. Mom was diligent about speaking regularly with her brothers and sisters. We can remember countless trips up and down I-55 between Sallis and Coffeeville to stay with Momma Sallie and visiting with all our aunts, uncles, and cousins. During the summers, we took vacations to Chicago to visit Aunts Onia and Elnora and Uncle Winfield. One favorite trip was to visit Uncle Bubba in South Carolina. At the end of that visit, our parents surprised us and took us to Disney World in Orlando. In showing us how to love our mom also taught us how to smile. She kept a smile on her face – even in the hardest moments and even when she disciplined us.

Lesson 4 – She taught us how to support one another. Mom supported us through all our extracurricular activities while we were in school (football, basketball, band, choirs, track, and countless clubs and organizations). She frequently dropped us off and picked us up from practices before we could drive ourselves. She also attended our games and events regularly and sometimes ended up helping or leading parent support committees for many of the organizations.

Mom taught us the value of hard work and how to be resourceful. Teaching is one of those all-encompassing jobs that doesn't allow you to leave your work at work. So, on many days she would come home, prepare a meal for us, and get back to grading papers and developing lesson plans. As we got older, she was able to use us as her teacher's aides, grading papers for her while she cooked dinner and completed other household duties.

She was always supportive of dad whether it was his career in education, public service, or any of his "serial entrepreneurial adventures." We grew up attending NAACP meetings, Attala County Beat 4 Improvement Club meetings, and Alcorn State alumni chapter meetings. All these meetings planted seeds in us that would help us understand the importance of giving back to the community and making it better. This has helped shape our lives as we continue to work in our churches and communities in Tennessee and Arkansas.

Lesson 5 – She taught us about the Savior. Our mom set a perfect example of a God-fearing mother and wife. She is a Proverbs 31 virtuous woman. She also spent time teaching Sunday School at Mt. Olive M.B. Church, and she and dad kept us in church. On our family road trips, we only listened to sermons and church songs. Mom looked at these trips as sleeping pills, nodding off soon after we were on our way.

When I was 10 and Jeff was 6, we sat in the backseat signaling the big trucks passing by to blow their horns. This scared mom, and she would jump out of her sleep and grab the dashboard. My dad would just laugh, and she would fall back to sleep, not knowing we were signaling the trucks to blow. But when we signaled the trucks about three more times, she figured it out and gave us a warning: "If I hear another horn again, you are going to meet your Savior." To this day, I don't blow my horn when she's in the car!

Lesson 6 – She taught us how to sacrifice and share. She continues to teach these values to her five grandchildren, attending baptisms, kindergarten, elementary, and middle school graduations, and soccer and basketball games. She is always a willing host for any of them during the summer and for holidays.

These are just a few of the many lessons that we learned from mom over the years. Even after her "official" retirement from the classroom, mom still pours into the lives of students, family, and friends each and every day. She is a Superwoman!!!

Linda Jamison, now a retired librarian and teacher residing in Kosciusko, also taught Jesse and Jeffery in school. So, she, too, can take some credit for their successes. Jesse is a Baptist minister, who works as a technical associate/test engineer for Wright Medical, an orthopedic company in Memphis, Tenn. Jeffery is an executive in Carrier Compliance and Administration with Walmart in the corporate headquarters in Bentonville, Arkansas.

The lessons these sons described are great examples for today's young mothers. Juanita's life and influence impacts others way beyond Yalobusha and Attala counties. She gives a whole new meaning to servanthood and motherhood as she continues to serve others non-stop day after day.

She is probably driving someone to the doctor right now. It is no wonder and no surprise. She was raised that way. A SUPERWOMAN, INDEED!

Reader Comments

I continue to enjoy your stories about the women of Yalobusha County, and I have been thinking lately about a lady whose name I don't remember but she was Dr. Spears's nurse. What I remember most is going to his office and she would be there in that nice white uniform, looking so professional, when most of the African American women I knew as a child were domestic workers. This lady was always friendly and welcoming to us, and just seemed so "together," for lack of a better word. I just remember being so impressed with her, and I think she would make a good subject for a story if she hasn't been featured already.
Camille Dautrich,
Branson, MO

Oh! Juanita is a SUPER WOMAN! I enjoyed the six lessons. I got it – this is not about me.
Dorothy Middleton,
Jackson, MS

Ruby McKie Turner
A Hidden Treasure Shares Her Memories

A few months ago, Cleveland Joseph introduced me to his cousin, and I soon discovered one of the best resources on the history of Water Valley's black community in the 1930s, 40s and 50s. Ruby Turner was born in Water Valley on October 30, 1928 and lived here until 1956. "We were known as the Mackeys," she quipped, "but our name was McKie. You know how the white folks called you what they want to call you." She said her brother and sister had to make a special effort to correct their last name when they worked for the federal government years later.

At 91, she remains active as a pianist and soloist in her church in Phoenix, Illinois. She recently played piano for the male chorus for Men's Day and is now rehearsing for the 18th annual Christmas Cantata. Her first book, Lights of Another Color – Out of the Darkness of Slavery, is near completion.

While her relatives are long gone, she stays in touch with her husband's cousins who still live in Water Valley: the Turners, the Josephs, the Whites, to name a few. They are planning their 2020 family reunion in Oxford, and I hope to meet her there in person and get a copy of that book.

Two previous columns about black maids noted that the authors did not know the last names of some of these women. This upset Ruby, and she was quick to give me the last name of her cousin, Etoile Winters, in our very first conversation. I would love to share more about our long conversations, but I happily yield the space to her.

Recollections and Reflections
By Ruby M. Turner

I was born in Water Valley, Mississippi to Alfred E. McKie and Genora Morgan McKie, the youngest of eight children. My paternal grandmother, Eliza Kelly McKie, was born a slave on the Kelly Plantation in rural Coffeeville, Mississippi. She and her husband, Joshua McKie, moved with their family to Water Valley in 1879. In 1883, they purchased their home adjacent to the land on which the Everdale Missionary Baptist Church later would be built. Eliza and Joshua played significant roles in founding this church, which previously had been a Bush Harbor church. This area became the center of the colored community and included the colored school and Miles CME Methodist Church.

Former slave women and their children actively engaged in social activities, especially those among the first free-born generation. The churches and various organizations sponsored musical events and trips that formed a key part of the colored community's social structure. Parents - newly freed – set a cultural standard for their children, laying the foundation for future generations. And strong, influential women from this generation influenced my life and the generations that followed.

This central community that I lived in was also the home of four women school teachers, including the principal of the Water Valley Colored School. The leading pianists also lived in this community.

My first memories of my surroundings come from the 1930s. I was enrolled in the Water Valley colored school shortly before my fifth birthday, in 1933. It was also the year my oldest sister, Eliza, began her teaching career and when I became involved in church activities. Both school and church provided the beginning of rewarding and enriching experiences.

The women who lived in the neighborhood and influenced me and the other children in the hills and valleys around town were Theresa Davidson, Ethel Curry, Minnie Nickolson and Alberta Weir.

Theresa Davidson, the wife of Principal E.C. Davidson, was a teacher at the Water Valley Colored School and had multiple duties. She taught English literature and geography. She was also the director of the glee clubs and in charge of the extracurricular department, producing operettas, musicals, dance and plays. While doing all of this, she raised four children.

Ethel Curry was the primary teacher and later taught science and biology. The Water Valley Colored School housed both an elementary and high school, and the teachers had to work in all the grades.

Minnie Nickolson was the assistant Sunday school superintendent of the Everdale Missionary Baptist Church.

Alberta Weir was the pianist of the E.M.B. Church, and like the other women, led a life of service to young children, teenagers and adults. More than once they all went the extra mile beyond the call of duty.

As a little girl, I became involved in the extracurricular activities at school. Mrs. Davidson produced the "Tom Thumb Wedding," a pageant where children act out the marriage ceremony of the 1863 wedding of General Tom Thumb (Charles Sherwood Stratton) and Lavinia Warren.

I was six years old and played the part of the bride. Melvin Kennedy, the son of Laura Turner, was the groom. Classmates filled out the other roles. The wedding was held at the E.M.B Church, and it was a huge success. Ethel Curry photographed the wedding cast on the school campus the following morning.

Another production Mrs. Davidson directed included a chorus line. We wore black shorts, white blouses, and shoes with taps on the toes and heels. The program also featured solo acts.

We performed one of the more memorable dance routines to the popular "A Tisket a Tasket," which had catapulted Ella Fitzgerald to stardom. My sister Eliza played the piano for us. The plays required memorization, and the poise and confidence of acting before a large audience translated into the classroom and benefited the students tremendously.

In addition to her work as a teacher and producer, Mrs. Davidson used her talent to arrange sing-a-longs at the school on Sunday afternoons. She also introduced music appreciation featuring the glee club at the E.M.B. Church.

Black history was not a part of the school's curriculum, and our teachers were prohibited from including it in class. However, Mrs. Davidson believed that the students should know about their heritage, and she made sure the subject was part of English class. She also took this opportunity to teach the students how to use circumvention when interacting with white people. Certain responses to questions asked by white people, she explained, had to be answered in the correct way, meaning a simple "yes" and "no" were not tolerated. The former slave way of answering "yas-suh" and "nah-suh." "yes-sum" and "no'om," she told her students, were not proper words. She instructed the class to reply "yes" with emphasis, putting a little distance between "sir" and the same for females. By doing

Ruby M. Turner

this, she noted, we would preserve our self-respect and dignity. It was a lesson well taught, given that as people of color we faced laws that governed every aspect of our lives. It took courage for Mrs. Davidson to defy this system.

Minnie Nickolson, the assistant Sunday school superintendent, and Alberta Weir, the pianist of the Everdale Baptist Church and also Ethel Curry left their mark as strong leaders in the church and community.

Mrs. Nickolson sponsored an annual Easter program that was a part of the Sunday school youth and children department. It required several weeks of preparation with rehearsals at the end of the school day. Children and youth attended these rehearsals to learn the songs from Mrs. Weir and the speeches with special dramatic readings assigned by Mrs. Nickolson. They worked out the logistics of the marches, which were executed with military-like precision.

Families looked forward to the Easter programs, which always brought an overflow crowd to the church. White guests sat in a special reserved section. The dedication of these two women instilled pride and confidence in the students.

Ethel Curry provided an essential part of the personal care for the neighborhood's girls. On the afternoon before Easter, she used her beautician skills to give the girls hair styles of their choice – free of charge. As one of the younger participants, I requested Shirley Temple curls!

On Easter afternoon, Miss Curry decorated the choir stand with colorful streamers of crepe papers and fresh bouquets of flowers to provide a beautiful background for the program.

Additionally, Miss Curry, as a science and biology teacher, extended her school day to arrange nature walks outside of town on late fall days. She pointed out how the trees were changing, becoming bare, and noted the different kinds of foliage. As a reward we were allowed to gather holly berries and mistletoe for the Christmas holiday.

Miss Curry did not forget her students during the summer months. As a segregated town, Water Valley did not provide recreational facilities for the colored residents. Community leaders, including Miss Curry, sponsored safe, interesting activities, such as house parties or outdoor events. She organized late evening strolls on warm summer nights when the moon was full. A group of children of all ages would meet at her house, and the walk would lead to the farm of E.M.B. Church members Mr. and Mrs. L. Z. Hervey. They hosted a party after the walk in their expansive front yard so the children could play games without fear of the police – who were always suspicious of gatherings by colored people – showing up. At the end of the party, Miss Curry served refreshments that she had prepared.

Her dedication along with others gave the colored children and youth beautiful lasting memories.

Three other women deserve recognition for their service to the community and their churches.

Annie Kelly was the "jeans" teacher and supervisor over the colored schools in Yalobusha County, though no one ever explained what "jeans" meant. She had an office on main street and visited all of the colored schools. Miss Kelly's parents were among the county's first free-born generation in the post-Civil War era. Black residents with a high school certificate could teach school but had to attend Rust College in the summer to pursue a college degree. Miss Kelly was also a leader in the Miles C.M.E. Methodist Church and later on the conference level of the C.M.E. Church, where she worked in the various auxiliaries to improve and grow the church nationwide.

I remember Miss Kelly's congenial personality, always putting the interest of children first. On one of her visits to the Water Valley Colored School, she assigned me the task of memorizing the Twenty-Third Psalm with 10 cents offered as a reward. I met this challenge, and a week later I proudly recited the psalm. Miss Kelly motivated many children, encouraging them with her words of wisdom to pursue higher goals.

After her marriage later in life, she continued to devote her time and energies to motivate and inspire those who sought higher education – the very model of a strong and intelligent woman not to be forgotten.

Annie Givens, featured in the December 13, 2018 article in this column, and her husband, Reverend S. J. Givens, lived next door to me when I was a child. When we played outdoors, Mrs. Givens kept a watchful eye over us. She later moved to her home on Wagner Street. Her niece, Faye Thornton, and I were best friends, and I often visited the Givens. Mrs. Givens continued to attend the E.M.B. Church and became the Sunday school superintendent after Mrs. Nickolson retired and moved to another state.

As Sunday school superintendent Mrs. Givens kept abreast of the current materials published by the National Baptist Publishing House. She attended the annual convention each year as a delegate of the E.M.B. Church. World War II drastically changed the makeup of the communities as so many young men were drafted to serve in the armed forces. Camp McCain, an army camp, was located in nearby Grenada. When some of the young soldiers visited Water Valley on weekend passes, they helped fill the void left by the men who had been drafted. The community welcomed these soldiers, and when they came to the E.M.B. Church Sunday school and worship service, Mrs. Givens assigned them to the adult class that my mother taught. They eagerly participated and were a positive addition to the church.

Over the years, Mrs. Givens faithfully worked with the children and young adults in various programs, and the Sunday school grew under her leadership.

She was a beautician, and she showed the same interest in her clients as she did with fellow congregants. Her door was always open.

Lou Avant was a strong, influential leader of the church. She was the president of the Everdale Missionary Baptist Church Women's Missionary Department. Her leadership abilities extended beyond this department and included the needs of younger women. In the early 1950s, she organized a young Matron Missionary Society in the Everdale Missionary Baptist Church. I was a part of this group, and we worked with the children of the church and did outreach services for the sick and shut-in. The work was rewarding, but we felt the need to do more and approached Mrs. Avant with the idea to form the Young Matrons Gospel Chorus. She readily agreed, and we put the plan in motion. I served as the pianist for the junior choir for several years, and I became the pianist for the Young Matrons Gospel Chorus. As a choir, we were successful, but we did not have choir robes. We raised the money, including donations from the white business community, and became the first choir to be robed.

As young married and single women we wanted to have a social outlet that was not church affiliated. Again, we approached Mrs. Avant with our idea to form a social club. Always progressive, she supported us in this new endeavor. We organized the Sweetheart Social Club and soon held our first afternoon tea at the Miles C.M.E. Church. The good attendance reflected the community's support. We soon became recognized as young leaders and decided to include benevolent duties to help the elderly, especially on holidays, with food donations.

In May of 1956, my oldest sister, who lived in Chicago, was in the final stage of her illness, so I left Water Valley to be with her. After she passed, my husband and I, with our two daughters, moved to Chicago and later to Phoenix, Illinois, a suburb of the city. Most of the women involved in the aforementioned activities moved to various states in the mid-1950s, ending a special Yalobusha county era.

On March 10, 1974, the committee for "A Tribute to Theresa Davidson" met in Chicago at the home of Lorine Turner to plan a dinner the next month at the Pilgrim Baptist Church Community Center. On the evening of April 20, 1974, former students who lived in the Chicago suburbs and in other states gathered at the southside building to reminisce about their experiences under Mrs. Davidson's leadership. The highlight of this memorable evening was the surprise visits of her sons Drs. E.C. and Kerry Davidson.

The women featured in this article - each of them a leader - dedicated their lives to enriching and inspiring the children and youth of the colored communities that are now a part of the African-American experience. This is their well-earned legacy.

Reader Comments

Thank you, my aunt is a history book of her own.
Cleveland Joseph,
Oxford, MS

I just had a chance to read your article about Ruby Turner. She had a lot of influence from those whose names are names of people who helped many through some difficult days of our history. Much has changed since then and it's good that what you do is to remind us of their importance and influence in the lives of so many.
Harry Neal,
Winona, MS

Article 34 was once again breath taking and inspiring. So much attention to her children, community and so many others during a real time of suffering and being abused and bullied.
Jim Brzoska,
Deltona, FL

If at 91, Sister Turner can play the piano and sings, surely, I can complete what I started last year--piano lesson. And, she can write! I SHALL do better. It was an enjoyable read.
Dorothy Middleton,
Jackson, MS

I am beginning to catch up with your wonderful articles. They are filled with so much history, this one reminded me of when my daughter was the Kindergarten bride (when Q marries U). I'm reading from the most recent back to where I missed.
Cheryl Johnson,
Lithonia, GA

35

All Our Names Were Freedom
Agency, Resiliency, and Community in Yalobusha County

This was the title and outcry of the oral history program the UM Southern Studies graduate students presented December 7th in Water Valley. If I had a video, perhaps I could recapture the emotional highs of the occasion. The presentation left the approximately 70 in attendance in awe and me in tears. How fitting to be at Spring Hill M.B. Church North on Martin Street, directly across from the black funeral home that was once the site of an adult only club, The Blue Room, on what was known as The Block. It was the center of black entertainment, black businesses and way too many tragedies years ago. Strangely enough, while there is little to no business there now, men still socialize under the trees near the funeral home, even on Sundays.

The interviewees present were Lillie Roberts, Emma Faye Gooch, Dorothy Kee, Marjorie Moore, Katherine Roland Pollard, and Luther Folson, Jr. James Wright and Luther Folson, Sr. were unable to attend. Had they been present they would have heard the interviewees whispering, 'That's me!" and seen the faces light up as they recognized their quotes.

When I was younger, I admired 88-year-old Lillie Caldwell Roberts. She dressed like she could have been on the cover of Ebony Magazine and carried herself just like that - a grand and elegant lady – ahead of her time. I often wondered where she found such beautiful clothes. By now my readers know that she was the first black to register to vote in Yalobusha County, her husband, Joe Caldwell, accompanying her to the courthouse with a gun in his pocket. She and Dorothy Kee were featured in Dr. Alysia Steele's 2015 book, Delta Jewels, In Search of my Grandmother's Wisdom, and also in this column.

Retired Army 1st Sergeant Emma Gooch has returned home after extensive service to our country and describes herself as a lone community activist, most concerned about the lack of social activities or facilities for the black youth in the community.

Every time I speak with Marjorie Moore I learn more and more. Her mother, Elvira Jackson, was one of Coffeeville's leading black female educators. On Saturday, I learned that Roosevelt Hervey, one of the early principals of Davidson High School, was her mother's brother. One of the young preachers that my mother mentored and carried around from church to church across north Mississippi was Reverend Johnny Roland, Katherine Roland Pollard's grandfather. My mom also influenced Luther Folson, Sr., and that, in turn, influenced, his son. Luther Folson, Jr. is currently awaiting a legal review of the recent county sheriff's race where he lost (to his white opponent) by two votes.

As I mentioned at the church, James Wright was the youngest I remember in his strong God-fearing family. Nobody

The interviewees attending the oral history program on Dec. 7 included (front row, from left) Dorothy Kee, Lillie Roberts, Marjorie Moore and Katherine Pollard; (back row, from left) Colton Babbitt, Keon Burns, Brittany Brown, Emma Gooch, Dottie Reed, Rhondalyn Peairs, Michelle Bright, Luther Folson, Jr. and Jessie Wilkerson.

messed with his dad, Ed Wright, Sr. The Wrights, the Gooches, the Boldens, the Sanders and the Chapmans rode the same school bus driven by Kenneth Carothers, Harry Campbell, Fred (Pee Wee) Harris and Lincoln Shields and others. Their stop was next to last. Saturday night Annie Gooch Longstreet told me she was a little girl on that bus, and she looked up to me because I was so confident. "I wanted to be just like that," she said. From what I saw, she accomplished that, and I was left shaking my head.

Special thanks to Dr. Jessie Wilkerson and her outstanding graduate students. I am so proud of them and honored to have worked with them: Colton Babbitt, Michelle Bright, Brittany Brown, Keon Burns, and Rhondalyn Peairs – future PhD's.

The interviews these millennials have documented are preserving the legacies and black history of Yalobusha county. This information will lead to more stories, expanding, on what we have already accomplished. The interviews are being transcribed and will be presented to the participants. With their permission, the university will archive them. "I couldn't have been happier with the way things turned out, and we're looking forward to future collaboration", said Dr. Kathryn McKee, the Director of the UM Center for Southern Culture.

The university has promised continued support for this oral history project and the *North Mississippi Herald* column. During the December 7th event, I gave Drs. Wilkerson and McKee a $3,000 donation from the Sylarn Foundation, which is based in Michigan. This matches UM's funding of the oral history project to date. One of the foundation board members has ties to Mississippi and read about the project.

Continue to check my website and the column for updates. We are still accepting stories and recommendations of individuals who would like to participate.

Sincerest thanks to all who attended the program, with special thanks to Pastor Samuel Townes and Spring Hill North for the use of their facilities and the extreme hospitality shown. Now back to the presentation. I could share more of my response and feelings but want to give you the perspective of four attendees:

Classrooms are both public spaces and strangely private ones. As professors, we seldom see what our colleagues or their students are doing; we hear anecdotes about discussions that went well and, just as often, about activities that veered comically off course. But on December 7, I joined some of my co-workers and many residents of Yalobusha County in peering into what had been going on all semester in Southern Studies 560, "Oral History of Southern Social Movements," taught by Dr. Jessie Wilkerson at the University of Mississippi.

Five students from that course (Colton Babbitt, Michelle Bright, Brittany Brown, Keon Burns, and Rhondalyn Peairs) treated us to a staged reading of the oral histories they had been collecting all semester from African American residents of Water Valley, Coffeeville, and the wider county. Although we saw a seamless performance, akin to being at a play or watching a radio drama, the students tell me that it was harder to put together than it might seem. They weren't just reading the "best" or most "interesting" lines from what they heard. They were curating what they'd heard by putting moments from the transcripts in conversation with each other around particular topics that ranged from religion to outright discrimination. The result was a powerful retelling of stories that have not been often told, told in the words of people who have not always been heard. At the Center for the Study of Southern Culture, we are excited to continue mapping and recording the experiences of African American residents of Yalobusha County. Thank you to Dottie Reed for initiating this important project and for recognizing in the first place that everyday experiences in small town Mississippi are the very essence of history.

Kathryn B. McKee
Director, Center for the Study of Southern Culture
McMullan Professor of Southern Studies and Professor of English

---

While I was born and raised in the City of Atlanta, I did see a strong thread in my past and the stories told at the presentation. Education was the overriding theme for me. I was raised to believe that education was the key to having a successful life. The roads to that much desired goal were different, but the goal was the same. I have to admit my road was not as arduous as the stories I heard, I am still proud of the results. We have all been a part of the "southern mystique", however I must say it took heartier efforts from the stories I heard in Mississippi.

Thomasenia P. Robinson
Retired HR Manager

The students presented a unique perspective of African Americans they had interviewed, and they did it in a way that was totally unexpected. Most people with whom I spoke expected to watch a presentation on the video screen. When the students did an oral presentation, it took them by surprise, but I and those I spoke with enjoyed the method of presentation and its content. To take the time to review hours of interviews, digest the information, then narrow the scope for presentation was well done. Then to write a script was wonderful.

Having heard about some of the individuals in the beginning of the program, I was able to recognize them as the student did the oral presentation. That made the presentation even more meaningful. I hope the students will consider that type presentation again, maybe as a short play where they could learn the lines and expand the production. I thought they were all great.

> *Earl Warren Richard*
> *UM Graduate*
> *Bachelor's 1978*
> *Master's in Education Administration 1996*
> *Ph.D. in Educational Leadership 2016 –*
> *Emphasis in Administration, Leadership & Management*
> *Research Specialty: Acting White Phenomenon*

It was a great experience. I honestly was not expecting it to be so rich in history and culture. I am grateful and honored to have been a part. In addition to its being a rich and informative event, I'd like to add it felt nostalgic. To have the opportunity to listen to some of the stories - some great, others not so good, was priceless and reminded me so much of the stories my grandmother often shared with me while sitting on her lap as she relived the glory days and expressed her fondest memories of how the black community was tight knit and dependent on each other and its institutions. Again, it was an awesome occasion. I look forward to hearing about where this project goes in the future.

> *Joshua D. Harper*
> *Coordinator of Diversity Recruitment*
> *The University of Mississippi*
> *Office of Admissions*

Closing Thoughts
By Dottie Reed

A repeat performance has already been scheduled in February at the university, most appropriately timed – Black History Month. I am confident parents, high schoolers and youth could enjoy and learn from this experience.

This column and the Black Women of Yalobusha project started 16 months ago, in June 2018, and continues to grow exponentially. I thank all those who have been featured, those who have written and for all contributions. Finally, special thanks to David Howell and the *Herald* for providing this venue. We look forward to sharing more stories of the many outstanding black women of Yalobusha county in 2020 and documenting oral histories of the black community. Merry Christmas and A Happy and Blessed New Year to All!

Dr. Katie McKee, Dr. Jessie Wilkerson and Dottie Reed with a $3,000 donation to the University of Mississippi from the Sylarn Foundation for the Yalobusha Oral History Project.

Reader Comments

Such a wonderful article regarding Water Valley history.
James Reed,
Greenville, SC

Thank you for your article on the Oral History presentation! The work that local residents and Dr. Wilkerson's students did has nurtured my desire to work on more oral histories in my own work.
Jasmine Stansberry,
Memphis, TN

I read your article today with interest. In particular, I saw a mention of "Coffeeville." My maternal mother was born in Coffeeville. I am interested in knowing more about the early 1800s for blacks at that time surrounding her birth. Thanks, and congratulations on a very successful project.
Jim Simmons,
Stone Mountain GA

I spoke to Kirsten Dillinger, who was present at the event and she told me that the experience was powerful. I hate that I was unable to attend, but I am so glad that Southern Studies will continue to work on the project and that the archive will chronicle the sacrifice and commitment to justice that continues to thrive in that community.
Katrina Caldwell,
University, MS

Thank you for sharing this column with me and for opening the doors of your home community to my colleagues and I. Working on this oral history project the past semester has been an honor, and I'm grateful to have been welcomed into the community to document the life histories of the outstanding black community in Yalobusha County.
Brittany Brown,
Meridian, MS

36

Good Triumphs Tragedy
A Story of Forgiveness

Every now and then a story causes me to deviate from the column norm. I pondered for days and sought spiritual guidance about how I would start this first article of 2020. One friend suggested that I share some of the many thought-provoking comments I have received from across the country. Another friend suggested contacting my white homegirls who have written for this column to get their thoughts as we have reached Article 36. Both suggestions seemed too self-centered and not befitting the first column of 2020 - A new year that in my opinion finds most average Americans a bit above concerned – more like worried.

Beware worrying is considered a sin.

My mind and heart rested on a Facebook post sent to me by a Yalobusha native now living in Jackson. The post was written by Dr. Hilliard Lackey, a native of Marks. He writes about a personal, tragic incident in Water Valley many years ago, when he was only five years old. I felt compelled to share it here with Dr. Lackey's permission. "We study about Moses, George Washington, and even Martin Luther King," he says, "but we don't know a thing about (our) grandpa and grandma."

Listen carefully to the timely challenge he issues at the end of the story.

A Facebook Post
By Dr. Hilliard Lackey

When I was five years old in 1947, November 11 became a day to remember....

My mother said in the kindest tones that Daddy won't be coming home. He was sleeping at the hospital. He was going to heaven and sleep there.

Confused. Confounded. Bewildered. Pick a word and then add a million more. This was all messed up. My Daddy was not coming home? Ever?

I was not exactly sure what die, dying and death meant. But it (they) had to be bad and somehow good because everybody was crying and yet making a fuss over us.

They were trying to explain that Daddy was gone to heaven and wouldn't be coming home again. Then, they would embrace and cuddle us while making promises like if you ever need anything.... Well, I wanted some cookies and candy like my Daddy used to buy for me on our trips to the store. Nobody could understand my descriptions (Of course, I ate my loot before returning home to keep from sharing with five brothers and sisters) and Mom didn't know either. The solution was to take me shopping at Garmon

Farms Sabino plantation store. Sure enough, there was that big jar of cookies, and down the counter a bit was the nectar of the gods - orange slices.

My Dad may not be coming home, but in his name came more cookies and orange slices. It would take me years to understand that my Daddy sleeping in that bed on wheels they called a casket would (really) not be coming home.

Years later I found out where, how and why Daddy died in Water Valley, Mississippi.

Black Lives Matter is one way of reminding some that black lives have seemingly not mattered. Some of us have vivid memories and testimonies...

My father, Hilliard Lackey, was born on October 25, 1916. Racism killed him in the Dr. George Brown Water Valley, Mississippi Hospital on Panola Street and Elm Street November 11, 1947. He was 31. Over the years I have vacillated between seeking revenge and vengeance or vindication. He had ulcers from the stress of being black in the Mississippi Delta. He left Marks to have his ulcers removed by Dr. George Brown in Water Valley, Mississippi after the family finished its cotton crops that year. The only doctor that would see him lived in Water Valley. However, the hospital had a racial policy of no blacks allowed in rooms inside the main building. They surgically removed my father's duodenal ulcers in the hallway but had to place him in the garage behind the hospital to recuperate. There was no heat, and a November cold snap rolled through causing temperatures to drop drastically. My father died out there in the cold garage shivering from exposure. Perhaps, that's the main reason why I recruit vals (valedictorians) and sals (salutatorians) who aspire to be doctors!

I spent Saturday afternoon September 20, 2014 visiting that old hospital and the new integrated Yalobusha County Hospital. Water Valley has come a long way. My father would be pleased. Happy birthday Dad! I am no longer angry just inspired!

History should be prologue to the logue we are currently living and writing. Each of us has a story. My father's plight was the norm rather than the exception. Almost all older people can weave a tale of woe about the way we were. Sadly, few young people will listen. Our schools teach pseudo history or HIS-Story while living black history is in our midst and fading away as our children strap on earphones and our elders slowly die off. We study about Moses, George Washington, and even Martin Luther King, but we don't know a thing about grandpa and grandma. Knowledge is power! If we only knew the road trod to get each of us to our respective present, we would perchance be inspired to try harder in our own endeavors!

Final Reflections
By Dottie Reed

I must acknowledge the outstanding unsung black woman, Cora Lackey Long, who raised an accomplished and respected educator in Hilliard Lackey. Stay tuned to learn more about her in an upcoming article. Dr. Lackey was taught the importance of forgiveness and had the courage to find out what happened to his dad and where. What can we learn from his story – from his life accomplishments?

Can we try harder in our own endeavors in 2020? Can we forgive the atrocities of the past and deal with the current rise in racism in this country, in Mississippi, in Yalobusha County, in Water Valley in a positive way? Could exploring your heritage provide insights that could perhaps make you a better person and the world a better place?

A bountiful New Year to All!

Hilliard L. Lackey, Ph.D.

Associate Professor / Coordinator of Doctoral Student Development

Hilliard L. Lackey serves as Visiting Professor of Urban Higher Education for the Jackson State University (JSU) Executive Ph.D. Program. He earned degrees (B.A., History and Political Science, MS.Ed. in Educational Administration and Supervision, and the Ed.S. in Educational Administration) from Jackson State University and the Ph.D. in Higher Education Administration from University of Mississippi. He has been an administrator/professor at JSU including; Director of Alumni Affairs, Director of Development and Alumni Affairs, Special Assistant to the Executive Vice President. He has also served as Associate Dean for Academic Affairs and Director of Enrollment Management at LeMoyne-Owen (Memphis, TN). Dr. Lackey is a 2008 inductee into the National Black College Alumni Hall of Fame, 2003 Thurgood Marshall Scholarship Fund HBCU Alumnus of the Year, 1997 NAFEO Distinguished Alumni Award honoree, and in 2004 the McCormick Freedom Museum of Chicago placed his quote on a monument. He was a Fulbright Fellow to North Africa (the Maghreb) and is an authority on the Historical Geography of the Mississippi Delta.

Reader Comments

A very touching, sad, but very informative article. I was two years old when Dr. Lackey's dad was murdered. Water Valley was just like the rest of the south, very prejudice and racist. Thank you for such a good job.
Fred Harris,
Seattle, WA

How grand would it have been to have Dr. Lackey speak at ETSU and to speak today at every college and university within the southern sector? This article was so throbbingly poignant.
Charlene Crouch,
Boston, MA

What an inspiring story by D. Hilliard Lackey! And an excellent choice for your first writing in 2020.
Dianne Prince,
Orlando, FL

Thanks for the article about Dr. Lackey. He is a "living legend" at Jackson State University.
Eddie Sanders,
Detroit, MI

This column really speaks to me – both because it acknowledges that many of us aren't feeling so great (read: are depressed) right now, and because it challenges and inspires us, through Dr. Lackey's moving story, to try harder in our own endeavors. I think that's the perfect message to usher us into 2020.
Adrienne Harris,
Atlanta, GA

37

When Race Took The Back Seat
Friends To The End

One of the gratifying byproducts of this column is the exploration it has fostered of our shared history in Yalobusha County – beyond the lives of the extraordinary black women already profiled. Last year two white women - "my white homegirls" as I call them - were moved to write about their own recollections of the black women who influenced their lives.

Camille Fly Dautrich and her friends wrote about the black women who worked as maids and babysitters for their families. Dorothy Wiman wrote about Cora Folson. These are among many familiar stories about relationships that developed when further socialization outside of white homes was prohibited or frowned upon. In most instances, the white children barely knew the last names of these caretakers, where they lived or if they had children of their own. Today, we still wonder about the authenticity of the love for these women.

An eloquent remembrance from Dr. Hilliard Lackey several years ago about his experiences within and across the racial divide portrays genuine admiration and friendship.

In April 2007 Dr. Lackey spoke to an International Women's Day program at the Clarksdale Exchange Club and chose to salute the 70-year friendship between his mother and her white friend in the Mississippi Delta, from 1940-2010.

Cora Lackey Long and Betty Tubb Garmon, both born in 1920, spent childbearing years on Garmon Farms and final years in Clarksdale. He called his presentation his personal salute to black and white women in the Mississippi Delta during and after segregation.

He acknowledged that his presentation included information that "may be sensitive material to members of both families, and for that I offer sincerest apologies. Yet, my soul won't rest until and unless I share this story which is meant to be complimentary and not negative."

Here is his presentation reprinted with his permission with minor edits for clarifications and consistency.

Pair of Great Dames Accompanied Him
By Hilliard Lackey

When the Clarksdale Exchange Club invited me to serve as guest speaker on Wednesday, I put up one stipulation: my two grand dames would accompany me. One is my mother, Cora Lackey Long and the other is the matriarch of Sabino Farms, Betty Garmon.

They are about the same age. Both married men on the Garmon Plantation in Quitman County, also known as Sabino Farms. Both have sons named for their fathers. Both are now widowed. My mom is black. Betty Garmon is white. That alone is recipe for a great story, but it gets much more interesting; they love each other. They are friends across the chasm that society imposed between them and have found ways and means of negotiating that chasm through methods akin to extrasensory perception.

These women of the Delta were born around 1920 during an era when black was black and white was white. There was no in between. Their worlds were distinctively different. One was the lot of the plantation owner and the other was the plight of the tenant farmer. When and if the twain met, the Southern way of life was invoked.

My mom finished the sixth grade and married at age 15 in 1935. That was the norm for little black girls in that day. The year you started wearing a bra was the year you were ready for marriage. Going on to high school was not a notion, let alone an option for black girls on Delta plantations. High schools for colored children were in towns like Clarksdale, Marks, and Lambert. There would not be school buses for non-white children until the 1950s. Almost no one of color had an automobile. Everybody walked or rode a mule to work, church, school or to visit neighbors. Few or no doctor visits were made as home remedies and midwives were widely used. Rural life had its culture, its way of doing things and its limitations.

Mrs. Betty, as we called her to distinguish the younger Mrs. Garmon from the elder Mrs. Garmon, married the plantation heir around 1940 and in 1942, gave birth to my friend and soul brother, Judge Ollie Laurence Garmon, III. The Garmons epitomized the paradoxes of segregation. First and foremost, they were white. There were white societal standards of conduct they were bound to respect and observe, at least publicly. This was not their druthers. The young Mrs. Garmon was as gracious, as nice and as kind as any Christian ought to be. Her husband, the late State Senator O. L. Garmon, Jr., was fair, considerate and generous to a fault. Their three children were cut from the same cloth.

Their public stance was separation of the races especially when around peers and business associates. Many an afternoon, early evening or late night, little colored boys slipped through the side door of the big house and shared desserts, toys and comic books with the Garmon boys. The sound of a car coming into the driveway occupied by a visiting peer was a signal to scat and scatter. That's just the way things were.

My dad died when I was five years old. My mom remarried, and my stepfather was an avid reader who loved comic books and sports pages in newspapers. We were too poor to even pay attention, so paying for a newspaper was way beyond our imagination. The Garmons received two or three newspapers daily: *The Memphis Press Scimitar*, *The Commercial Appeal* and, I believe, *The Clarksdale Press Register*. The younger Mrs. Garmon made sure that my stepdad brought us the second-hand newspapers every day or they were stacked and saved for later pick up. We had stacks of comic books, *Readers Digest*, *National Geographic*, everything. We were blessed with a bountiful supply of reading materials. We would come to read our way from abject poverty to relative prosperity.

Senator Garmon had part ownership of a car dealership in Shelby. In a moment of benevolence, he said to this writer, "Whenever you need to get over to Lambert or Marks for a school event, just come by and get one of our cars." My proms were the bomb!" I had a new car to drive the nine miles from Sabino to Lambert for major school events. God knows I was a happy fellow on those occasions. I am eternally grateful.

The reality of segregation became quite evident when it was time to go to college. My friend, and soul brother, was going off to study agriculture (against his will) at Mississippi State University. He and I lamented that we both would like to go to the University of Mississippi and become lawyers. He was a victim of plantation expectations and I, the victim of racial discrimination since UM was not yet integrated. Instead, he went to MSU and I went to Jackson State University. Ironically, we both got our wishes. He was able to transfer to UM and eventually got his law degree while I finally found my way to UM and got my doctorate.

Our mothers were still in touch, asking each other about the whereabouts and well-being of children. Senator Garmon passed away, and soon the younger Garmon clan relocated to Clarksdale. Eventually the Lackey-Long family also made its way to Clarksdale. Still the Southern-Way-of-Life chasm between the families loomed as large as ever. Yet, through the miracles of telephones and the mythical magic of bonding, there remained that sense of friendship and family.

So, at noon tomorrow, April 11 at the Clarksdale Exchange Club, at long last on this side of Jordan, these two matriarchs of families on different sides of the plantation chasm, will sit at the same table as friends, in public, before God and witnesses. Somewhere their deceased husbands, their scattered progeny, and an understanding public will be smiling.

Cora Lackey Long

Born May 22, 1920 and raised in rural Quitman County between Marks and Clarksdale, Cora Lackey Long was the eldest of ten children of Matilda Mumford Anderson and Jerry Frank Anderson. At 15 she married 18-year-old Hilliard Lackey and had six children between 1936 to 1946. Widowed at age 27 in 1947, she and her children remained in Mississippi as sharecroppers. She remarried to Samuel Allen Long, Sr. in 1949 and had five children. The 11 siblings were raised with Christian values. She was widowed again in 1998.

Cora Lackey Long only reached the sixth grade in elementary school but decided

Cora Lackey Long

early on to support the educational pursuits of each child. She instilled in her children to be all they could be while having a personal relationship with the Lord. Her progeny numbers 11 children, 29 grandchildren, 42 great grandchildren, and 33 great-great grandchildren.

She knew all 115 birthdays, full names, and personal progress. Cora called each one to say Happy Birthday, congratulations for graduations, marriages, new jobs, and other special occasions. She kept a mental log of most items and a master list of telephone numbers. As the Family Tree Information Center, she visited or called to give uplifting encouragement to any of her lineage having personal challenges.

Cora drove her own car visiting the sick and shut-in until turning age 88. Never one wanting to worry others, she hid her own illness as long as she could. Finally, she wore down physically and with grace and dignity smiled and ascended peacefully to glory. A virtuous woman dwelt amongst us for more than 88 years. To God be the glory!

Dr. Hilliard Lackey is a native of Quitman County, a college administrator and professor at Jackson State University. His extraordinary credentials were listed in this column earlier this month. I am so appreciative of his contributions and his legacy. Thanks to Dr. Lackey for sharing his stories and his life as he continues to promote the educational endeavors of the students at JSU and beyond. Eddie Sanders, Davidson High Class of 1968 and JSU graduate, notes that Dr. Lackey is a legend at Jackson State. I can see why.

The story of his mother and Betty Garmon connects with stories previously shared in this column. The University of Mississippi continues to be a factor – both positive and negative. Isn't it ironic that we now are working in collaboration with the University to document the history of black families in Yalobusha County? With that support we strive to continue to explore, discover and preserve these untold stories. We want to inspire and engage the current and upcoming generations to understand where they came from in order to clearly see where they are going.

I hope that young parents, millennials and youth will be moved by something they read in these stories to ask about their ancestors, to explore family history and move beyond relying on social media as their main source of information. I hope, too, that they will be motivated to select a cause, a community need or a service to honor the blood, sweat and tears shed by black people that allow us to enjoy the lives we are living today.

I have read the transcripts from the oral interviews conducted by the UM graduate students, and I have been unable to garner words to describe my reaction to the openness and honesty versus the pain, hardships and discrimination; the strength, endurance, pride and love of family; the ultimate success in achieving goals, becoming positive role models and just plain good people. How do you at five-years old miss three years of schooling because there were no buses or other transportation, and yet end up with a master's degree? How do you recover from losing your home, sharecropping two or three years to buy it back and then still be willing to serve your country? How do you sit in a classroom at the flagship university where the professor refuses to acknowledge your raised hand and go on to teach public school for 28 years? I don't know how they did it.

Can we forgive the murders, the rapes and the discrimination? Can we forgive, as Dr. Lackey did, his father's preventable death in Water Valley? As the saying goes, "We have come a long way baby, but we still have miles to go before we sleep." I wish I could share each of their stories in full detail. They are being archived so that one day others can read them and learn about Yalobusha County's exceptional black residents. They fill me with pride.

Reader Comments

I am blessed again by your publication. The "Great Dames" story is moving and parallels so many untold experiences. Keep up the relevant and important work of documenting our history.
Dianne Prince,
Orlando, FL

Just finished reading article 37! I enjoyed it almost as much as 36. What you are doing is transformative.
Jim Simmons,
Stone Mountain, GA

An enjoyable read, growing up I read a second-hand newspaper, The Commercial Appeal. Mrs. Mable Williams, a white woman, saved them for us.
Dorothy Middleton,
Jackson, MS

Great article. Very sad but explains the reality of the time.
Cheryl Wheeler,
Ellenwood, GA

Dr. Louise Baker Brown
Clothed With Strength and Dignity

Just like my experience reading about Emma Gooch, my friend and classmate, I thought I knew Louise Baker Brown. I was wrong, and now I want to tell you what I have learned about yet another outstanding black woman of Yalobusha County. I will start by noting what I knew or thought I knew: that she was from Coffeeville and that she was smart, according to my late sister, Faye, who taught her in high school.

I remember one day running into my Hi-Y and Tri-Hi-Y friend, Thomas Brown from Oakland, who was also a student at the University of Mississippi. Hi-Y and Tri-Hi-Y was the negro branch of the YMCA school program. It was sponsored by schools and allowed us to attend district and state events and develop oratorical and leadership skills. The friendships, associations, competitions and skills we developed helped many black students in Mississippi excel in college and in our careers. For many of us this was the only socialization with multiple peers outside of our hometown communities.

Thomas told me he had finished Northwest Junior College in Senatobia and was married to Louise. He and I loved, worked with and hung out around the little one room store run by our UM black student advisor, the late Reverend Wayne Johnson, called the Co-op. I don't know if Thomas was preaching then or thinking about it. Next thing I knew he had gotten his undergraduate degree and headed to Atlanta to seminary.

Fast forward to the early eighties and somehow Thomas and I reconnected by phone, discovering we were both in Georgia and living in the same county. We ended up in the same area, and our sons attended the same high school. That is when I got to know Louise a little better. By then she was a highly respected teacher with a doctorate in education, and she and Thomas were very involved in the parents' association – all this in addition to rearing a highly recruited footballer headed to the University of Georgia and then to the NFL. Thomas, an established preacher in the Christian Methodist Episcopal church and the dean of Phillips School of Theology at the Interdenominational Theological Center, asked me to help with a conference. It was there that I observed Louise in her role as the wife of a dean and a pastor.

Life of Louise Baker Brown

And now my enlightenment, as I call it, on the life of Louise Baker Brown. Walls and Lura Baker gave birth to Louise on October 3, 1952 in Coffeeville, the fourth of their seven children.

They lived about four miles from downtown on 80 acres of land inherited from the Baker grandfather. Of the seven siblings, five are still living, and her brother, Bobby, resides at the original homestead. The family lived out of their garden and raised livestock. Both parents could read and write but had little formal education beyond the third or fourth grade. Mrs. Baker is known as one of the best cooks who ever worked at the Yalobusha County Hospital. She now resides there in the nursing facility.

Though the Bakers did not grow cotton, they earned money picking for other folks. "I could pick 200 pounds," Louise said. "I am very competitive when I do something, I want to be the best. Coupled with the fact that I was getting paid." Mr. Baker worked as a laborer for 20-plus years in soil conservation around Enid Dam. Prior to that he worked for a few weeks at plant in Grenada and discovered he could not tolerate being in an enclosed space. Then he tried a local chicken plant for a brief stint, but that did not last long. And from that day forward he never ate another piece of chicken.

As Louise and I talked, we soon realized the similarities in our life stories. We both graduated in the last class from the all black high schools in 1970. She graduated from Central High School as valedictorian of her class. Just as I did after graduation, we both set out to find jobs in the big city. Louise went to Chicago and worked to earn the money that she needed for tuition at Northwest Junior College. I went to Detroit with no plan of returning, had zero luck job hunting, came back and went to college with nothing.

Louise had earned $800 that summer but needed $812 for tuition at Northwest. With tears in her eyes now, she recalls telling her dad the morning she was leaving for college that she needed $12. "It never occurred to me that I should ask for more," she laughs. "I thought all I needed was the 12 dollars." She chokes up again at her dad's response. He told her that he didn't have the money, but perhaps seeing the disappointment on her face – even if he didn't understand the importance of college – he said he would borrow the money. Louise said from that day until the day he died, she never asked her father for another dime, and she made sure that he never wanted for anything.

Many of us avoided asking our parents for money while in college because we knew they simply did not have it. Nor did they really understand the costs of college. This poverty and deprivation forced us into an independence, a drive and the determination to be self-sufficient and successful. Years later, Louise would jokingly say to her dad many times that the 12-dollar investment in her was the best investment he ever made.

At Northwest Louise worked at the snack bar and lived on campus. "I learned to trust in God at an early age and was determined to get an education and never expected a handout" she said. She credits her Central teachers, especially Monroe Walton, for inspiring her love of science and education. Even though the books were outdated, and teachers had to use their personal funds to supplement supplies, time and time again those teachers proudly told her and her classmates that they were going to be somebody. But in her college classrooms Louise realized she and her Central schoolmates had received an education that was inferior to her fellow students. Her black roommate from Patton Lane High in Batesville was more advanced and often helped her understand concepts that she had never been taught.

All the schools in Yalobusha County had integrated in some fashion by the fall of 1970, and while Louise does not recall any of the strife associated with school integration, she believes that the transition was detrimental to her three younger siblings and many other black students who, for whatever reasons, dropped out of the new school by 10th or 11th grade. I cannot help but believe that administrators showed a distinct lack of care and concern for the marginal students then as well as today.

Louise graduated from Northwest Junior College with an Associate Degree. In July 1972, she married Thomas Louis Brown.

They had met in high school at a Social Elite event. This was a club established by black women to mentor young girls. Thomas had driven his mom to the meeting in Charleston and participated in the session. When he said he wanted to be a doctor, Louise was intrigued. But they didn't see each other again until their paths crossed at Northwest.

When Thomas asked her to marry him, he also told her that he had been called to ministry. "I was scared because I had no idea how to be a preacher's wife," Louise admitted. "I was raised in the Baptist church and our attendance was infrequent. I knew this was a serious commitment – he would have people's lives in his hands. I wanted to know if he was sure. He told me that he did not have any expectations of me and assured me that he would support my educational goals. So, I took a chance, and he kept his word."

Both enrolled at the University of Mississippi where Louise completed her junior year and Thomas graduated. They moved to Atlanta, and Thomas attended Phillips School of Theology at the International Theological Center. Louise enrolled at Spelman College, graduating in 1974 with a Bachelor of Arts in Sociology. She worked for the Atlanta Police Department for a year as a police officer. In 1978, Louise completed her Master of Education from Columbus State University, Columbus, Georgia. Her daughter, Nicole, was born in 1979 (a son, Thomas, would come seven years later), and even as a new mother, she supported her husband in his pastoral assignments. Louise taught high school social studies in Talbot County for four years and was named Talbot County Teacher of the Year in 1980. The couple returned to Atlanta in 1982, and Louise resumed her teaching career with the Dekalb County School System.

In 1990 Louise was named DeKalb County Teacher of the Year. She earned her Specialist of Education in 1994 from the

Dr. Louise Baker Brown

University of West Georgia, in Carrollton. In 1998, she became an Instructor Coordinator with DeKalb County Schools working on a team supporting middle and high school educators. She completed her Educational Leadership Certification in 2000 from the University of West Georgia and earned a Doctor of Education degree from Nova Southeastern University in Fort Lauderdale, Florida in November 2006. Louise retired in 2007 after 30 years as an educator.

Louise continues to be active in the work and mission of the CME Church. She has joined Thomas in conducting marriage retreat workshops in several Episcopal Districts. As a highly respected couple, they have set a strong example for many in and outside of their denomination. For 12 years – from 2006 to 2018 - she and Thomas were based in Jackson, assigned to the Fourth Episcopal District covering Louisiana and Mississippi. She has received awards and numerous accolades for her leadership and work in the church and greater communities, specifically in Christian education.

In 2019 the couple moved back to Atlanta.

Louise now serves alongside Thomas, the bishop in the Sixth Episcopal District, which covers the state of Georgia. Many of the pastors they supervise were students under Thomas when he served as dean of the Phillips seminary, Louise often acting as mom, friend, mentor and advisor to any who needed the support while away from home. Their work in the CME Church has sent them to Mexico, Jamaica, Brazil, Nigeria, Kenya, South Africa and London. Currently, she leads the Ministers' Spouses, implementing training, teaching and support. And she is also a member of the Power of Good News CME Church in Lithonia.

Just like my family Louise, her mother and her siblings have held on to their portion of the 80-acre Baker Farm. When I asked her about experiencing discrimination in Coffeeville, she said she believed that "land ownership protected us in a way. White men often came by trying to buy our property or wanting to hunt and my dad always stood his ground. We children were sheltered from a lot."

Of life challenges, Louise says that motherhood was much harder than teaching – which was easy by comparison. She did not want her children to be deprived. It always surprised her to hear some folks say they did not realize they were poor until they got to college. "I am not sure what took them so long," Louise said. "We were never hungry, but I saw early on how much we did without." Education became and remained a priority. When her son, Thomas, played football at UGA, she was concerned about the white environment but stressed to him that above all, he would get his degree. She knew everyone on the academic support team for the athletes and stayed on top of her son's progress. Thomas graduated, went on to the NFL and is now coaching on the collegiate level.

In addition to being the proud mother of Charisa Nicole Jefferson and Thomas, Jr., Louise loves her role of grandmother to six grandchildren: Ariel Moriah, Kingston Albert and Alana Joel Jefferson, and Orlando Thomas, Tyson Louis and Judah Elizah Brown.

All this is in keeping with her commitment to helping young folks when she was teaching. Louise told her students to expect to succeed. "Don't take low achievement as something we aspire to here" was her mantra. She had her students sign contracts to aim for an A or B in her classes. Anything less than a C in her view meant that the student was not going to even try to do well in the class. Her doctoral dissertation focused on preparing students for standardized testing because she believed that most black students needed assistance. She developed a program to provide noontime and after school tutoring to help them.

Louise has embraced the church with the same commitment she gave to education. She is clear-eyed about the present challenges. "It is the effort required to be relevant to our time without looking like the world. I didn't grow up in the church, but it was always important to me. Church is not a real concern or priority like it used to be. We see so many people who do not think church is relevant. Our culture is now saying that church is not important. As blacks we cannot forget where we came from. We must assume some responsibility for each other. We have gotten away from that – if we are okay - we don't think about others. Sunday is just like any other day, perpetuated by tv talk show hosts and announcers who talk about everything except what they do on Sunday. There are so many who have never been in a church and feel there is no need. Those of us who are in ministry must keep presenting the more excellent way."

Proverbs 31:25- She is clothed with strength and dignity as she laughs without fear of the future.

Reader Comments

The residents and citizens of your hometown should be proud of your talent and research. When will someone write your story?
Lee Williams,
Moca, Puerto Rico

Another inspirational and heartfelt story of life in very tough times. All your articles I realize are about folks who lived in very difficult situations with discrimination a major road block to many opportunities and yet they have all faced the facts, raised large and productive children, faced the hardships and all went onto fantastic educations and contributions to their families, the community and their religious beliefs. God bless them all!
Jim Brzoska,
Deltona FL

I appreciate the excellent article about Dr. Louise Baker Brown, the beloved wife of Presiding Bishop Thomas L. Brown, Sr. of the CME Sixth Episcopal District which provided an awesome profile of the extraordinary life and faith journey of Dr. Brown.
Theresa Duhart,
Tacoma WA

Congratulations on your journalistic work in The North Mississippi Herald. Wish I was going to be in Oxford, Feb. 19th, to hear your talk on the oral history project you inspired. Am proud for you and to know you.
Gwynne Brunt,
Atlanta, GA

Thanks much for another great article detailing the Browns and their connection to Yalobusha County and Ole Miss. I was about 8 when James Meredith integrated Ole Miss and probably 16 when Coolidge arrived. Well do I remember those days as well as the efforts to integrate the white schools in Meridian. As you may know, my brother Sam, who played at SIU with Tommy Thompson, and Robert Bell, who along with Frank Dowsing integrated MSU football, were among first to play football at Meridian High School. I was also the first black kid to play sports, i.e., Football, basketball and track, at Kate Griffin Jr High School in 1968. Lord knows I did not want to go. I protested and protested, but the good Lord, and mother and father had a plan I could not see. If course for me it was on to MHS, Ole Miss, the Cleveland Browns, and subsequently a 36-year career in local, state and federal law enforcement.
James Reed,
Greenville, SC

We have a really fantastic newspaper in Water Valley, North Mississippi Herald, I encourage you to subscribe. Tremendous paper. Dottie Chapman Reed's bi-monthly column is one of my favorites. She profiles impactful black women in Yalobusha County.
Lauren Nail Swindol,
Water Valley, MS

39

Mildred Faye Polk
Answering The Call - Chosen

In Matthew 22 verse 14 Jesus ends the parable of the wedding feast by saying, "For many are called, but few are chosen."

The Bible uses the word calling many times in different contexts. This verse often refers to the call to ministry or discipleship. The interpretations are so many that I asked my pastor, Dr. Vance P. Ross of Central United Methodist Church, for his thoughts. "In this verse," he says, "following a troubling parable, Matthew finds Jesus making this perplexing statement. I read it this way: many are called generally. Few dare to embrace it. Everyone gets God's call. Certain ones answered God's call. Fannie Lou Hamer, Martin King, Ed Nixon, Rosa Parks, Fred Shuttlesworth, Diane Nash answered— as did many others. Most did not."

It is rare, I feel, when ministers will openly and clearly explain their calling. The woman we feature today has done just that and again left me impressed by the gifts and talents coming out of Yalobusha county. My loyal readers will recognize the last name Polk as that of not one but two prominent, highly respected families of Yalobusha. While working on a past article, Mildred mentioned her call to ministry and at my request, she is sharing her story. Enjoy!

The Ultimate Call
By Mildred Faye Polk

We have all heard our name called in one type of setting or another. We are called to dinner. We are called because someone wants to speak to us on the phone. We've been called because someone wants to get our attention, etc. We have many different calls that we can get in our lifetime. However, some of us have had to answer 'The Ultimate Call' on our lives. That call is from a higher power for us to do the impossible; and that is, "to go into all the world and preach the gospel to every creature." (Mark 16:15) That's the unexpected call that came to me, a nobody, from God Himself to take up the blood-stained banner for my Lord.

Who am I? My name is Mildred (Faye, my family's way of calling me) Polk. I was born to James and Gencie Polk in Oakland, Mississippi, the 15th of 17 children. I lived in Oakland until I graduated from Walker High School in 1968. I attended Davidson High in Water Valley for 10 years when the powers that be sent us to Walker High because we lived between Oakland and Water Valley. I suppose they called it re-districting. I worked in the area for approximately ten months after graduation and then headed for Milwaukee, Wisconsin. I did not want to go but, due to family circumstances, I did not have much of a choice in the matter. I went to live with my oldest sister in Milwaukee.

Although I did not want to leave home, I believe it was God's will that I take a leave from where I was raised. You see, I did not know another world existed different from the one where I grew up. It was only after I went to Milwaukee that my world view expanded, and I now thank the good Lord for that exposure. Hindsight is 20/20, they say.

When God speaks to you, you must listen. God began to speak more precisely to me when I was in my early to mid-thirties in Milwaukee. As my pastor would read his text to preach the word, I would find myself preaching a completely different sermon in my mind while in my seat. (Too bad no one heard them because they were good sermons!) My Pastor, though, openly told us that "God doesn't call women to the preaching ministry." It really wasn't a problem for me because I never wanted to be a preacher, so I thought nothing of it as it related to me becoming one. On the other hand, I never had a problem with female preachers either. I thought that if God can make a donkey talk, then He can do anything else He so chooses to do.

It was a Sunday morning, during worship service at Providence Baptist Church, that God spoke to me, not about preaching, but letting me know that He wanted me to do more than I had been doing as His servant. My pastor announced that any church that had been supporting American Baptist College in Nashville, Tennessee with at least $5,000 a year could send a person, tuition free, to get a degree in Bible Theology. We had been doing that for many years by that time. His announcement troubled me so that I did not get much sleep until I spoke to the pastor about it. I expressed my desire to get the degree and told him if a younger person wanted to go, I would relinquish my interest. However, I thought I would be pretty sure to get the opportunity because not many 'Christians' want to go deeper in the study of God's word beyond their local Bible Study and Sunday School classes. Not me. Once I started feeding, I could never get my fill of the Word. I am always hungry for more. It all worked out.

Let's fast forward to the time after my graduation from American Baptist College, when God started to bug me again. He was speaking to me about preaching His word. However, I was not sharing this with anyone. Most of my fellow classmates at ABC assumed that I was already a minister since I was enrolled in a seminary. But after one of my instructors asked me point blank if I was a preacher, and I answered "No," God seemed to press me even more, anywhere, everywhere, any time of day and night until I just couldn't handle it anymore. I remained in Nashville after graduation, and one night following a church meeting, I cornered one of the female ministers and blurted out, "How did you know that the Lord had called you to preach?" She just laughed at me and said, "you'll know." But I still didn't know. A little while after that I probably did what I should have done in the beginning. I prayed to the Lord. I basically said, "God if this is what you want me to do, then you have to show me something so that I can know for sure."

It was in December of that same year, 2006, a few months after I uttered that prayer, that God sent me the answer by way of a total stranger, suggesting that God truly does work in mysterious ways. The first week of December I attended a three-day class at the Sunday School Publishing Board Conference in Nashville. After the last class, as the instructor and students were packing up and saying our goodbyes, the unthinkable happened. Our instructor was a lady from Nebraska whom I had never met before I joined the class. Usually a quiet and reserved person in classroom settings, I don't remember doing a lot of talking, but I did participate. When she called me up to her desk by name, I wondered why. I playfully said something like, "Yes ma'am. What may I do for you?"

Mildred Polk wears an outfit made by an Ugandan seamstress.

I was expecting the usual, "Are you a preacher?" as so many others had wondered. Before this moment, my answer was always, "No – and don't talk to me about becoming one."

But the instructor asked me something different.

"Have you accepted your call to preach?"

Shocked and surprised, I laughed and told her, "No! I'm running."

Her reply is etched in my memory forever. "You may as well do it because it is all over you."

God had sent the answer to my prayer, and I stopped running and totally committed to His plan for my life: to preach the gospel!

When you accept God's will for you, it feels like the weight of the world has been lifted from your shoulders. You become at peace with that thing you did not want. If He calls you to it, then, He will equip you to do it. I had to trust that God knew better than I what I could do and, to whom He wanted to endow His gifts. Thus, I accepted His call and haven't looked back. And I'm so happy and elated that I did.

God is so, so amazing! After I accepted my call, I could see and do things that were not even on my bucket list because of Him. A few months after accepting my call, God allowed me to join pastors with the National Baptist Convention USA for an eight-week mission trip to the U.S Virgin Islands. This was in a teaching capacity, not preaching, but it was an opportunity of a lifetime granted to me, His humble servant.

I moved back to Mississippi –Southaven – in 2011 after having spent five years in Nashville. The very next year I was afforded a trip to the Holy Land of Israel with my church, New Hope Baptist. For that I wish to thank my family, friends and church members. And that's not all. A few years later I had the chance to fulfill one of my own bucket-list items, which was a true blessing from God and a dream come true.

It was in the year of our Lord 2016, and by

divine intervention, that I met Dr. Dwight and Solome Quinn, missionaries to Uganda in East Africa, who were recruiting men to go and encourage the Ugandan pastors. We found this out after we got there that they had been looking for men to work with the Africans, who were facing many challenges in spreading the gospel. The trip ended up being four females plus the Quinns who made the trip. Thank God that I was one of them. Never in my wildest dream would I ever think I would be preaching and teaching on the soil of any African country. I have been blessed to have two opportunities to minister in Uganda, returning in 2018. God works all things out for the good of those who love and trust Him with their whole heart, soul and mind.

"In everything give thanks, for this is the will of God in Christ Jesus concerning you." (1 Thess. 5:18). This scripture my mother taught me when I was nine or ten years old and it's still one of my favorites. Thank you, mom. I thank God for all the many, wonderful blessings He has allowed me to see, to do and have. Blessings!

Mildred currently serves as one of the associate ministers at New Hope Baptist Church in Southaven with a congregation of approximately 400. She is responsible for outreach, which includes serving communion, visiting nursing homes and working with missionaries. Her goal moving forward is to be a full-time missionary locally, in the field or overseas. She would like to be a consummate missionary. We wish you God speed!

Reflecting on Mildred's life, I am reminded of my Aunt Mary Hester Pritchard's signature song that went like this:

Time oh time, Time is winding up.
Destruction in the land, God's gon move his hand.
Time oh time, Time is winding up.

Reader Comments

What a neat article and what a blessed lady this is. Love that she finally accepted her calling.
Margaret Walters,
Tucker, GA

Thank you so much for the article on Mildred Faye Polk. It is an interesting account of one of God's chosen. I've wondered often about women preachers. This story of Ms. Polk makes me think that God has women who can turn their world upside down when they surrender to that call from HIM. Would love to meet Ms. Polk. I'm sure she and I know a lot of the same people.
Harry Neal,
Winona, MS

Can any good come out of Yalobusha County? Yes! Faye is a living witness—Telling a dying world about Jesus, who can make a donkey talk...Feel a shout coming! What a wonderful God we serve! I was/is inspired. This write-up is awesome!
Dorothy Middleton,
Jackson, MS

40

Annie K. Montgomery
By The Work of Her Hands

Thanks to the work of the Women's Missionary Council and Leadership of the Christian Methodist Episcopal Church we can celebrate the legacy of a woman whose parents were among Yalobusha County's first free-born generation in the post-Civil War era. Annie Kelly Montgomery was born on February 20, 1890 to George and Mattie Kelly in Water Valley. She was a life-long member of Miles Memorial CME Church on Simmons Street, near the courthouse. And as I have so proudly said about many others, she was an outstanding black woman of Yalobusha.

Annie Kelly was educated in the black public schools in Water Valley, completing high school and then a teacher training course at Mississippi Industrial College, located at that time in Holly Springs. Next, she earned a bachelor of arts degree in home economics from the college in May of 1930, after being admitted in 1926. Aside from teaching eight years in Water Valley public schools, substitute teaching throughout the county, especially in Oakland, the smallest and most disadvantaged of the three towns in the county, she taught at Mississippi Industrial for 14 years and served as a trustee at the college.

All this was in addition to working as the Jeanes Supervisor in Yalobusha County for 20 years. These supervisors worked for the Jeanes Foundation, which had established a fund to support education programs for black children in southern rural communities. It was named for Anna T. Jeanes, a white philanthropist and a Quaker from Pennsylvania, who worked with Booker T. Washington. From her office on Main Street in Water Valley Mrs. Montgomery, then known as Miss Kelly, oversaw the growth and development of the black schools and personnel in the county.

According to 90-year-old Ruby Turner, now living in Illinois, who grew up in Water Valley, most of the black teachers during this time could teach with a high school diploma but were required to pursue continuing education and a college diploma. Thus, most of them attended college in the summers or as often as they were able to keep their jobs and still advance their careers. It could take years to obtain that first degree, and their options were limited to black colleges. Many of them were far away, which required travel and possibly relocation and tuition costs. Mrs. Montgomery took her advanced studies at Tennessee State College in Nashville, Hampton University in Virginia, and Tuskegee College in Alabama.

To encourage black high school girls to aim for college, she helped organize and served as president of the Social Elite Club, a group of black women in Yalobusha County who mentored and provided scholarships.

Annie Montgomery's tombstone at Oak Ridge Cemetery in Water Valley shows only her year of birth, 1890, and year of death, 1974, the year I graduated from college.

I cannot remember where I was when her funeral and burial were held on April 29, 1974. I wish I had attended the service.

I knew Mrs. Annie Kelly Montgomery because she was the superintendent of the Sunday School at Miles Memorial CME, where my family were members. And she was another one of those like Mrs. Lucy Kelly that I must always address as Mrs. out of respect. I was afraid of her! Every Sunday all the youngest children had to kiss her on her cheek. I hated that and would ask my mom and siblings why I had to do it. Of course, she was a kind lady, but I did not come to appreciate it until I picked up a book in the mid 2000s about the history of the CME church written by Retired Bishop Othal Lakey.

He noted her involvement and leadership in the CME church, and I was astounded. At the recent annual meeting of the Women's Missionary Council, Bishop Lakey said, "She was the secretary to the episcopacy and the general board of the CME church, which was a very important role." I only knew she substitute taught when I was in elementary school, and I hated when she subbed in my classes. She was a strict disciplinarian, and while her fellow missionaries considered her a master teacher, I felt intimidated because she had such high expectations of me.

Annie was married to the late Rev. D. M. Montgomery, a CME church pastor, who died before she did. He was known as Doc or Dock and had at least four children with his first wife, Beulah. He was listed as a college teacher in Holly Springs in the 1930 US Census.

Beginning in 1953, Annie lived with Pearline Butler Cody for 21 years. Annie considered her as a daughter. Pearline was a beloved and respected first-grade teacher and my first Sunday School teacher. We studied from a book called the Catechism. It sounds like it might have been a publication based on Catholicism. All I know is I remember the word. I loved Sunday school and still do! My mom usually gave me a nickel to put in the offering, I was so proud to be able to contribute and of course thought that was a lot of money. As time passed, Mrs. Montgomery and I became sort of friends. But I was not aware of her prominence and significant contributions to Water Valley, Yalobusha County and the entire state of Mississippi.

Annie Kelly Montgomery is best known for having developed and designed what she called the Missionary Hand. Each finger has its own designated action label: Give, Work, Talk, Study and Pray. And each has a specific biblical reference. The hand's purpose was to remind the missionary women of the organization's focus. The Hand was presented to missionary council members and is still used today.

Annie Montgomery began her years of service to the CME church in 1922, when she was 32. Her positions included local missionary president, local church trustee, and district missionary president. Mrs. Montgomery was a member of the committee that wrote the first Council Handbook, serving with Mrs. L. A. Story and Mrs. Rossie Thompson Hollis. In 1923 Mrs. Montgomery completed an unexpired term of the Council's first treasurer, and in 1926, she was elected as the second treasurer in Council history. She was elected Mississippi State president in 1928 and organized women's missionary societies throughout the state. Other positions she held included, statistician, registrar, finance committee member and secretary of town and country. Her involvement, dedication and work at the state, district and national level strengthened connections among CME member churches.

Reflecting on her Council work in 1971, Mrs. Montgomery looked to the future, writing, "It is our prayer that our mantle of service will fall on younger and more succinct shoulders, who will carry on in whatever is the design of the congregation."

Annie K. Montgomery

The second line on the front of her tombstone reads:

Co-organizer Women's Missionary Society of CME Church - Organizer of Missionary Work in CME Churches in Mississippi.

The engraving on the back of her tombstone reads:

Donated by the Four Mississippi Conferences of the Fourth Episcopal District, Bishop Joseph A. Johnson, Jr., Presiding Bishop.

What a suitable epitaph!

Remember the saying that goes something like this? "It matters not the years that you live but what you accomplish between the dash." Mrs. Annie Kelly Montgomery accomplished a lot and influenced many lives between 1890 and 1974 – 84 years. Her legacy shall live on! She was 62 years old when I was born, probably 65 or so when I remembered her demanding those cheek kisses from me and my Sunday school mates, and then going on to teach us life lessons and about Jesus. She was much older when she mentored Dr. Louise Brown, Beth Brown Whiting and the other girls in the Social Elite Club. Maybe that was the magic that sustained these faithful outstanding women. They never stopped giving, they never stopped serving and never stopped caring. They were achievers who demonstrated the strength and fortitude to rise above the limitations and confines of Yalobusha County. They made a way. A friend up north often prods me to think about the contributions these outstanding black women of Yalobusha could have made had they been allowed to participate as full citizens of society, of Water Valley, of Yalobusha County, of Mississippi and of the United States in the prime of their lives. Can you imagine the difference their skills, talents and contributions could have made for a greater society if they were not plagued with racism and discrimination?

Now as a grandmother of four grandsons, a mother of three sons, one currently on active military duty overseas – another a veteran - a widow, retired, living in a red state and very concerned about our country and the future. I am afraid we might have to start marching again or that our numbers may be too low and too late to make a difference. I understand that "woke" is a word young folks use meaning informed, aware and cool, I think. Consider the other meaning of the word, and if I am asleep, please don't wake me up until all this chaos is over. Another friend who was born at McClendon – a black hospital in Atlanta – earned a bachelors in history from Morris Brown - a black college - earned a master's degree in public administration from the University of Denver, Colorado and was raised in the black African Methodist Church as a PK (preacher's kid) says, "World history is repeating itself, as we saw with the Roman Empire, which deteriorated from within; now America has become more amoral as a country and is headed down the same path."

We have just said goodbye to another Black History Month and a February like we have never seen before, God help us all! I believe Mrs. Annie Kelly Montgomery would be disappointed in where we are today, but she would want us to keep the faith. Her obituary states that her greatest joy came from her untiring work in the church. Asked how she wanted to be remembered, she said, "When God calls me home, rather than long speeches about me, let my work speak for the deeds I have done." I wish our hometown could have given her accolades while she was alive. While she had no children of her own, many, many children and families in this county, state and country were influenced and enriched by the unforgettable Annie Kelly Montgomery. In this month where we are celebrating the history of women nationally and internationally, how proud I am of the black women of Yalobusha County.

Reader Comments

Wow. She was a legend.
Bernice Bland,
Decatur, GA

Thank you for your persistency and excellent research. You are making an indelible contribution to the legacy of women of color in Yalobusha County and beyond.
Thomas Brown,
Stone Mountain, GA

I truly enjoy reading about black women of Yalobusha County. Lives of so many have been influenced by and rightly formed by these precious ladies like Mrs. Annie K. Montgomery. I know of one here in Winona, a black lady who has a heart for children in her neighborhood. She does a lot for the children's needs, clothing, food, etc. and tries to help steer them in Godly ways. It's ladies like her and Mrs. Montgomery who I know will hear and have heard from Jesus himself. "Come on in you good and faithful servant."
Harry Neal,
Winona, MS

The 40th on Annie Kelly Montgomery is once again breathtaking. I think you and Annie are "woke"! (First time I've heard this.) Fantastic article.
Jim Brzoska,
Deltona, FL

Elvira Hervey Jackson
An Educator Extraordinaire

It is no secret that black teachers had a major influence on the growth and development of black children before and after school integration in the South and perhaps across the United States. Some of us remember every teacher that we ever had – teachers who made indelible impressions and gave us the tools we needed to be successful beyond high school and college. I still have all my report cards and certificates!

These teachers inspired us to further our education, inspiring some to become teachers themselves and leaders in the community. Among Yalobusha County's black residents, teaching was the most honorable and respected profession aside from preaching.

Most of our teachers came in town to teach for the week and then returned to their hometowns for the weekend. Several local families provided boarding rooms and accommodations. I recall the Spencers, Webbs and Currys opening their doors to these teachers. Eventually, Principal Joseph H. Ford designated a house near the new Davidson High for these young teachers who came from black colleges and brought with them a freshness, cultural exposure and excitement. They made us eager to learn and anxious to see what lay beyond Water Valley. I knew I wanted to get some of what they had – an education, a job, independence. They made us curious about the colleges they had attended and their hometowns. We were blessed with some of the most excellent educators in the area, and in Coffeeville's Colored System, Elvira Mae Hervey Jackson stood out.

Elvira was born in Yalobusha County on Valentine's Day in 1915, the youngest of eleven children, six boys and five girls. Her parents, Ned and Ella Paris Hervey, were farmers and descendants of slaves. She attended school in Water Valley completing the 8th grade. Then she earned her high school diploma from Rust College in Holly Springs and completed her Bachelor of Science in Elementary Education in 1958. She obtained her Master's Degree in Secondary Education in 1965 from Tennessee Agricultural & Industrial State College in Nashville, Tennessee, now known as Tennessee State University.

In 1934 Elvira married Henry Hessie Jones, the son of John and Mattie Jones. Mr. John was a logger, known for his ability to handle a team of mules and for the distinctive two walking sticks that he used when he went out and about. Elvira and Henry had one daughter, Marjorie, who lives in Coffeeville today.

The Jones family sharecropped on a farm in the Bryant Community, living in a house that had no electric lights and heated only with an old wood stove. Elvira was Marjorie's first teacher in a one room school where she taught first through sixth grade. Marjorie and her cousins and neighbors often walked four miles to school. But in the wintertime, her dad, Henry hitched his mule to a buggy to give them a ride. To keep

Elvira Jackson

warm on the way, the children heated rocks, wrapped them in blankets or old rags, put them in a bucket and put their feet on this homemade heater. As soon as they arrived at the Pine Grove Baptist Church School, they would build a fire in the school's wood stove.

Marjorie remembers that all the children were close, going through their lessons until recess time. They brought their lunch in buckets or paper bags - often peanut butter sandwiches or whatever their parents had on hand. They drank water – no one had juice or milk. They played basketball outside, with no gym and no inside toilets. Then it was back to their studies and an afternoon recess before being dismissed for the day.

In addition to teaching at Pine Grove, Elvira also taught at Rocky Mount Baptist Church School, at Antioch Baptist Church School and the Williams School before she became principal of Pleasant Grove Baptist Church School in the Bryant Community.

Elvira and Henry eventually moved to 128 acres of land, east of Coffeeville, which they bought from a black man named Frazier whose health was failing. While the land had some timber, the couple used most of it to farm, making sorghum molasses, raising livestock, horses, cotton, and vegetables. Elvira taught at Pleasant Grove School until the schools were consolidated into the public-school systems around 1952, when her daughter, Marjorie was entering 8th grade.

After Elvira and Henry divorced, she and Marjorie lived with her sister, Hattie Berry, who was the principal of Central High School where Marjorie attended ninth grade in 1953. Their brother, Roosevelt, was the principal of Davidson High in Water Valley – evidence of the family's commitment to Education.

Marjorie graduated from Central High in 1956. Elvira married Sam Jackson in 1957. By then she had moved up to teaching high school social studies and English and remained in the Coffeeville school systems until she retired in 1980 - a 40-year career that made an immeasurable impact on the greater Yalobusha community.

Sam Jackson passed away in 1970. Henry Jones passed away in 1989.

Elvira's commitment to teaching paralleled her commitment to Pleasant Grove Baptist Church, becoming one of its most active members. (She had attended Mt. Moriah in Water Valley as a child.) She served in numerous roles including Sunday School teacher, president of the Missionary Society, financial secretary and treasurer, yearly program coordinator, and member of the senior choir. She served for 24 years as the dean of the Mt. Moriah Baptist District Association, responsible for educational classes, teacher certifications and workshops. She attended both state and national sessions for years and assisted in implementing many district strategies and practices. The Pleasant Grove Church website singles her out as "a prominent member of our congregation."

Annie Givens, who was profiled in the December 18, 2018 column, trained Elvira for her dean's duties, and she in turn trained daughter Marjorie, who served as dean for 12 years.

In addition to her teaching and church activities, Elvira participated in community networks, retirement associations, and other committees and boards. Among her most prominent activities was her work with the women's division of black Masons, known as the Royal Arch Masons. She achieved the high honor - or degree- of "Heroine of Jericho," the name deriving from the Book of Joshua, and the woman, Rahab, known as the Heroine of Jericho. Beyond this honor she was a lecturer of the Fifth District Heroines of Jericho Lodge.

Annette Hervey Westmoreland, featured in the November 29, 2018 column, shares the following:

My great Aunt Elvira was a soft spoken woman and did not mind helping anyone. When I had to ride the bus home from Jackson State College, she would pick me up at the bus station and carry me to her house to wait there until my dad, her nephew, would pick me up. Aunt Elvira inspired me to become a certified dean for a Christian Leadership School under the Sunday School Publishing Board in Nashville, TN. I took her advice and completed the necessary courses to become a dean.

When I played the piano for their church, my dad would drop me off at their house and I would ride with them to Pleasant Grove Church, which was located off number 7 highway. The building they are in now is new. She was a great dean and speaker for the Mt. Moriah Baptist District Association.

Aunt Elvira gave me a lot of encouragement. Every time I came home, my mom and I would drive to Coffeeville to visit her, and if my mom was not in the city, my husband and I would drive by to see her. I never heard Aunt Elvira speak negatively about anyone. She would always say, "well, we just have to pray for him or her." Her daughter Margie was also inspired by Aunt Elvira to become a dean, because she always traveled with her mom to the different National Congresses and the December Sunday School Publishing Board Conferences in Nashville.

The last time Aunt Elvira was able to attend the SSPB in Nashville, my daughter urged me to go to her hotel room with pen and paper to record as much about the family as I could. This is when I found out that our great, great grandfather was killed by the Klu Klux Klan. My dad never told me that or perhaps he didn't know. It is so important that we try to get all the information from our older ancestors that we can. I regret I didn't do better recording family history from all my older family members who are now gone.

From Dorothy and Syreeta Key, featured in the March 28, 2019 column:

Mrs. Elvira Jackson was one of the first teachers who captured my attention and gained my admiration. I was awed by how firm she was, but still managed to be so caring and nurturing. If you did something wrong or could even be perceived as wrong, she could make you feel 12 inches tall. Thankfully, she did not leave you that way. She would let the reprimand sink in and then build you up to do better. I loved that and really came to understand and appreciate it when I became an adult and began my own teaching career.

Mrs. Jackson was a role model, not only as an educator, but in the community and the church as well. She was most influential in my career. As a matter of fact, she even taught my dad in classes offered to veterans as well as in seminary. She also motivated many of us in our church and the surrounding area to pursue Christian education. To sum things up, we could simply say that she was an awesome lady who personally achieved much but always encouraged everyone she encountered to do their best in whatever they endeavored. With her, there was no half-stepping!

-Dorothy Kee

When Mrs. Jackson passed away, many people wondered whether she was really my godmother. She was so endeared and had such far-reaching influence that people were suspicious that anyone they were not aware of being connected to her were clout-chasers. (Now that's star status.) Only then did I find out that she had been my godmother since birth. Actually, I never thought about it until then and realized what a blessing she had been to me and many of the people I knew.

Although she was still teaching when I was in first or second grade, she was never my teacher, officially. Even so, she taught me much. She did the usual godmotherly things such as gifts on birthdays and holidays, secretly pressing tightly folded bills in my hand when I was home on weekends from college, etc. But I give her credit for many things I know and do today. She was a master at delegating tasks and responsibilities, and you always wanted to be sure your performance met her approval. She could easily discern who was best suited for what tasks. When she asked, you just did it!

Because of one of her assignments when I was around ten years old, I taught myself to type, incorrectly at first, but I was one of the fastest and most accurate four-finger typists in town. I guess I passed her inspection because her requests and golden nuggets of advice kept coming. My grandmother was so happy that she was allowing me opportunities to learn that she bought me a quiet, fancy new electric typewriter (the predecessor to the personal computer)."If you're going to be doing things for Mrs. Jackson," she said, "you need a better typewriter than that old, noisy, clunky Brother one your mom has. You may need it for school, too." So, you see she was respected by everyone, but at the same time, she remained down to earth, approachable and concerned for others. A couple friends and I quickly realized that she really did not need us to do the things she asked us to do, but she wanted to make sure we learned to do them. She was concerned about the welfare of future generations.

- Syreeta Key

Elvira Mae Hervey Jackson died February 15, 2011, the day after her 96th birthday. This heartfelt tribute from her grandson, Tyrone Moore, is but one example of her enduring influence.

Big Mama,
I just want to say thank you for being the best grandmother anyone could ever ask for. You taught me the meaning of love and forgiveness. Most of all Respect. I will always love you. I really enjoyed spending the moments I had with you before you left me. I must truly say coming to your house was really "BIG MAMA'S HOUSE," one always filled with love and smiles - never a dull moment. May you rest in peace and I will see you again one day.
I love you Big Mama.

While all the colleges are closed because of the coronavirus crisis, our oral history project in collaboration with the Center for Southern Culture at the University of Mississippi moves on. The interview that Colton Babbitt, the UM graduate student and Water Valley resident, conducted with Marjorie Moore contributed to this article. The transcript of her family history will be archived at the university. The Albany Southwest Georgian featured a second article about the oral history project during Women's History Month. A draft of the article is posted on my website.

Sharing the lives of these black women shows that we are more alike than different. As Eduardo Porter wrote in a recent article in The New York Times, "We must build an understanding of what it is to be American that includes everyone." It is my hope that when this crisis is over, we will have gained that understanding and have an America that does includes everyone. Perhaps we can be inspired and encouraged by this quote that appears on an online obituary for Elvira Hervey Jackson.

"Knowledge by suffering entereth, and life is perfected by death. When she started walking in the light, she kept going through."

Yes, she kept going through.

Reader Comments

For 5 years 1965 – 1971, I worked at the Bank of Coffeeville and I think I met Mrs. Jackson through that connection though time has dusted my memory. However, this article about her makes me wish I could dust off my memory and recall her. This article about her was a WOW article. I enjoyed reading about her and am sure she and I knew a lot of the same people. One day perhaps we can sit down on a cloud and share about those good ole days in Yalobusha County. Oh yes, you are invited.
Harry Neal,
Winona, MS

I really appreciate all of the wonderful articles. Each person's story reminds me of some possible comparable person in my native Tunica County. All of your articles are being kept and compiled into a book, right? So that all of the future posterity interested in glimpses into Yalobusha County's History of Color, will see.... It will be an important book.
Kenneth Weeden,
Raleigh, NC

Great article about a great woman.
Pamela Simmons,
Stone Mountain, GA

My favorite teacher!
Juanita Fleming,
Sallis, MS

42

Mamie Herron Shields
A Sower - Planting Seeds - Bearing Much Fruit

My appreciation for Mamie Herron Shields and her important work in Yalobusha County first came through her husband, Lincoln. Mr. Shields was a teacher and basketball coach at Davidson High School in Water Valley. He was also my bus driver during my high school years and like other drivers filling a very important role. They are caretakers in jobs that require meeting safety requirements, maintaining discipline and delivering students to and from school – the first school representative that some students encounter each day. As a teenager I vividly remember seeing my bus going down one road, circling around for 3 or 4 stops before getting to mine, which was my cue to head up the hill to be picked up.

In an earlier column I mentioned that the bus for Water Valley's white students passed by my stop first. My protection and security came with the second bus - my bus and my bus driver. You see, in the South a young black girl standing alone in a curve on a country road with no neighbors in sight could be a target, as I was. One afternoon when I got off the bus and headed down the hill towards our house, I heard yelling and looked back to see a white man standing at the top of our driveway being most obnoxious. I ran. He had stopped in the middle of the road. I was maybe 14, afraid, but so disgusted that I never mentioned it and never tarried after that when getting off the bus.

Mr. Shields was always on time, alert and well dressed, a different shirt ironed and pressed every day when most of our wardrobes were far sparser. Like many drivers, Mr. Shields had to stop at the school to pick up his bus to begin his route, which made me wonder what time he left home, how his children got to school, and if they had a hot breakfast. The way he presented himself and the few times I saw his wife, Mamie, whose job as a home extension agent I barely understood, made me think of her as the ideal mother of well-manner children in a perfect home – theirs was made of brick on highway 7 in Coffeeville.

Mr. Shields was a great educator, administrator and coach. I am sure that he and his wife went into their pockets, closets and pantries many, many times to assist others. Though decades have passed since Mr. Shields picked me up in Water Valley, it is never too late to offer thanks and appreciation on behalf of myself, Davidson students, faculty and the communities for his leadership, guidance, support, service and love.

Mamie Shields worked for the Home Extension Agency, an outgrowth of 1914 legislation that cemented a cooperative effort between the U. S. Department of Agriculture and land grant colleges. Extension office personnel held informal educational programs and hands-on demonstrations designed to enrich local communities. Mrs. Shields conducted demonstrations at our 4-H Club meetings and in our home economics class at school. I believe she also visited folks in their homes throughout the county and gave demonstrations at the extension offices. I took note of how she managed her job and her family. She always had it together.

I was in college before I came to know her children, Suzette, Derrick and Jeffery, who attended Coffeeville public schools. I tried to recruit Derrick when I worked at the University of Mississippi, and he did attend a conference for national merit and achievement students. But he decided to go elsewhere. Mr. and Mrs. Shields are now enjoying each other in that same house on Highway 7. With each column I learn, grow and am encouraged through the lessons gleaned from these women's lives. Below Mamie's children offer detailed insights into yet another outstanding black woman of Yalobusha County.

Mamie Lee Herron Shields
By Suzette and Larry Ware

For more than 50 years, Mamie Lee Herron Shields has been an integral member of the Yalobusha County community not only through her professional life but also from the example she set raising her family - as noted in the introduction, her husband Lincoln and three children. Derrick, her oldest son, (married to Andrea Smith Shields, a realtor with Keller Williams Realty River Cities), serves as senior pastor of Christ Community Church in Columbus, Georgia. Her daughter, Doris Suzette Ware, (the wife of Pastor Larry W. Ware of the Bethlehem Missionary Baptist Church of Coffeeville), worked in banking for many years and as a certified housing specialist in housing management in both Iowa and Florida. Her youngest son, Jeffery, (married to Angela Williams Shields, an electrical engineer at NASA in Huntsville), is senior program analyst at the Space and Missile Defense Command at Redstone Arsenal in Huntsville, Alabama.

Mamie Shields' success as a wife, mother, grandmother and great-grandmother illustrates her lifelong commitment to excellence and the moral foundation laid for her by her late parents, Beulah Newsome Herron and Reverend M. H. Herron of Prentiss, MS. Mamie is the tenth of eleven siblings, all of whom are now deceased, leaving her as the only survivor of the close-knit and loving Herron clan. She is the grandmother of 11 and the great-grandmother of 4. She is the aunt of 40 nieces and nephews and the great-aunt, great-great aunt of over 100, many of whom call her frequently to check on her and her family or to seek counsel.

Like so many of her generation, Mamie left home to go to college after graduating in May 1949 from Prentiss Normal Institute in Prentiss. Her elementary education was at the Pine Ridge public school in White Sand. Mamie completed a Bachelor of Science Degree in Home Economics at what is now Alcorn State University in June 1953. She completed further studies in home economics at Michigan State University in East Lansing, MI, and extension education at Prairie View A & M University in Texas. In May 1974, she completed the Master of Arts Degree at the University of Mississippi. She received the Award for Distinguished Service from the National Association of Extension Home Economists in November 1980.

Before arriving in Coffeeville and Yalobusha County, Mamie served as a home economics classroom teacher in Hattiesburg in 1954. She taught home economics in Columbia in 1956. In 1959 Mamie's work took her to Winston County and the Cooperative Extension Service, which was administered by Mississippi State University. As the county home demonstration agent, Mamie worked with rural residents, showing them how to take care of their property, inside and outside, cook, can and make crafts. During a visit to the Winston County Fair Mamie met Lincoln Shields, a native of Noxapater who had also graduated from Alcorn. It proved to a fortuitous connection - they subsequently married and moved to Coffeeville.

Mrs. Shields extension service work in Yalobusha County began in 1963 as Negro Home Demonstration Agent. In 1967, she became the area home demonstration agent in a pilot program known as the Expanded Food and Nutrition Education Program. Her territory initially covered Panola, Tallahatchie and Yalobusha counties and later Grenada and Tate counties. She also served as County 4-H agent for Yalobusha County. In 1974 she became Mississippi's first African American county extension home economist. She spent the remainder of her cooperative extension service career in this position, retiring in June 1989.

From her office in Water Valley, which was next to the county courthouse, Mrs. Shields built a network of clubs around both black and white families, including 4-H and Future Farmers. The goals were to help participants improve their nutrition and homemaking skills and to foster stronger relationships within their families and the community. When her children were students in the Coffeeville School System, Mrs. Shields served as PTA president from 1979-81, and she could often be found walking the halls of the schools as a concerned parent.

The impact that Mrs. Shields had on all those she encountered in her extension work is virtually impossible to measure. What is certain is her profound effect as a role model for many in need of mentorship. She not only patiently taught basic skills around the house but on more than one occasion served as an emergency counselor for families in crisis. The Shields were the first African Americans in Yalobusha County to be FHA homeowners, and Mamie and Lincoln used their experience to aid those seeking to build new homes.

After her retirement in 1989, Mamie Shields remained dedicated to her community. A fine cook and seamstress, she was often consulted for weddings and other social events. She willfully gave service to those in need of them without reservation.

Mrs. Shields also brought her talents to a number of organizations including Epsilon Sigma Phi, the extension professionals' organization; Mississippi Council on Family Relations (MCFR); district, state and national extension home economist associations; Yalobusha County AARP chapter secretary; Central Mississippi, Incorporated (CMI) personnel and advisory board; Yalobusha County American Cancer Society, secretary; Mississippi Action for Progress board member; Yalobusha County Library board member. Mrs. Shields served as coordinator of the Yalobusha County diabetes wellness support groups affiliated with churches of the Mt. Moriah District Baptist Association. She was largely responsible for administering a $10,000 grant to bring diabetes education throughout Mt. Moriah District Churches. This was in association with the Appalachian Diabetes Coalition of Marshall County, West Virginia.

Mamie Shields' spiritual life was as important to her as her professional and community pursuits. When the family arrived in Coffeeville, they joined the Bethlehem Missionary Baptist Church under the leadership of the late Reverend William Murphy Brown. There, she served as a Sunday school teacher, youth director, deaconess, and the mother board. She organized the first Baccalaureate Service for Coffeeville

High School graduates at Bethlehem in 1979 and the one in 1980. Her ministry reached into the Mount Moriah Baptist District Association where she served as youth director coordinating activities throughout the district and as an assistant to moderator Amos Sims. She also earned a Bachelor of Theology in 2006 from the Coffeeville extension of Mississippi Baptist Seminary and a Bachelor of Religious Education in 2011. These followed courses of study in Christian education in 1993 and 2006.

Mrs. Shields also served as class secretary of the seminary and later, served as dean of the Coffeeville Extension to continue the organization's reach into Yalobusha County.

Beyond their professional work, Mamie and Lincoln Shields have often assisted neighbors who suffered losses from storms or fires. And every year, since the late 1960s, they have planted turnip and mustard greens that the community can take free of charge – no restrictions on the amount and only one request: break the leaves off so that the plants can continue to reproduce and grow and therefore be a blessing to others. It is a perfect metaphor for their lives of service.

In this last year of her eighties, Mother Shields remains a devoted wife, homemaker and grandmother and still a source of encouragement to her three children. You can find her at times teaching her great-grandson how to cook or bake or providing leadership among the women of the church. Her latest project was teaching the deaconesses to bake communion bread. Many people continue to visit her, seeking her wisdom on raising a family, homemaking, and general life lessons. Mamie Shields has served a long time. More importantly, she has lived well by serving others well.

Through Her Children's Eyes

Jeffery – *Mom always taught me the importance of having a relationship with God. She did more than "talk it" – we lived it by regularly attending Sunday School, Church and Baptist Training Union on Sunday evenings. Mom taught us to treat everyone with love and respect. She taught us to be accountable in life with our schoolwork and always insisted "if you said you were going to do something, always try to do it." Mom stressed giving your best in whatever you do and trust God to do the rest. Mom is so devoted – I watched her and her sisters taking care of their father as he got older. Mom, during her 70's, mastered the computer and mastered Microsoft Word. She could perform operations as well as I could. Mom is always up for the challenge of learning and doing new things.*

Angela – *Mrs. Shields is a wonderful mother-in-law. She always had encouraging words when our boys were little. She said, "Angie, if you feed them, you can get along with them." I did just that and still do it because it really works! She also taught me to make homemade biscuits and I take great pride in making them for my family and for the whole family when we are gathered in Coffeeville.*

Derrick – *My mother always exhibits a balance of grace and truth. She invests deeply and relationally in the lives of everyone she encounters. Her love for people and family is exceeded only by her love of God.*

Andrea – *My mother-in-law has been an inspiration to me from the beginning of my marriage to Derrick. Being an African American female in the US Army and full-*

time student at that time brought a unique set of challenges when planning and setting career goals. She has a way of motivating you with one conversation and making you feel that you can accomplish your goals with hard work, good organizational skills, the passion to move forward and most importantly, with the help of God. She is a positive role model in my life.

Suzette – *(Mom or Mommy, as I sometimes still say!) is such a huge influence in my life – always has been. It is exceedingly difficult to talk about her alone and not mention Daddy because they did so much together down through the years, and it's even more difficult to express my thoughts about her in a small paragraph! It has been and still is such a gift from God to have Mamie Shields as my Mom - and to have benefitted from all that she has been and still is to enrich my life. She helped me bring up our daughters, teaching them as I saw her teach others in her career. When we returned to Mississippi to live, we heard countless stories from people, seemingly from everywhere, telling us of how Mom and Dad blessed their lives – furniture after a house burned, help with talking to their children, with recipes and with cooking meals for their families, with church programs' order of service, with flower gardens, the blessedness of getting greens free from their garden every year - the list goes on. I watch as they happily help others. Mom loves to keep track of who picks greens – just to know how many people are blessed from the garden.*

The example for all of us is of dedication and loyalty to whatever her family is doing. The grandchildren talk of how awesome it is for her to still tuck them in, especially when they are not feeling well. Her touch is truly special! I learned that she once considered becoming a nurse. Mom writes in a daily journal and has photo albums depicting family members over the years,

Mamie and Lincoln Shields

demonstrating both her love of history and her pride in family members' achievements. Grandchildren and great-grandchildren are all here at Christmas time – her pound cakes and banana puddings are a hit with the entire family. Great-grandson, Justin, gets a cookie pudding because he does not want bananas in his dessert – and she does it especially for him. Lord willing, we look forward to gathering around Mom and Dad at Christmas 2020!

Mom inspired my life verse Colossians 3:23: "And whatever you do, do it heartily, as to the Lord and not to men." No one is perfect, and Mom is no exception. But she is definitely one who loves her family, loves people, loves her Church, loved her work in training and teaching, and loves to keep current (she has gotten herself a Facebook page) and learn more about the Bible so she can keep teaching others.

When I read of the Proverbs 31 woman – I think immediately of her, which culminates in verse 31 which says, "Give her of the fruit of her hands, and let her own works praise her in the gates".

> *"Give her of the fruit of her hands, and let her own works praise her in the gates".*

Larry—*Mamie Shields and I have had a special relationship since August of 1978, when she welcomed me into her home to visit her daughter for the first time (Of course, I called first before I just 'showed up'). She not only has strong ideals but also exerts a strong influence on others. Taking seriously the Lord's instructions to His disciples to "compel them to come," she reaches out to others to consider the Lord and the church. Without apology, she seeks the Lord and offers Him to everyone within her reach. She knows from her own experience overcoming challenges that God is the absolute necessity one must have in this life to succeed and make a difference.*

MAMIE LEE HERRON SHIELDS . . . a woman of great achievement, singular influence and dedicated to purposes beyond herself. Coffeeville and Yalobusha County are stronger because of her unselfish generosity toward others. And while many in the community may be unaware of her contributions, they are not unnoticed by a righteous judge who rewards all of those who demonstrate the commitment to faithfulness in service to others.

My Closing Thoughts
By Dottie Reed

Oh, how I wish we were simply getting ready to purchase a red rose or a white one for church this coming Sunday – a red rose to indicate your mother is living and the white to honor a mother no longer here, and then heading out to a Mother's Day brunch.

Instead our churches are closed, and we are in a global pandemic, in a country where black and brown people are the most vulnerable. We are suffering and dying in higher percentages, yet we must continue to pray and seek to worship in our own ways, through television, radio or via live stream on our phone or computer. Even for some that is a struggle, especially where technology is limited. Many of us are on lock down, practicing social distancing and looking out for friends and neighbors while others seem oblivious. Many of us, too, are separated from our mothers, able to see them only through a window or video screen. The number of mothers and individuals we continue to lose to the Covid 19 virus is overwhelming and devastating. Yet, we must not despair. We must be encouraged by the faith of our mothers - mothers like Mamie Shields, who continues through faith to sow positive seeds that bear fruit. She has learned, earned and returned! Thank you, Mamie Shields! Happy Mother's Day to you and all the mothers of this world!

– break the leaves off so that the plants can continue to reproduce and, therefore, continue their growth and be a blessing to others.

Reader Comments

I read about Mamie Shields tonight. She sounds like she is right about my mother's age. And she has the same name as my great grandmother (who would have been a generation before Mamie Shields and my mom. She is truly an inspiration and a role model. I can see how she influenced her large family with her Christian character and her quest for knowledge. Did I see that you are concluding this series of articles soon? I am really going to miss reading your insightful mini biographies. I am going to save reading about the next lady for later this weekend as I like to savor the details of each black woman's history and ponder the article for a while. I wish more people could read your articles. I wish more people had your heart for your fellowman.
  Margaret Walters,
  Tucker, GA

Your website and such articles are a wonderful way to get a tiny glimpse of your world.
  Ron Chen,
  Princeton, NJ

A wonderful story. It's remarkable how much this woman was involved in and able to accomplish in her life – and still is! A great role model.
  Adrienne Harris,
  Atlanta, GA

Well done good and faithful servant!
  Clarence Brown,
  Falls Church, VA

Thank you for introducing me to Mamie Herron Shields. I love the title of the writing. The content blessed me and took me back to memories of our county 4-H worker, Mrs. Martin.... keep the articles coming.
  Dianne Prince,
  Orlando, FL

I lived in Coffeeville when the Shields moved to Coffeeville. I knew them fairly well and they were impressive people in the area. I knew Mr. Shields better than Mrs. Shields. I knew them to both be very respectable people. It was good to find out about life for them today and It was good to see the picture of their family. Their family picture speaks well of them as parents. They are good folks.
  Harry Neal,
  Winona, MS

I was in tears...I wish I could be half the woman she is.
  J. Charity Ware,
  Coffeeville, MS

Ora Lee Polk Phillips
Loved by Many - An Inspiration to All

By now you might have noticed the prominence of the Polk family in Yalobusha County and in this column. The second article published, August 23, 2018, featured one of the family's grand matriarchs, Sallie Ann Polk. Then we featured Alma Polk Nicholson, Juanita Polk Fleming and more recently Mildred Polk. Now I feel we have come full circle to the highly respected and sought-after Ora Lee Polk Phillips. When I called her one day back in 2018 asking about who knows what, she told me she was glad that I was sharing stories about the black women of Yalobusha. "Someone sent this white man to me, who was in town looking for anyone who knew Hattie Turner," she recalled. "He said that she came and stayed with him and his dad when his father was ill – she helped raise him. They moved to Memphis and lost touch with her. I was sorry that I could not help him."

Even though she didn't have an answer that day, the moment showed Ora Lee Phillips in a familiar role because of her long and dedicated service to the community: the go-to person for valuable information about Water Valley.

Now her youngest sister Juanita pays tribute to this living matriarch of the Polk dynasty.

Sister - Matriarch - Servant
By Juanita Polk Fleming

As I started to formulate a synopsis of my oldest sister, Ora Lee, I realized I really don't know a lot about her early childhood because she is the second child and I'm the ninth child of ten. There is quite an age difference between the two of us. I was only five years old when she graduated from high school. Thus, I have learned even more from researching my oldest sister.

Ora Lee was born in Water Valley to Willie Winfield and Sallie Ann Winters Polk. As the oldest girl, she quickly learned how to cook and clean and became Mom's helper. As a child she had to work before and after school, feeding cows, hogs, and chickens.

Ora Lee's education started at Bayson Chapel School during the time our parents were sharecropping in the Mudline area. We then moved to Oakland where our parents were still sharecropping, and she attended the Leigh Branch School. After several years we moved back to the Water Valley area, and Ora Lee attended Bayson Chapel School until the eighth grade. Then she went to live with cousins Charlie and Victoria White, who lived closer to Water Valley, so she could attend Davidson High School for ninth grade. It was two miles to the school. When the weather was cold, they would stop about half-way at Uncle Stokes

A young and beautiful Ora Lee in the mid-fifties

and Aunt Alice McFarland's house to warm up and then continue on.

We then moved to the Upchurch Farm in Coffeeville, still sharecropping. Finally, our family had electricity and our own well for water, which meant that we did not have to carry water from long distances for all the family needs. And we were able to ride the bus to school. Ora Lee attended the tenth through twelfth grades in Coffeeville, graduating from Coffeeville Colored High School in 1954. The principal at that time was Hattie Berry. (Hattie's brother Roosevelt Hervey was the principal at the Davidson Schools in Water Valley and her sister, Elvira Hervey Jackson, was a school principal in the community schools in the county. See Article 41, published April 8, 2020).

After high school Ora Lee attended Mississippi Valley College, now Mississippi Valley State University in Itta Bena. She left college in 1955 to marry Raymond Phillips. At their 25th anniversary the couple started an annual celebration, and for the next 40 years the entire family has gathered at Alma Polk Nicholson's house for the January event. This most recent January marked the couple's 65th wedding anniversary. They are the proud parents of eight children, grandparents to twenty-three and great grandparents to twenty-eight.

Ora Lee's hobbies include cooking and baking for family and friends, especially holidays and birthdays. She loves spending time caring for her flowers, and she especially likes competing with her husband and son Wayne to see who has grown the prettiest flowers each summer.

Ora Lee's diverse work history shows she was never afraid to tackle whatever was assigned to her – except for her very first job at the Valley Motel. She was hired to clean rooms after occupants checked out. "Day one went really well," she recalled. "On day two the owner carried me to the room to be cleaned and she gave me a white towel and told me, 'The person that stayed here last night had a dog, and I need you to get down on the floor and catch and kill all the fleas as they jump up.' When my ride came, I left the white towel on the floor and never went back."

Ora Lee worked for the Water Valley Head Start Pre-School Program from 1968 to 1980. "Mayor Watson Hunt came to me with an application and asked if I would like to work at Head Start," she explained. "I completed the application and was the first person hired as a teacher in the first group of workers. The late Bernice Minor was program director during that time. At the same time, I worked after school and on weekends at Woods & Miller, a department store, operated by Jerry & Sharon Surrette. While working at Head Start, I was up for being promoted to head teacher. For this position I really needed to be able to travel, but I didn't have a driver's license."

Ora Lee's former Head Start co-worker, Juanita Cox (featured in Article 4, September 27, 2018) submitted this account which she labeled **"Two Clever Women."**

One beautiful day, two women – Ora Lee and Juanita Cox – were chatting at their Head Start jobs, talking about how Ora Lee needed to go to the Department of Motor Vehicle (DMV) office to get her driver's license. The problem was that they only had a manual transmission - stick shift type car. Ora Lee knew how to drive but knew nothing about how to change gears with a stick shift. To Ora Lee's surprise, Juanita could shift gears like a pro. They quickly came up with a great idea to get Ora Lee her license.

They set out on the journey to the DMV with Ora Lee in the driver's seat and Juanita shifting the gears. While in route, Ora Lee suddenly thought, "Oh my! I sure hope they don't ask me to drive when I get there." If she was asked to drive, she probably would have run like...well, on with the story. They finally made it to the DMV, Ora Lee went inside and came back out a few minutes later with a brand-new driver's license in her hand and a big smile on her face. Thankfully, she was not asked to test drive!

The two then headed back to work the same way they had gone to the DMV – Ora Lee steering and Juanita shifting the gears! After they had safely returned, they laughed and laughed and still share that laughter today. These two clever women put their heads together to accomplish a goal: allowing Ora to get that job promotion and making a memory that will last a lifetime.

Fortunately, Ora Lee did find a car with an automatic transmission for her work travels! After her promotion to Head Start's lead teacher, Ora Lee wanted to enhance her skills, and in February 1971 she earned a certificate from the Lincoln School of Attendant Nursing, based in California.

The Bathroom Encounters
The first encounter as told by Ora Lee.

One Monday morning on my way to meet Head Start Director Alice Faye White for a trip to Jackson and a weeklong workshop, a gentleman I knew flagged me down and told me that a new bank was coming to town and the president was looking for an outstanding black person to work in the branch. I told him that I was going away and that I would get back to him when I returned. All week in Jackson, I wrestled with the two positions - whether to stay with Head Start or to apply to work at the new bank. On that Thursday my nerves got the best of me, and I went to the bathroom. I cried and prayed and wondered what to do. Faye realized I had been gone for quite some time and came to check on me, afraid that something was wrong. I finally told her that I was considering applying to work at the new bank. Faye assured me that if that was what I wanted, she would support me, and she encouraged me to apply. When we got back to town, I told the gentleman I was interested in the job and soon I received a call from a woman named Yvonne Vance.

The second encounter as told by Yvonne Vance.

In November 1980, I was asked to open a new bank branch in Water Valley for my employer, the Sunburst Bank located in Grenada. Soon after making the decision to locate in Water Valley, we hired a realtor to find a *good location for the branch. Hershel Howell was the realtor and we had already purchased a lot on Central Street, which had a small building that, with minor repairs, could serve as a temporary bank until we were able to make plans for the new and larger building.*

Naturally, I was anxious to begin building my staff. As we already had prominent people in Water Valley who had been instrumental in our getting approval from the state banking board, we leaned on them for help and advice in local matters as well, especially in the hiring of the best employees. One day in late November Cecil (Buddy) Walley, a well-known local pharmacist, told me that he had a lady by the name of Ora Lee Phillips who wanted to apply for a banking position. I called Ora Lee and we agreed to meet at a home that I had bought in Water Valley, which was undergoing renovation. After she arrived, we looked for a place to sit and interview. As it happened, carpenters and painters were all over the house making all kinds of noise. The only quiet place was the upstairs bathroom. So, the bathroom became our interview office. As you can guess, there are only three items permanently located in a bathroom and the sink is too high to sit on, so the other two items became our interview chairs (And we still laugh about it to this day!).

I was very impressed with Ora Lee and immediately made her a job offer. She accepted and quickly learned a lot about banking including how to run the proof machine and how to run a teller window. After proof machines were no longer needed, Ora Lee became a full time Teller. Being the friendly and helpful lady that she is, and knowing everyone in Yalobusha County, Ora Lee became one of our most valuable employees. She was a friend to everyone who walked through the door and was well respected by all the customers and employees alike.

While I eventually went to Oxford in 1987 to start another new branch, Ora Lee worked for several more years at the Water Valley bank. I will always treasure my time there and will always consider Ora as my friend. (And the original interview site will never be forgotten).

Ora Lee started working at the Sunburst Bank, now known as Regions Bank, in 1981 and explained how that job led her to another endeavor. "I was often approached by customers about their need for daycare," she said. "After much thought, prayer, and encouragement from my children, I started looking into the possibility of opening a daycare facility. I had a long talk with Wayne Harris, the president of the bank at that time. He was very helpful and supportive. I found a potential location, applied for and received the loan from the bank and the rest is history."

On January 3, 1991, Ora and her daughter Kathleen opened Rainbow Kiddy World Daycare. She continued to work at the bank while her daughter operated the daycare. Ora spent many afternoons after leaving the bank and most of her weekends at the daycare making sure things were ready for her babies each day. She reluctantly made the decision to retire from the bank in 2005 after twenty-four years to help her daughter run Rainbow Kiddy World. Through those years they provided services for hundreds of children and low-income working parents. Kathleen made the decision to close Rainbow World later in 2005 so she could become a full-time servant of God in her church and the community.

Ora Lee is a lifelong active member of Bayson Chapel M. B. Church, where Reverend Amos Sims is the pastor. She has served faithfully in numerous capacities including Sunday school and bible study attendee, former choir member, and former

My Closing Thoughts
By Dottie Reed

Ora Lee Phillips

Role models like Ora Lee Polk Phillips are so needed today. She is a great example of what can be accomplished in life through perseverance and kindness. With a high school diploma and a year of college she has accomplished more than some with advanced degrees. She has used the skills that her parents taught her, the knowledge her teachers gave her and the tools she acquired in her career to be successful in her life journey. Nurturing is the word that comes to my mind when I envision her face. We have talked about what she has done at work and in the community and for others. Lest we forget, while she forged her career, she was also a wife raising eight children - no easy task.

Being the youngest in my family and having to tag along with my mother and sisters throughout the community when I grew up, I acquired a lot of big sisters who encouraged me and set high expectations through their examples. I can still rely on them now. They are the catalysts for the work that has gone into this project, how it has become a vehicle to document the stories and achievements of black women and to preserve the oral histories of black families. I am privileged to be able to write about them, name them in this column and even the unnamed know who they are. Ora Lee Phillips means home to me – meaning that I can call her and other women in Yalobusha County and get what I need. I know that I can go to the black churches and see someone who will welcome me because I am a child of that community and they will know my name. I am glad Ora Lee Phillips knows my name.

director of the Youth Department for many years. Currently she serves as a member of the program committee, director of the Mother's Board, organizer of the Bayson Chapel Prayer Ministry, and wherever else she is called upon to serve. In the community Ora Lee served on the Water Valley Chamber of Commerce, Yalobusha County American Cancer Society, as an active poll worker for the Sylvia Rena community where she lives, and as a board member of the Yalobusha County Dining With Diabetes.

That driver's license she obtained so many years ago has proven to be invaluable. Ora Lee now drives many senior citizens to their doctor appointments and/or other errands whenever needed.

In 2013 Ora and Raymond were honored to serve as grand marshals for the Water Valley Christmas Parade. My sister has been a great role model for me, my other siblings and cousins. We cherish her advice and wisdom and for being that guiding light. For the love, laughter and good times there is no comparison.

Reader Comments

Very nice write up on Ora in the paper this week. I am finding more about our black women now than when I was living there, we were kind of sheltered from learning about each other. Thanks again for your contribution.
Annette Westmoreland,
Buckeye, AZ

She has been getting plenty of calls, from blacks and whites.
Juanita Fleming,
Sallis, MS

Just finished reading your article about Ora Phillips, an interesting one indeed. I have enjoyed so much your articles about Yalobusha Black Women. Hopefully these articles will inspire all, black and white, women and men, to heights these ladies have accomplished and make Water Valley and Yalobusha County an even better place.
Harry Neal,
Winona, MS

Another excellent article in your series. Each has been so informative and inspirational about the strong Black Women in the city, county and state you grew up in and the powerful impact they have had on your life and others in the community.
Robert Simpson,
Atlanta, GA

Has it really been two years that you've been writing this column? Congratulations! You should be proud of the work you have done to celebrate the women from your hometown and, by extension, all black women who embody the values of faith and service to their families and communities.
Adrienne Harris,
Atlanta, GA

Another great story for Yalobusha County to hold dear to their hearts. I must say very politely that Ora Lee was a very beautiful woman in both the pictures in this article. God bless all these women of Yalobusha who God blessed them with so many children and the additional energy to accomplish so many things and teach and take care of so many things. My Mom always had us two boys as assistant house cleaners on every Saturday, so there was no going outside with friends until the cleaning got done and I always thought that was punishment. When I read these articles and see the things children and adults alike did growing up, I'm ashamed of myself! While I am so disappointed that this column will be ending, a break in all this research, conversations and compiling these articles will be well-deserved after making sure The Outstanding Women of Yalobusha go down in a wonderful history!
Jim Brzoska,
Deltona, FL

44

Ezra Captain Davidson, Sr.
Principal of the Water Valley Colored Schools

Growing up in Water Valley, I often heard mention of Professor E. C. Davidson, the principal and founder of Davidson Schools. He seemed bigger than life to me even though I had never seen a picture of him. He was honored and revered as a phenomenal educator. Recently, Brittany M. Brown, a graduate student in the masters program in Southern Studies at the University of Mississippi completed a brief documentary on the last class to graduate from Davidson High School in 1970. It featured Army veteran Emma Faye Gooch and me, referring to us as the last graduates of the segregated Davidson High, which sounded strange to me as I had never heard it referred to being segregated. While true of course, it was the black school or the white school to us. Davidson was indeed all-black and segregated and we loved it.

The documentary is short but powerful, and it is posted on my website and YouTube. This summer Brittany is working on the oral history project launched through this column with the hope of expanding the documentary. She has received a fellowship to continue the interviews of black families and individuals in Yalobusha County. These interviews are being archived at the university to document and preserve our stories, our black history. The Davidson High Class of 1970 was small in comparison to those that preceded us. We graduated 50 years ago, and I appreciate what Brittany has done. She has and will reach out to other classmates and Davidson graduates to get their input.

In honor of the Class of 1970's 50th anniversary, the end of an era for Davidson High and Father's Day, I have chosen to deviate from the standard focus of this column to pay homage to Professor E.C. Davidson. He was born Ezra Captain Davidson on September 24, 1886, one of six children, four brothers and one sister, in Tillatoba, MS. His tombstone in the Oak Ridge Cemetery in Water Valley reads "Rev. Ezra Captain Davidson, Sr." and shows the year of his birth and 1957, the year of his death. His funeral was held on August 31, 1957. We, members of the DHS class of 1970, were just five years old. Professor Davidson started the Davidson school in 1924 located in a red brick building on the corner of Simmons and Cemetery Streets across from Miles Memorial CME Church.

Around 1931-32, Professor Davidson married Theresa Wood Cogburn, then a widow and he a divorcee. She brought two girls to the union, Hazel and Gwendolyn. They had three boys together E.C. Jr., Lester and Kerry. According to Gwendolyn Sherrill Morgan, one of Theresa's daughters, 98, and now residing in Chicago, her mother was born April 18, 1900 and grew up in Water Valley. "My grandfather, Louis Wood, who worked for the railroad in Water Valley, sent my mother to a private school, Mary Holmes All-Girls School in West Point for her early educational training," she said. Theresa completed high school at Lane College Preparatory in Jackson, TN in May 1916. Thirteen years later, in 1929, she attended Alcorn Agricultural and Mechanical College, now Alcorn State University in Lorman, and in 1932 she took classes at Jackson College, now Jackson State University in Jackson. In 1937 she enrolled at Rust College in Holly Springs and earned her degree in August 1943. There is not one C on her transcript!

"Mom was just a semester or so away from finishing her masters from New York University when she had to come back home for medical reasons," Gwendolyn recalled. Professor Davidson also completed his college degree at Rust College. He worked in a factory in Ohio before he answered his urge to return to Water Valley to begin his lifelong work in education. "When dad was not running the school, he was preaching," Kerry said. "He often preached at churches in the area. Dad was very religious and totally committed to serving the Lord." Professor Davidson pastored Kind Providence Baptist Church, now known as New Providence Baptist Church on Pope Road in Water Valley.

Kerry describes their house at 501 Calhoun Street as always filled with boys and girls seeking help with academics and extracurricular activities. "My mother played a critical role in the development and success of the Davidson school, he recalled. "She taught English, sponsored the Tri-Hi Y clubs, directed the choir and presented many cultural programs. She was an excellent writer and worked with students year- round especially when school was closed to allow time for picking cotton. She never complained."

Ruby Turner, a native of Water Valley, is a very active 91-year old now living in Illinois who remembers much about Yalobusha's earlier black community. In Article 34, December 8, 2019, which profiled her, she described an event in April, 1974, when she and former Davidson students living in

Professor E.C. Davidson
1886 - 1957

Professor E. C. Davidson, principal of the Water Valley colored schools since 1924, died Thursday night at his home on Calhoun Street after an illness of several months. Had he lived until Sept. 24, he would have been 71 years old.

Funeral services were conducted at Everdale Baptist Church, Water Valley, Saturday afternoon, August 31, at 2 o'clock, with Rev. Eugene Burley, pastor, delivering the funeral sermon. Burial was in Oak Ridge Cemetery with Water Valley Funeral Home in charge. His body lay in state in the chapel of Davidson High School from 10:30 Saturday morning until the time of the funeral, and a large number of his friends, both white and colored, visited the school to pay their respect.

During the service resolutions were read as follows: In behalf of the Yalobusha Teachers Association, by Annie Kelley Montgomery; In behalf of Davidson High School, by John Dowsing; and In behalf of Kind Providence Church, by Bertha Mitchell. Prof. Davidson was also a minister, and served as pastor of the Kind Providence Church for a number of years.

He leaves his wife, Theresa Davidson, who has taught with him in the Water Valley colored schools for a number of years; three sons, E. C. Davidson Jr., a senior at Meharry Medical School, Nashville, Tenn.; Kerry Davidson, Water Valley; and Lester Davidson, Chicago; two step-daughters, Hazel May, Benton Harbor, Mich., and Gwendolyn Sherrill, of Chicago; four brothers and one sister.

Prof. Davidson was born at Tillatoba, and had spent the greater part of his life in Yalobusha County. Before coming to Water Valley he had taught school for ten years elsewhere, and previous to his teaching career he had worked in an industry in a Northern city.

To Professor Davidson, more than any other person, goes the credit for the building of the Davidson High School to its present position of honor and respect, and very fittingly the school was named in his honor.

When he came to Water Valley, the colored school of the city ended with grammar school, and those who desired a high school education had to go elsewhere to continue their schooling. Little by little, he was able to enlarge the curriculum of the school, and a source of satisfaction to him was the fact that the school was raised to a full four-year high school.

Professor Davidson emphasized to his people the principles of Christianity, and the need for upright conduct. He had the highest respect of his people and of the white people of the community as well.

He often told his friends how he came to his decision to teach school and to preach. He said that while he was working in a Northern city, he felt a strange call to return to his native state and help his people. "It was a hard decision to make," he said, "as I was making $5.29 a day (top-rate pay in those days) and also teaching an independent night school.

"I promised God that I would do my best. How well that job is being done, I rest the ultimate case with Him and the people."

the Chicago area honored Theresa Davidson. The surprise attendance of her sons, Drs. E. C. Jr. and Kerry Davidson, was a highlight of the event. According to Ruby the 12th grade was added to Davidson High in 1941, much of the help for the school coming from fundraisers at Everdale Baptist Church. The first graduating class in 1942 included the Davidson's daughter, Gwendolyn, who recalled that of the fourteen students, thirteen finished. "One girl went to Chicago and did not come back," she said. Gwendolyn, herself, went to Chicago after she graduated. Most of her career was in retail until she became the primary caretaker for her mother, who passed away in 1986.

The Davidson school buildings where I attended were on Calhoun Street. Only the elementary building, now privately owned and in dis-repair, still exists. The class of 1970 started first grade in the building in 1958. Very few official records remain. Many trophies and artifacts were destroyed when the high school building on the hill above the elementary school caught fire. We never got our group graduation picture. As an elementary student I was always excited when we were able to go up the steps to the high school auditorium for any reason, but especially for an assembly that we called chapel. Each class was given a turn to present during a chapel program, and I remember reciting the pledge of allegiance and my class singing "I want to be a Sunbeam" when it was our turn. And here are the lyrics to another song we performed that still comes to mind.

We were filled with hope and optimism about our future. We often sang "God Bless America, " and yes, there was still prayer in school.

Have faith, hope and charity
That's the way to live successfully
How do I know,
the Bible tells me so
Do good to your enemies and the Blessed
Lord you'll surely please
How do I know,
the Bible tells me so
Don't worry bout tomorrow
Just be real good today
The Lord is right beside you
He'll guide you all the way
Have faith, hope and charity
That's the way to live successfully
How do I know,
the Bible tells me so.

Moving up to the high school building was always a motivating thought and a goal for sure. By now, John Dowsing was the principal. Dollie Ann Henderson oversaw the elementary school.

Joseph Ford was the principal when a new high school was built on Goode Street with a cafeteria and gymnasium, and we were quite excited. We elementary students were bussed over for lunch each day and for other varied activities. The gymnasium became the home of the Mighty DHS Tigers basketball team where the boys' team won the division title in 1966 and earned a trip to Jackson for the state championship. We were so proud! Today a plaque honoring Professor Davidson hangs in the entry way of the building. It is now called Davidson Elementary and is a part of the Water Valley School System.

Kerry and E.C. Jr. graduated from Morehouse College in Atlanta, GA. E.C. Jr. graduated from Meharry Medical School in Nashville, TN and was an obstetrician-gynecologist in Los Angeles, CA. Kerry taught at Fisk University in Nashville then went on to earn his doctorate in Modern European History from Tulane University in New Orleans, LA. In 2016 he was recognized by the Louisiana Board of Regents for more than forty years of outstanding service. He joined the board in 1975 and held positions of Deputy Commissioner for Academic Affairs and Deputy Commissioner for Sponsored Programs, retiring from the board in 2016. Kerry spoke at the dedication of Davidson Elementary School, formerly Davidson High on Goode Street and the fifth Davidson

School Reunion on July 7, 2001. The Herald published his entire speech October 4, 2001.

"My childhood years in Water Valley have shaped so profoundly who I have become as an adult," he said. "In a very meaningful sense, none of us who grew up here have ever really left Water Valley – the playmates, friendships, food, values and landscape endure as attributes which influence our thoughts and behavior. Many of the indelible memories, not surprisingly, are related to the period that Davidson High School was located on Cemetery Street." In what sounds like a charge to all gathered and still relevant to us today, Kerry added, "My father's generation struggled to create opportunity in an environment of educational deprivation and despair. We must continue this struggle, while maximizing the advantages which currently exist."

On May 17, 1990, The Herald printed an article recognizing Ezra C. Davidson, Jr., MD as the first African American president of the American College of Obstetricians and Gynecologists. We are including this article (right). Dr. Davidson passed away on March 12, 2018 at age 84. His nephew, Kerry Davidson Jr., recalled recently that Dr. Davidson did not want a funeral or memorial service. The accomplishments of the Davidson children and grandchildren speak for themselves as do those of the many students who attended Davidson Schools over forty-six years, including those from the twenty-eight graduating classes that began in 1942.

In the fall of 1970, thirteen years after Professor Davidson died, the doors of the all-black/segregated Davidson school system were shut. All students had to attend what were the practically all-white schools in the Water Valley School system. Three black students, Dorothy Boston, Dorothy Neely Middleton and Annette Hervey Westmoreland, had enrolled at Water Valley High in 1966 through the freedom of choice option. They were featured in Article 9, November 29, 2018. Many white students refused to attend school with blacks and enrolled in newly formed private academies, several of which still exist today.

Professor Davidson defines leadership, organizational development, fortitude and fatherhood. In an era of strict segregation, he refused to let any obstacle deter him from his vision. Just think how desolate our community would have been had he not provided an opportunity for blacks in Yalobusha County to get an education. Let's salute him on this Father's Day by sharing his story with our little ones who may be students at Davidson Elementary this fall or have gone through there without knowing its history. Let's continue his legacy. The epitaph on his tombstone reads, "To live in hearts we leave behind is not to die."

The obituary that appeared in the Herald on Thursday, September 5, 1957 sheds even more light on how much Professor Davidson meant to the Yalobusha Community and the many students who passed through the halls of Davidson. Hail to thee our dear old Davidson and to thee be true. We will love our Dear Ole Davidson, Hail oh Hail to thee!

My Closing Thoughts
By Dottie Reed

On May 28th I got the best news from a military official informing me that my son deployed in Kuwait will be returning soon – by Father's Day the notice said. I hope by the time you read this he and his fellow soldiers will be back at Fort Bragg, NC. We were asked not to jeopardize their return by posting the information on social media so that is all I can say. I can say he lives in Raeford, N.C. where George Floyd was born. While I watched the memorial service for George that was held in Raeford, I realized why the name George Floyd flutters in my head when I say it. Beyond thinking it sounded like two first names, it dawned on me that the idea for this column was born at my cousin George Adams' funeral. And my late brother's name was Floyd. So, there you have it – George Floyd – Perry Jr. is what they called him.

George Floyd was loved, and he was a father, his youngest just six years old, with two children. Dr. Christoppher Stackhouse, whose church I have attended with my son and grandson in Fayetteville, N.C., said during his eulogy of George that there was something different about the day he was killed – that his death sparked a fuse that is going to change this nation. I pray he is right! Speaking to mourners, Dr. Stackhouse repeatedly invoked his name: "George Floyd, Perry Jr. is what they called him."

I must admit that in the midst the social justice protests and the pandemic I remain self-quarantined or on lock down because I fall in that critical group where if infected, I don't believe I could survive. I am forever concerned about my other two sons and all black boys and men who live with the fear of being singled out because of the color of their skin anytime, any day as they go about their daily lives here in America.

This inequality and racism must end! Folks like Professor Davidson, his family and our parents have been fighting too long for equal treatment for Black America. I applaud the current efforts that are underway to overturn the systems of racism, police brutality and discrimination. We must all do our part. Change is going to come, but it will be slow. I truly believe that a new America is indeed on the horizon for my people and for all people.

Reader Comments

He was such a blessing to get to know through your writing. He reminds me of a man by the name of Richard Wilson who was our elementary principal and school bus driver and janitor. The things they did to make our lives better. I was so moved by the depth of your research and the way it was presented. I hate to see the series come to an end. Nevertheless, I know the Lord has a greater plan for you and where he is taking you.
Dianne Prince,
Orlando, FL

I really enjoyed reading the article and thank you for including me and my work in your article. I'm honored.
Brittany Brown,
Meridian, MS

Thanks for this history lesson. I remember as a child, before I was old enough to attend school, my stepsister, Zelma Hervey took me to Davidson School (on the hill) with her and introduced me to Professor Davidson. He gave me a dollar because he said my head looked like his head (smile). It's funny how some things you never forget.
Eddie Sanders,
Detroit, MI

Thank you! From Professor Davidson's mischievous son who was frequently whipped harder than others before the entire class.
Kerry Davidson, Sr.,
Baton Rouge, LA

Like always another great article. Professor Davidson was almost bigger than life. I can remember going to assembly at the Calhoun Street location and Professor Davidson would bring the students who had gotten in trouble and punish them in front of the whole assembly. I love these stories from our past.
Fred Harris,
Seattle, WA

Two Years Later
Black Women Project Moves To The Next Phase

After two years of featuring outstanding black women of Yalobusha County here in this newspaper, I have decided to end the series to focus on the oral history segment of the project, "Black Families of Yalobusha County, " and wherever else life may take me. My column has given me an opportunity to show my appreciation to the many wonderful black women of Yalobusha and the many other deserving candidates. It was my vision to feature the unknown and the lesser known, connecting their stories to the history of the county. In reality, the list of who and what has been written about is far from complete. Our oral history project, through the Center for Southern Studies at the University of Mississippi, captures the stories of women, men and families and can be viewed and followed at *https://egrove.olemiss.edu/blkfam_yalo/* Thus, our goal to preserve the history of our black community continues. Due to the Covid-19 epidemic the bulk of the interviews may be virtual or socially distanced until better days come. To escalate the project, I am providing the team of graduate students and their advisor a list of individuals who could participate in oral history interviews, which will be archived at the university.

Our stories are joining an extensive repository at the university that includes B.B. King's personal record collection as part of one of the largest blues archives along with collections from Fannie Lou Hamer, Freedom Riders, John Grisham, Elvis Presley and, of course, William Faulkner. I must exhale! Finally, we black folks are taking part and being included in the exceptional technological resources just up the road – thirteen miles from Water Valley. And rightfully so!

On my first and only trip a few years ago to the National Museum of African American History & Culture in Washington, DC, instead of going up the escalator, I went down to the bottom floor to see if I could find anything about my ancestors. I did find one article about someone with my maiden name. It was painful to see all the pictures of lynchings and black women in Parchman prison and the display surrounding Emmitt Till's murder, including his coffin. However, I was so proud when I found a piece of art on display on another floor by my late husband's cousin, Claude Clark. Artist and Educator is how he described himself. You know I did the mom thing, took a picture and texted it to his daughter, Alice TOforiAtta, my three sons and my eleven-year-old grandson. I urge you to take advantage of this opportunity to tell your story, to record your family history, to leave a record behind for your heirs.

The Yalobusha team consists of students working on masters and doctoral degrees. Returning graduate team members are Brittany Brown, Colton Babbitt, Michelle

Bright and Rhondalyn Peairs, now under the direction of Dr. Brian Foster. Dr. Jessie Wilkerson, who had the vision and initiated the collaboration with the university, has gotten a promotion and in July will be joining the West Virginia University history department as the Robbins Chair in Appalachian and 20th century U.S. History. We will continue to rely on her input and expertise during this transition.

I want to thank her, express my sincerest appreciation and wish her continued success. She will be sorely missed.

Foster, who now leads the project, is a native of Verona. His first book will be published at the end of the year. He is bright, talented and energetic, teaching both graduate and undergraduate classes this summer. Students from all his classes will be intimately involved in this project. To broaden our reach, he will be adding social media. That's the beauty of working with young folks – so hold on to your hats! I hope that you will welcome him and the new students as they reach out to the Yalobusha community.

It is my hope that these interviews will result in an occasional article for this column. Otherwise, this is the last one under "Outstanding Black Women of Yalobusha" for a while. I thank you for your support and encouraging feedback over the past two years. Yes, it has been two years since I wrote a letter to the editor at the Herald and this column was born. Special thanks to David Howell, who was open to my cry. Thanks to all of you who have allowed me to invade your spaces, asking all sorts of questions, and digging up the past. Thanks for sharing or writing about your loved ones and revisiting joyful and sometimes painful memories. I also want to thank my angel editor who insists on remaining anonymous and who has made me look like a writer while tolerating my limitations.

I must admit I have learned a lot and hope that many of you have also. The comments and feedback have come from around the country and from a diverse readership. I hope these stories have been enlightening and helpful in understanding in many ways why we are witnessing social justice protests here and around the world. I was proud to see the peaceful protest in Water Valley. Perhaps more of us now better understand that Black Lives Matter and that the point former NFL quarterback Colin Kaepernick made was not about the flag or the national anthem but that racism, more virulent than most would admit, runs rampant throughout our neighborhoods and communities. We must continue to work to eradicate it or it will eradicate us all. Just think about the parents out there who continue to teach their children to hate and, in many cases, show them how. Let us not forget those who have lost their lives. Their names continue to fuel the movement for positive changes in our justice system and an end to systemic racism.

The question still looms: What can we do to make a difference? In the midst of our 2020 struggle for social justice, an end to voter suppression, police brutality, unjustified killing of black men and women and poverty, it is difficult to determine what and where efforts are most needed. Political activism, with the November election in the forefront of many of our minds, and the everyday stress of the current moment could overwhelm us. But we must not let it. To borrow from Sam Cooke, a change has got to come!

In a June 19th article for *Essence Magazine*, "Juneteenth and National New Beginnings," Dr. Tera W. Hunter said, "We are at another crossroads in the nation. The direction we choose to take at the ballot box, in the streets, in the boardrooms, in places of worships, in the mom and pop shops, in schools, in police stations, in governmental bodies at all levels, in our health care institutions, and in media will determine the extent and shape of democracy for

Dottie Reed admiring a painting by her husband's cousin, renowned artist Claude Clark on display at the National Museum of African American History in Washington, DC.

coming generations. Long may the struggle persevere until justice for all prevails." Dr. Hunter, professor of History and African American Studies at Princeton University, is a scholar of labor, gender, race, and Southern history.

While Covid 19 continues to challenge us and places obstacles in our path, we forge ahead. One of our journalism students, Brittany Brown, created a video on Davidson High School for a project this spring semester. Here is the link, *https://youtu.be/o3jkXIeUySU* and it is also posted on my website. Brittany has obtained a fellowship to continue this great work this summer. It is my hope that she will expand the video to include information from Article 44, June 19, 2020, about the principal, Professor E.C. Davidson Sr., his family and legacy. Wouldn't we love to see and hear more from his son, Kerry, and his stepdaughter, Gwendolyn. Not to mention the former teachers and students who were a part of the 48 years of the Davidson School era. These are the stories that we have begun to archive and preserve as black history.

Your feedback and comments have always been important to me. Let me hear from you if you have ideas or suggestions. All 44 articles including this one can be found on my website. Also check there to keep informed as the Black Families of Yalobusha County project moves forward.

Since my last article, just barely three weeks ago, where I spoke about watching the Raeford, North Carolina memorial service for George Floyd, I found myself watching the funeral service here in Atlanta for another black man killed by the police. As the eulogist, Pastor Raphael Warnock, said while the two cases are different, both men are dead. Dr. Bernice King mentioned how she could relate to Rayshard Brooks' eight-year-old daughter, Blessing, because she was only five when her father, Dr. Martin Luther King, Jr. was assassinated. The names of Rayshard Brooks' children really resonate with me: Blessing, Memory, two-years old, and Dream, only one year old.

As this column goes on hiatus, I pray that we do not have to add another name to the already much too long list of Rayshard Brooks, George Floyd, Breanna Taylor and Ahmaud Aubrey. While many of us are wearing our masks, washing our hands, staying home and social distancing, I leave you with this prayer by Ruth Padilla Deborst, a Latin American-born theologian:

May we who are merely inconvenienced remember those whose lives are at stake.

May we who have no risk factors remember those most vulnerable.

May we who have the luxury of working from home remember those who must choose between preserving their health or making their rent.

May we who have the flexibility to care for our children when their schools close remember those who have no options.

May we who have to cancel our trips remember those who have no safe place to go.

May we who are losing our margin money in the tumult of the economic market remember those who have no margin at all.

May we who settle in for a quarantine at home remember those who have no home.

As fear grips our world, let us choose love.

During this time when we cannot physically wrap our arms around each other, let us find ways to be the loving embrace of God to our neighbors.

I had intended to end this column on this high note until Dr. Jessie Wilkerson shared the following letter to the editor of The South Reporter published last week about the current state of affairs at our neighbors to the north, Holly Springs. I felt most compelled to include it (left side of the page) because Holly Springs is the birthplace of not just an outstanding black woman but a journalist, an anti-lynching advocate, a suffragist, and an activist - Ida B. Wells-Barnett. She was born July 16, 1862. The letter is entitled, "Historic preservation: What it means for black lives to matter in Holly Springs."

It was written by Gracing the Table (GTT), a racial healing and discussion group in Holly Springs, who organize events designed to get local citizens to think about the African American past's impact on the present.

Historic Preservation: What It Means For Black Lives To Matter In Holly Springs

To the Editor:

The public protests as responses to the shooting deaths of Ahmaud Arbery, George Floyd, Rayshard Brooks and countless other black people in the contemporary U.S. have become points of reflection for many of us. Race is at the center of private and public discussions in ways that it has not been before. As those who believe in historic preservation as one form of reparation for slavery and its sustained impacts, we reflect on what this moment means in the context of historic preservation in Holly Springs.

What have we witnessed?

In the past 10 years, we have observed several significant efforts to publicly address the systemic silencing of black history in Holly Springs. Behind the Big House, a slave dwelling interpretation program which prioritizes the experiences of those enslaved in Holly Springs, is one of them. The program, managed by Preserve Marshall County and Holly Springs Inc., began in 2011 and remains the only multi-site historic preservation entity sustained by local community members. Out of that came Gracing the Table, a racial reconciliation group charged with helping to repair the impacts of slavery and its manifestation of systemic racism in the present.

Most recently, we had the unveiling of historical markers to honor the lives and contributions of people who attended the Rosenwald School and W.T. Sims School, the first public schools for African Americans in Holly Springs; and dedications of two markers in honor of journalist, antilynching advocate, suffragist, and activist Ida B. Wells-Barnett. These efforts, and others, reflect a public desire to preserve and personify the significant contributions of African Americans to Holly Springs. These efforts are not only meaningful to local historic preservation but respond to a nationwide gap in recognizing the contributions of Africans and their descendants in the U.S. This disparity is a real one with a long history of historic preservation efforts in the U.S. valuing the histories of those able to record it, mostly rich White men.

Why is this important?

Holly Springs is no different than many other antebellum cities with a cultural landscape that honors early White settlers who built their wealth through the enslavement of others. After the region's Chickasaw occupation, the city was founded by White men and women who either economically benefited from the institution of slavery on the East Coast or who moved West to frontier Mississippi to profit from the free labor of enslaved people. Holly Springs, and its historical prominence, are here because slavery mattered.

This cultural moment is an opportune time to reflect on what that history means to residents and descendants of Holly Springs, and whether the historic preservation landscape in Holly Springs reflects how much slavery really mattered, and how much of an impact the institution has on how we see ourselves today.

What does this opportunity offer?

This opportunity offers a chance for the people of Holly Springs to think about the individuals and institutions that reflect not only who we are but who we hope to be. If we really want black lives to matter in the present and future, as many expressed at the march on June 12, then the black lives of our city's past must also matter. What memorials (historic sites, street signs, parks, etc.) are dedicated to African American individuals and institutions in Holly Springs? Where are they in the city and why are they in certain locations? Are they prominently and equally featured when guests visit Holly Springs?

This is not a question about the ecumenical costs of making long-overdue changes, but whether our willingness and agency exist to repair nearly 200 years of damage to black residents and their ancestors in Holly Springs.

We must ask ourselves what we want to collectively remember and why? This question cannot be separated from an ongoing national campaign for black equity, or from local economic opportunities associated with heritage tourism. We have made some small strides in the latter but have neglected to frame our community development discussions about what it means for Black lives to really matter to heritage tourism in Holly Springs. What might it matter for Holly Springs to not be "All Kinds of Character," but "The Birthplace of Ida B. Wells," a black woman who is also one of the most significant historical figures in the world? What about her would we not want to be? What can the Rosenwald and W.T. Sims schools tell us about the long history of inequity in education in Mississippi from slavery until the present-day? What can they tell us about what fortitude it takes for black Americans to survive despite systemic racism? What might it mean for Holly Springs' antebellum mansions to not be disconnected from the slave dwellings that made them matter, from the enslaved men and women who labored in spite of being policed in every facet of their lives? What can they tell us about how black Americans are policed today? If the slave dwellings do not matter as much as the big houses, then doesn't that indicate that the descendants of enslaved people don't matter as much as the descendants of those who enslaved them? These are just a few questions. There are too many to ask in this space. What we do hope is that our reflection helps give voice to those already thinking about these issues and provides a starting point for others.

To know history is to understand the

times you find yourself in. It is to be aware of what is taking place in your environment and being a cognizant participant. Our country is in a defining moment for us and our future. It matters what we do. What each one of us chooses to do in this moment will determine the future of our country for generations. The drafting of the Declaration of Independence, the three-fifth compromise, and the 1965 Civil Rights Act were all moments in history where our leaders made decisions about who we were. What kind of country will we choose to be? What kind of city will we choose to be?

To know history is also to understand the responsibility of your contribution to it. In a just society, one's thoughts and actions matter and equitably affect everyone else. This is an awesome inherent responsibility of being alive, of being human. Life grants us all this opportunity to affect one and another. We make history in our communities every day. What will be your contribution to our history? Will you be a cognizant active participant for the greater good? Will you act in what you perceive to be your self-interest alone? Will you choose to be silent, not pay attention, not participate. We all have a choice. How do we want our community to move forward from this moment? Do we want to create a society that is conducive to the benefit of all its citizens?

Since 2012, Gracing the Table has worked to help Holly Springs tell and talk through uncomfortable truths about the history of our community. We plan to continue that work with others, thinking more specifically about history's impact on contemporary Black lives and what that means for all of us.

Sincerely, Wayne Jones
Gracing the Table

A Note From A Northern Reader

Mississippi's most well-known outstanding black woman is surely Fannie Lou Hamer, the political activist who demonstrated profound courage at great personal peril. Her national prominence is both understandable and well deserved.

The outstanding black women of Yalobusha County featured in this column, while less heralded beyond their community, showed their own courage day after day. In a segregated world for much of their lives, they kept families intact, nurturing them along with friends and neighbors. Through organizations, civic and religious, they displayed their manifest talents and leadership.

Special Note: Ruby Turner pointed out the following errors in the article about Professor Davidson published in the Herald on June 18, 2020. The title of founder was used incorrectly as Davidson was a public school. According to her, Professor Davidson started as principal of the Water Valley Colored School, 1st through 8th grade in 1919. His oldest daughter, Gwendolyn, is only 97, born in October 1923. We received conflicting information from sources and the obituary as printed. His youngest daughter's name was Hazel not Helen as reported in error.

Epilogue
The Mississippi Hill Country Oral History Collective

IG: @MSHillCountry
Twitter: @MSHillCountry
Web: MsHillCountryCollective.Com

Co-Facilitators:
Ms. Dottie Chapman Reed
and Dr. Brian Foster

Mission

The Mississippi Hill Country Oral History Collective records, archives, and shares the stories of events, individuals, organizations, and institutions with historical significance to black, indigenous, and other communities of color in the "Hill Country" region of Mississippi.[1]

About

In 2019, Dottie Chapman Reed—a native of Water Valley, Mississippi (class of '74)— and Dr. Jessica Wilkerson, Assistant professor of History and Southern Studies at the University of Mississippi, had an idea. Reed had been working on an oral history project in which she profiled various "outstanding black women" in her native Yalobusha County. Reed published those histories in the North Mississippi Herald and to her website. Wilkerson's scholarship, professional pursuits, and community work had also prioritized recording and sharing community histories, especially those of women involved in post-1960's labor movements in Appalachia. Reed and Wilkerson wondered how they might build a collaboration where their work met. The result was the Black Families of Yalobusha County (BFYC) Oral History Project.

In the fall semester 2019, Wilkerson and students in her graduate oral history methods seminar, began working on the BFYC oral history project, documenting the stories of elder African-American women and men in Yalobusha County. In total, they collected interviews with nine narrators. At the end of the semester, Wilkerson and students translated parts of the interviews into an embodied performance, which they shared with the project's oral history narrators and other community members in an embodied performance at Spring Hill North Missionary Baptist Church in Water Valley, Mississippi; and later as a part of a lecture series put on by the Center for the Study of Southern Culture.

In the spring 2020, Dr. B. Brian Foster, assistant professor of Sociology and

---

[1] In 2009, Congress designated the Mississippi Hills National Heritage Area (MHNHA)—a region that spans all or part of 30 counties Central and North Central Mississippi. These counties include: Alcorn, Attala, Benton, Calhoun, Carrol, Chickasaw, Clay, Choctaw, Desoto, Grenada, Holmes, Itawamba, Lafayette, Lee, Lowndes, Marshall, Monroe, Montgomery, Noxubee, Oktibbeha, Panola, Prentiss, Pontotoc, Tate, Tippah, Tishomingo, Union, Webster, Winston, Yalobusha.

Southern Studies at the University of Mississippi, joined as director of the project and, along with a team of graduate students and Ms. Reed, imagined ways to expand the Oral History Project. After a series of conversations during the summer and fall of 2020, they had a working vision: establish a dedicated community—comprised of university faculty, graduate students, and interested community partners—to do what the BFYC Oral History Project had done: record, archive, and share the stories of marginalized communities in the Mississippi Hill Country. They decided to name themselves The Mississippi Hill Country Oral History Collective.

The Collective's guiding mission is to record, archive, and share the stories of black, indigenous, and other people of color in the 30-county "Hill Country" region of Mississippi. They do this by working with community partners and local historians to identify events, individuals, organizations, and institutions with special significance to both the foregoing communities and the greater Hill Country region. Once a subject is identified, The Collective works to build an oral history collection, which generally include audio files and transcripts from oral history interviews with at least 20 narrators.

B. Brian Foster, Ph.D. (He/Him)
Assistant Professor of
Sociology and Southern Studies
University of Mississippi
My Book: I Don't Like the Blues:
Race, Place, and the Backbeat of Black Life
My Site: bbrianfoster.com

Working For A Better Tomorrow... A Better Future
by Dottie Reed

It has been said that the only history we have is what has been written. Yet, far too much of our history has gone untold and unwritten. It has also been said that if we do not know our history, we will repeat the mistakes of the past. The black women featured in this book made a way out of no way —-and not just any old way, - but a good way. They got in good trouble long before the late Congressman John Lewis coined the phrase – strong, black and southern and no doubt just like his mother.

They wanted more for their children than they would live to see or obtain. Just imagine how much better our society might be now had these women been given the rights and privileges of white Americans.

Black women were left behind, but they refused to quit. For if they had, we would not have former first lady Michele Obama, activist Stacey Abrams and Kamala Harris, the first black woman vice president of the United States of America. It is worth noting that each of them regularly pays tribute to her mother. Yet, the road ahead remains challenging as the fight for equality, justice, education, jobs and healthcare continues. We are still treated as not fully human, still being raped, hunted, shot often in the back or choked to death and still killing each other.

What's more, some seventy-three million Americans voted for a divided country, showing no love for black people.

The message is now clear, and the challenge is what will we do to make for a better tomorrow...a better future. We must move forward with vigilance to motivate, to educate and to empower young Americans to learn the true history of all people – blacks and indigenous people, in particular. Knowledge alone will not cure the evils of our society, but what better way to start?

One of the goals of the Black Women of Yalobusha project was to show the humanity of these women in the fullness of their lives. Let's not allow the sacrifices of our black mothers to be in vain. Let's pledge to continue to share their stories and the stories of black families and pass them on. We will.

Acknowledgements

Special thanks to my supporters, especially my friend and angel editor who insists on remaining anonymous. Thanks to my earliest supporters, David Howell, Hayward Cole, Linda Lewis Jamison, Thomasenia Robinson and Dr. Nicolas Trepanier. Hayward attended the very first meeting in Oxford with Dr. Jessie Wilkerson and Dr. Shennette Garrett-Scott and drove back and forth with me to Mississippi. Thanks to Dr. Wilkerson, Dr. Susan McKee and the Center for the Study of Southern Culture, the UM graduate students, the Sylarn Foundation for financial support, my high school classmate Emma Faye Gooch, friends, family and the outstanding women of Yalobusha. Sincerest appreciation to Marie and Larry Walker for their encouragement and financial support of my vision and projects. Lastly, sincerest thanks and appreciation to Barrett Smith my art and design editor.

"Outstanding Black Women of Yalobusha County" was some of the most quality reading I've seen in a long time."

**Coulter Fussell,
North Mississippi Herald**

Dottie Chapman Reed

A native of Water Valley, MS and graduate of the University of Mississippi now residing in Stone Mountain Georgia, Dottie retired from a career in education and corporate America. Aside from recruiting for her alma mater for three years she worked for East Tennessee State University, *The Wall Street Journal* and McGraw-Hill before starting her own business. She continues to work as a consultant and columnist. Additional work can be found at http://www.blackwomenofyalobusha.com.

Made in the USA
Columbia, SC
20 February 2023